Geriatric Dentistry

Geriatric Dentistry

Clinical Application of Selected Biomedical and Psychosocial Topics

Edited by
Carl J. Toga
Kalidas Nandy
Edith Nourse Rogers
Memorial Veterans Hospital
Bedford, Massachusetts

Howard H. Chauncey
Veterans Administration
Outpatient Clinic
Boston, Massachusetts

LexingtonBooks
D.C. Heath and Company
Lexington, Massachusetts
Toronto

Library of Congress Cataloging in Publication Data

Main entry under title:

Geriatric dentistry.

Papers presented at a symposium held in Boston, sponsored by Bedford VA Medical Center/Boston Outpatient Clinic and others.
1. Aged—Dental care—Congresses. 2. Aging—Congresses. I. Toga, Carl J. II. Nandy, Kalidas. III. Chauncey, Howard H.
RK55.A3G47 618.9'77'6 78-24646
ISBN 0-669-02806-1

Published simultaneously in Canada.

Printed in the United States of America.

International Standard Book Number: 0-669-02806-1

Library of Congress Catalog Card Number: 78-24646

This book is dedicated to Paul A.L. Haber, M.D., M.S., currently the Assistant Chief Medical Director for Professional Services at the Veterans Administration Central Office in Washington, D.C.

Foreword

Health problems associated with aging are currently of foremost concern in the United States. These problems have already had a serious impact on our health care delivery system and the resolution of many undesirable socioeconomic conditions. Therefore, it is vitally important to make a concerted effort to understand age-related problems and extend productive life span as well as our economic resources.

The impact that the health care demands of our geriatric population can have on the resources available now, as well as in the future, are unknown. Accommodations must be established to provide for the potential health care service demands and offer optimal dental care.

The goal of this book is to compile information gathered by scientists, educators, and clinicians in the fields of geriatric dentistry and gerontology relative to the state of the art and recent advances in these areas. A range of information covering the aging process as well as specific dental application is presented.

Florence Mahoney
Member, President's Commission on
Mental Health and
Member, Advisory Council of
the National Institute on Aging,
National Institutes of Health,
Bethesda, Maryland

Preface

In the last two decades the population in the United States has been markedly influenced both by an extension in lifespan and a reduction in birth rate. According to U.S. Census Bureau projections, there are 21 million people over 65 years of age. This number is expected to double before the turn of the century. Similarly, the number of older veterans is expected to increase from the current 6 million to approximately 12 million before the next century. This change in population composition has already had an impact on both medicine and dentistry. The Veterans Administration has been cognizant of impending associated problems for a number of years and has established eight Geriatric Research, Education, and Clinical Centers (GRECC) under the auspices of the Extended Care Service, directed by Dr. Paul A.L. Haber. The primary purpose of the GRECC program has been to develop a comprehensive understanding of the complex biomedical, psychological, and socioeconomic problems that elderly individuals encounter and to improve the quality of life for older veterans.

Although advances have been made in gerontological research and geriatric medicine, the field of geriatric dentistry has been, for the most part, ignored except by a small group of highly motivated clinicians. With the growth and improvement in preventive medicine and dentistry programs within the last few years, a larger proportion of the geriatric population have retained their teeth. These individuals frequently require specialized care for the treatment of problems related to the oral structures. In recognition of this need, leaders in the fields of dentistry, medicine, and gerontology gathered in Boston to discuss the current state of the art as well as future directions of geriatric medicine and dentistry. The symposium was sponsored by the Edith Nourse Rogers Memorial Veterans Hospital, Bedford, Veterans Administration Outpatient Clinic, Boston, GRECC, Harvard School of Dental Medicine, and the Veterans Administration Central Office. The meeting focused on a realistic approach toward the oral problems of geriatric patients, with reference to specific scientific and clinical aspects.

This volume is a compendium derived from the proceedings of the symposium and is divided into three sections. The first section deals with the biological aging of different organs and systems, providing a biomedically oriented overview. The second section is devoted to problems encountered in geriatric dentistry. It offers an in-depth coverage of oral pathology, structural and functional changes, various treatment procedures, and newer techniques utilized in dental medicine. The third section deals with an area often neglected by physicians and dentists, namely, the rather unique psychological, social, and economic needs of the geriatric patient.

A text in geriatric dentistry directed toward dental students, postgraduate students, clinicians, and investigators is long overdue. This book was prepared with that need as a foremost consideration. We hope that the material presented will be useful to the aforementioned individuals by providing the latest available information.

Howard H. Chauncey

Acknowledgments

Geriatric Dentistry: Clinical Application of Selected Biomedical and Psychosocial Topics is based on presentations given at the symposium entitled "The Geriatric Patient–Dentistry's Growing Challenge," which was recently held in Boston, Massachusetts. Many of the staff at the Veterans Administration (VA) Medical Center, Bedford; the Veterans Administration Outpatient Clinic, Boston; and Harvard School of Dental Medicine contributed to the success of the symposium and the preparation of this book.

We are particularly grateful to Michael J. Kane, Director; Charles G. Colburn, M.D., Chief of Staff; Edwin S. Busch, M.D., Associate Chief of Staff for Education, V.A. Medical Center, Bedford, and Eugene E. Record, M.D., Chief of Staff; James E. House, D.D.S., Chief, Dental Service, V.A. Outpatient Clinic, Boston; Paul Goldhaber, D.D.S., Dean, Harvard School of Dental Medicine; and Jean Mayer, Ph.D., Dr-ès-Sc, President of Tufts University; for their important contributions to the symposium.

Special mention is made of the efforts of Dr. Melvin I. Cohen, Dr. Robin Lawrence, Ms. Shirley Alford, Ms. Charlotte Gilman, Mr. Herbert J. Jacobus, Ms. Dorothea Malone, Ms. Patricia St. Cyr, and Ms. Claire O'Leary.

We are indebted to the American Society for Geriatric Dentistry and the U.S. Public Health Service for their cooperation. The symposium and the resultant book could not have been accomplished without the active support and encouragement provided by the Learning Resources Service, the Medical Research Service, the Office of Academic Affairs, the Office of Extended Care, and the Office of Dentistry, Veterans Administration Central Office.

This book could not have been prepared without the constant and persistent efforts of Ms. Susan Bulfinch who worked tirelessly as an editorial assistant. The authors are especially indebted to her.

Finally, we would like to thank Lexington Books for their understanding of the numerous difficulties encountered during the preparation of this book.

Introductory Remarks

Dentistry in the Veterans Administration (VA) is a unique service. It is primarily a hospital-based delivery system with a number of outpatient care facilities, but all are primarily focused on the ambulatory provision of care. It is an integral part of the largest health care system in our nation. A full time dental staff with a modern, well-equipped facility is present in almost all 171 hospitals and outpatient clinics. The professional staff exceeds 850 dentists, with approximately 300 residents on duty throughout the system. The VA dental staff provides an extensive range of oral procedures such as surgical, prosthodontic, and restorative. More than 40 percent of the two hundred specialists are certified by their specialty board.

VA dental services are affiliated with all fifty-eight U.S. Schools of Dentistry. During the past year, support was given to residency training programs in oral surgery, prosthodontics, periodontics, oral pathology, endodontics, and general practice. More than one-third of our staff holds faculty appointments in an affiliated institution.

It appears that now is an appropriate time to reassess the oral health needs of the geriatric veteran. The average life span has increased markedly, and many achievements have been made in the control of disease and the restoration of health. But, as dentists, we have not focused adequately on the multiple problems associated with aging. Although the VA is responsible for the administration of all dental benefits to eligible veterans, we have too frequently addressed primary concern for hospital patients and persons in extended health care facilities. How many ambulatory geriatric patients are there, and what is the outlook for the future? How can we best meet the oral health care needs of the aging veteran who requires treatment for a vast variety of conditions?

More patients are now receiving comprehensive dental care and more teeth are being saved. The number of root canal procedures increased by 85 percent in the period from 1972 to 1976; in 1976 more than 20,000 root canal procedures were reported. In that same year VA dentists completed approximately 270,000 cases and another 123,000 veterans were authorized for and received complete treatment by private practitioners under the VA fee-for-service program.

We have all been taught to be sensitive to patient needs. The geriatric patient may present a growing and special clinical challenge; yet, basic to this, there must be a warm and understanding concern for these individuals. How to live better while living longer is really the question with which we are presented.

A.J. Aaronian, D.D.S.
Assistant Chief Medical Director
for Dentistry, Veterans Administration Central Office,
Washington, DC

Teeth present a paradox. Their apparent indestructibility via fossilization has allowed paleontologists to use them to reconstruct the lines of vertebrate evolution and anthropologists to outline recent human history. Humans, as a species, are identified, in part, by their teeth. Yet during a lifetime teeth do age and may even be so worn as to be nonfunctional.

Our omnivorous ancestors, eating foodstuffs heavily laden with sand and dirt, frequently ground their teeth so that the pulp was exposed and apical abscesses developed. Considerable discomfort must have ensued. For these people, subsisting largely on uncooked meats and vegetation, adequate dentition may have been necessary for survival. In prehistoric times, survival time was much shorter, and it might be more apt to state that an individual was as old as his teeth. However, it is doubtful that an aged edentulous individual could have obtained adequate nutrition.

Gerontologists are now convinced that aging is a universal process independent of, but considerably modified by, environmental stresses. Not only are there anatomical and physiological changes, but there are psychological, social, and economic changes. Improving the life condition of the large and increasing numbers of older individuals within our society not only requires new information and additional resources, but their very presence is without precedent and is altering our social structure.

The VA has recognized these needs and is responding to them. This response has been planned to meet the challenge at all levels. We must evolve the requisite information and utilize it to train new practitioners who will supply these concepts and skills to improve the lives of our constituents.

Ralph Goldman, M.D.
Assistant Chief Medical Director
for Extended Care
Veterans Administration Central
Office, Washington, DC

How does research contribute to understanding problems associated with aging? A long list of basic and clinical problems must be investigated, both on a short- and long-term basis. Basic research on age changes in the biochemistry and function of connective tissue, epithelium, bone, and salivary glands is of extreme importance. Major problems, such as caries and periodontal disease, still require extensive basic research relative to the oral microbiota and the human immune system. Oral cancer, ulcerative mucocutaneous disease, diabetes, osteoporosis, nutrition, and diet are other important areas of study, as is the investigation of new restorative materials.

Problems in delivering health services to the aged are also important research subjects. These include behavioral patterns, such as motivation toward oral hygiene, acceptance of care, and attitudes toward oral health. In addition, there are many opportunities for studies dealing with delivery systems, methods of care, and financing. This is extremely timely, not only in its own context, but also because the findings can be applied to other fields.

There is little question about the desirability of increasing aging research, especially in the clinical area. To achieve this, however, it will be necessary to provide various training programs and clarify career opportunities for investigators. Information systems for practitioners, educators, students, and the public are needed and should be developed. The opportunities for aging research in dentistry are reflected by the broad range of subjects covered in the sessions described herein.

David B. Scott, D.D.S., M.S.
Director, National Institute of
Dental Research, National Institutes
of Health, Bethesda, Maryland

Part I
Organ and Tissue Changes

1 Biological Aspects of Aging

Michael J. Malone

The medical problems of the elderly are distinguished by two principal features: chronicity and multiplicity. Acute illnesses appear, but in a background of continuing disease, usually involving several organ systems. Pathological changes in genetics which may result in the aging process, are the major topic of numerous current studies.

It has been stated that age-related changes may occur as the result of a programmed series of metabolic events, which are specific for each species. Each organism seems to have a specific finite limit to life span that is encoded at the level of individual development and differentiation (Wilson, 1974). A corollary to this belief is the theory based on metabolic wear and tear. The theory proposes that there is an accumulation of metabolic errors or waste products during the life span and that ultimately certain essential metabolic processes cannot continue. There is general evidence for this theory, but the relationship between accumulation and interference with cell function is not well established.

These theories have been based on a variety of possible mechanisms. Some believe that spontaneous mutations occur subsequent to mutation-inducing factors such as ionizing radiation. These mutations can accumulate as metabolic errors within the cells and tissues (Wilson, 1974; Lamb and Maynard-Smith, 1964). Others think that a humoral immune system is active at a functional level throughout life and then declines with age (Makinodan et al., 1973). This is in contrast to the cell-mediated immune system and may result in altered ability to recognize and respond to viruses. Consequently, immune complex viral diseases develop, metabolic cellular changes appear, and neoplasia occurs (Adler, 1974). The cross-linkage theory suggests that double strand linkages of deoxyribonucleic acid (DNA) by small formaldehyde-like residues may "tie up" portions of the cellular template irreversibly. At least eight possible metabolic products aside from formaldehyde are capable of causing this type of irreversible tie up (Bjorksten et al., 1971). A final suggested mechanism is the free-radical theory, by which free-radical formation, possibly linked to ionizing radiation, can result in peroxide formation and to the formation of poorly degradable metabolic end products (Harman, 1956, 1961; Demopoulos, 1973).

Functional Disorders

A multiplicity of organic systems in the aged patient present clinical problems that involve every medical and surgical specialty. These disorders can be categorized according to the following functional classification.

1. Sensory. Deficits in visual, auditory, and gustatory faculties.
2. Motor. Deficits secondary to central nervous system (CNS) disease or disorders affecting muscle and joint function.
3. Visceral. Deficits in cardiopulmonary or hepatorenal function.
4. Functional. Affective disorders commonly arising from losses that impede the patient's ability to function in interpersonal relations or in daily living activities.
5. Cognitive. Disturbances in learning and recall that ultimately lead to an inability for self care.

Sensory

Visual. After the age of 40, most individuals experience a gradual and progressive outward movement of the near point of fixation. The condition known as presbyopia occurs when a convex lens is required for close work. This condition results from the progressive migration of the more dense fibers of the lens towards the lens center and, possibly, from changes in the ciliary muscle.

Cataract formation is the single most important cause of visual impairment in the elderly. There are two types of cataracts: cortical and nuclear. The cortical cataract follows a generalized breakdown in lens fibers and induces diffuse peripheral patches. Nuclear cataracts form from an acceleration of inward migration of lens fibers toward the center of the lens, with degeneration and central opacification.

Ultimate therapy is the surgical removal of the lens; modern operative techniques have greatly improved the prognosis for useful vision. Prior to definitive surgery, many elderly patients who show visual acuity determinations of 20/50 or better on Snellen charts may have significant visual impairment under certain light conditions. This is particularly true when facing direct light. Light diffusion caused by early cataract change limits the patient's depth perception and produces disturbing problems in reading or interview settings. Unfortunately, many patients may not advise the physician or dentist that this problem exists and simply become hostile or resistant in an otherwise inexplicable fashion.

In the aged patient, shrinkage of the vitreous commonly occurs; if opacities form, the patient may complain of floaters. These are usually insignificant, but in highly myopic patients, the problem may be greatly exacerbated and a source of continuing concern.

Finally, the most common form of glaucoma, chronic, simple, open-angle glaucoma, seems to have some genetic predetermination, with an increased incidence in diabetic populations. The course of this disease is insidious, and early changes such as enlargement of the blindspot and constriction of visual fields, are usually not noted. To avoid an oversight, tonometric evaluation of intraocular pressure should be a routine part of every physical examination of a geriatric patient (Kornzweig, 1973).

Hearing. After the age of 45 to 50 there is a gradual deterioration of hearing. This loss seems to have genetic aspects, since some families show loss in early adult life and progress to near deafness in old age. This hearing loss, presbycusis, is end organ in nature, reflecting changes in the cochlea and auditory nerve or both. Symptomatically, there is early loss of high frequency sounds with later loss in the lower frequencies. Patients often complain of problems in conversation, particularly in telephone conversations. An inability to discriminate between sounds is a critical issue, magnified by interview settings with a background of street noises, taped music, or office clatter. Such conditions may totally obstruct any communication and lead to feelings of anger and hostility on the part of the patient.

Motor

Central Nervous System. Damage to the CNS may result from a variety of causes. Vascular disease, trauma, infections, mass lesions, and degenerative processes can affect the pyramidal and extrapyramidal portions of the brain and spinal cord.

Cerebral thrombosis or thromboembolic disease represents the third leading cause of death among people who are 75 years of age or older (Vital Statistics of the United States, 1969). It has been estimated that over 2 million individuals live with residua of cerebrovascular disease and one-third of these people cannot function independently in society (Vital Statistics of the United States, 1969; Kurtzke, 1969). Strokes are grouped in several categories: transient ischemic attacks (TIA), where the neurological deficits clear in twenty-four hours; reversible ischemic neurological deficit (RIND), in which the deficits may last for two to three days; stroke in evolution, when the deficits develop in step-wise fashion over hours or days; and completed stroke, when the deficits remain stable with generally incomplete regression over days and weeks.

This classification is best made in retrospect and the specific type of stroke and prognosis may be quite difficult to determine in an acute situation. Generally, vascular incidents are sudden in onset and in some cases are precipitated by positional changes. A past history of hypertension, diabetes, or evidence of arteriosclerotic vascular disease affecting other organs suggest that a patient is at high risk.

A patient's mobility may be seriously affected by the residua of a stroke. Common clinical presentations are based on involvement of the carotid circulation and distribution of the middle cerebral arteries. These elements lead to greater functional loss in the upper than in the lower extremities and produce considerable difficulties in hand movement and coordination. If the ischemia involves the dominant hemisphere, problems in language and communication, particularly in an expressive sense, can be anticipated.

Parkinsonism, a disorder of the basal ganglia, is the most common movement disorder encountered in the elderly population, affecting 1 to 1.5 million people in the United States (Von Werssowetz, 1964). Parkinsonism may be idiopathic, postencephalitic, or toxic in origin, with three cardinal clinical features: tremor, dyskinesia or akinesia, and ridigity. In this era of improved pharmacologic therapy, proper diagnosis is essential for appropriate treatment (Cotzias et al., 1969). Affected patients frequently show considerable variation in the severity of their symptoms. Fever, dehydration, pain, and other metabolic disturbances often exacerbate dormant neurological symptoms. Treatment should be directed at the current infection or ailment and should not lead to poorly advised adjustments in medication or unnecessary hospitalizations.

Muscles, Bones, and Joints. Degenerative joint disease (DJD) is the most common form of chronic arthritis, affecting over 75 percent of individuals over the age of 70 (Simmons and Chrisman, 1965). In this form of wear and tear joint involvement, articular cartilage deteriorates and new bone forms at the joint surfaces. There is pain and stiffness without overt evidence of local inflammation. Joints commonly affected include the distal and proximal interphalangeal joints in the hands; the metacarpophalangeal joints of the wrist; cervical, thoracic, and lumbar intervertebral joints; hip; knees; and the metatarsophalangeal joints of the feet. Treatment should focus on decreasing mechanical stress, the use of muscle relaxants or analgesics, physical therapy, and the cautious use of antiinflammatory agents.

Motor disturbances greatly increase the patient's problems in routine activities. Offices or other settings intended for the care of such patients should be properly designed and make use of a lever-action bolt release for doorknobs and ramps with sturdy handrails rather than steps with ornamental, fragile balustrades. A simple stair system is easier to ascend than a curving, steep spiral system. Finally, consideration should be given to the traction problem of floor coverings and seat cushions. Waxed and slippery hardwood floors or linoleum surfaces are hazardous.

Visceral

In the presence of congestive heart failure, adequate cerebral circulation and perfusion of the brain may be compromised. The added feature of hypoxia occurs when chronic pulmonary disease is either superimposed or complementary. With some older patients, a confusional state, rather than complaints of dyspnea, may be the only clinical manifestation. When an elderly individual is already compromised or reduced to borderline functioning by the changes in senile brain atrophy, cerebral hypoxia and decreased perfusion may require total nursing care.

Myocardial infarction, particularly anterior wall infarction and congestive heart failure, are common manifestations of arteriosclerotic heart disease in individuals over 60 years of age (Pomerance, 1965). Treatment outcomes of myocardial infarction in the geriatric age group are reportedly good. It is important to give special attention to these people while in the hospital to avoid states of depression and confusion that stem from sensory deprivation in the evening hours (the sundown syndrome).

A gradual loss of elasticity occurs in the walls of bronchi, and bronchioli develop after the middle years. Some elements of emphysema can be detected in any patient over 65 years of age (Filley, 1967). It is essential that these patients receive continuing psychological support and an appreciation of the fact that many negative behavioral patterns may arise from their fear and depression. Increasing fatigue and exertional dyspnea are important symptoms of which to be aware. Patient education and avoidance of airway irritants such as smoke, fumes, and areas of high environmental pollutants are initial and essential measures in health care. The use of bronchodilators, special breath-retaining exercises (pursed lip breathing), and intermittent oxygen therapy are necessary in the more advanced cases.

Functional

Entering old age usually marks the beginning of major life adjustments for an individual. These adjustments follow a common denominator of loss. Personally, there is a loss of multiple physical capabilities and, for most people, the need to curtail active life styles. There may be loss in intellectual capabilities also, problems with memory, and in acquiring new skills. Interpersonally, there is loss of friends and family members as well as loss of economic position and social status. An individual's response to these losses is usually a depressive reaction of varying severity.

Depressions seen in elderly patients may appear as exacerbations of previously experienced elation-depression cycles or as an involutional reaction without a prior history of severe anxiety, feelings of worthlessness, or agitation. Finally, some patients seem to associate the onset of their emotional disturbances to a specific illness or loss (bereavement), and their response is reactive. These theoretical distinctions are difficult to make, however. Furthermore, many elderly patients will not present emotional complaints, but only present somatic or visceral symptoms. Atypical facial pain is one common presenting syndrome which may be symptomatic of an underlying depressive reaction. Tic douloureaux and other neurological disorders capable of causing facial pain are rare; depression is not. Recurrent complaints of bowel function, usually constipation, are often seen, and problems of insomnia and awakening in the early morning hours should alert the interviewer that the patient may be severely depressed.

Since depression can be treated effectively, it is important that this affective disorder be recognized early and treatment begun immediately. Pharmacologic treatment involves the use of two fundamental types of drugs: the monoamine oxidase inhibitors (phenelzine sulfate, nialamide, tranylcypromine sulfate) or the tricyclic antidepressants (amitriptyline hydrochloride, desipramine hydrochloride, imipramine hydrochloride). Full response to some of the tricyclic antidepressants may require several weeks (Overall et al., 1966). In some cases of severe psychotic depressive reactions, electroshock therapy can be lifesaving.

Cognitive Disorders

It is generally agreed that some mental changes occur in the normal aging human. Memory function, particularly information processing of complex tasks, lessens, and there may be some loss in highly abstract functions. These changes, however, have little relationship to the disorders designated as senile and presenile dementias. Onset may occur after 50 for presenile dementia and Alzheimer disease or after 65 for senile dementia. Onset is insidious, with such symptoms as forgetfullness, confusion, spatial disorientation, or behavioral aberrations. The time course of these disorders is variable, but cases with an earlier onset, such as Alzheimer disease, seem to have the most rapid evolution. From an early loss of higher judgmental and abstraction skills, the individual progressively loses all memory functions: recent, immediate, and remote. Ultimately, there is loss of basic orientation to space, time, and even to the self. Although frequently described as diffuse neurological disorders, these dementias are not diffuse in terms of clinical or pathological findings (Kaes, 1907; Langworthy, 1936). There is no loss of primary sensory or motor functions in senile and presenile dementia which affect only the secondary and tertiary association areas of the brain.

The brains from affected patients are small and atrophic. The atrophic change is regional, with primary involvement of frontal, frontotemporal areas, and the parietal lobes. A loss of brain substance involves both the cortical mantle (demonstrated by pneumoencephalograms, computerized axial tomography (CAT) scans, and autopsies) and the subcortical white matter. Microscopic examination reveals the characteristic findings of extracelluar senile plaques, intracellular lipofuscin deposits, and neurofibrillar tangles (Corsellis, 1976). The cause of these dementias is unknown. Although multiple familial cases have been reported, a lucid genetic link has not been established. The course is variable from onset to death, the duration being 3 to 15 years, with most patients requiring permanent nursing home or custodial care. To date, there is no known effective treatment.

Given this stark picture, it is essential that the treatable forms of neurological and psychiatric illness be excluded in the evaluation of any patient with a "senile" change. Such pseudodiagnostic terms as "organic brain syndrome" as opposed to an "inorganic" or "chronic" brain syndrome should not be used. Early distinction between the changes produced by depressive reactions and dementias may be extremely difficult. Early dementia and depression may coexist, possibly as cause and effect, in the same individual. Moreover, any person showing evidence of progressive intellectual impairment requires a complete medical, neurological, and psychological assessment. If the neurological and psychological testing support a finding of dementias, then further radiological and electrophysiological examinations are mandatory. The practice of casually using the label of "senility" followed by referral to a nursing home has no place in modern medical practice.

References

Adler, W.H. An "Autoimmune" Theory of Aging. In M. Rockstein (Ed.), *Theoretical Aspects of Aging* (New York: Academic, 1974), pp. 33-41.

Bjorksten, J., Acharya, P.V.N., Ashman, S.M., and Wetlaufer, D.C. Gerogenic Fractions in the Tritiated Rat. *J Am Geriatr Soc* 19:561-574, 1971.

Corsellis, J.A.M. Aging and the dementias. In W. Blackwood and J.A.N. Corsellis (Eds.), *Greenfield's Neuropathology* (London: Edward Arnold, 1976), pp. 796-848.

Cotzias, G.C., Papavasiliou, P.S., and Gellene, R. Modification of Parkinsonism—Chronic Treatment with L-dopa. *New Engl J Med* 280:337-345, 1969.

Demopoulos, H.B. The Basis of Free Radical Pathology. In *Proceedings of the 54th Annual Meeting, FASEB.* Fed Proc 32:1859-1861, 1973.

Filley, G.F. Emphysema and Chronic Bronchitis: Clinical Manifestations and Their Physiologic Significance. *Med Clin N Amer* 51:283-292, 1967.

Gass, J.D.M. A Fluorescein Angiographic Study of Macular Dysfunction Secondary to Retinal Vascular Disease I. Embolic Retinal Artery Obstruction. *Arch Ophthalmol* 80:535-550, 1968.

Harman, D. Aging: Theory Based on Free Radical and Radiation Chemistry. *J Gerontol* 11:298-300, 1956.

Harman, D. Prolongation of the Normal Lifespan and Inhibition of Spontaneous Cancer by Antioxidants. *J Gerontol* 16:247-254, 1961.

Harris, M.J. Mutation Rates in Cells at Different Ploidy Levels. *J Cell Physiol* 78:177-184, 1971.

Kaes, T. Die Grosshirnrinde Des Menschen in Ihren Massen und in Ihren Fassengehalt. *Fustav Fischer Jena*, 1907.

Kornzweig, A.L. Diagnosis and Treatment of Common Eye Diseases in the Aged: Guidelines for the Practicing Physician. *J Am Geriatr Soc* 21:512-518, 1973.

Kurtzke, J.F. *Epidemiology of Cerebrovascular Disease* (Berlin: Springer-Verlag, 1969).

Lamb, M.J. and Maynard-Smith, J. Radiation and Ageing in Insects. *Exp Gerontol* 1:11-20, 1964.

Langworthy, O. Development of Behavior Patterns and Myelinization of the Nervous System in the Human Fetus and Infant. *Contrib Embryol* 139:3-57, 1936.

Makinodan, T., Heidrick, M.L., and Nordin, A.A. In *Proceedings of the 2nd International Workshop on Primary Immunodeficiencies in Man* (California: Sinauer Press, 1973).

Overall, J.E., Hollister, L.E., Johnson, M., and Pennington, L. Nosology of Depression and Differential Response to Drugs. *JAMA* 195:946-948, 1966.

Pomerance, A. Pathology of the Heart With and Without Cardiac Failure in the Aged. *Br Heart J* 27:697-710, 1965.

Simmons, D.P. and Chrisman, O.D. Salicylate Inhibition of Cartilage Degeneration. *Arthritis Rheum* 8:960-969, 1965.

Vital Statistics of the United States II, B. Dept. (Washington, DC: Health, Education and Welfare, 1969).

Von Werssowetz, O.F. *Parkinsonism* (Springfield: Charles C Thomas, 1964).

Wilson, D.L. The Programmed Theory of Aging. In *Theoretical Aspects of Aging.* (New York: Academic, 1974), pp. 11-21.

2 Muscular Changes in Aging

Morris Rockstein

As Descartes once said, as thinking beings, humans are aware of their existence. However, unlike lower animals, humans are patently aware of the fact that they must grow old with the passage of time. The universal nature of the aging process is such that an old dog, an old lion, and an old human all exhibit similar manifestations of aging. These include graying and thinning of hair and diminished elasticity (and consequent wrinkling) of the skin as changes in outward appearance. More important from the standpoint of survival is the pronounced diminution in vigor and speed of movement. It is this significant manifestation of senescence and the senile state that is discussed here. The subject of muscle aging is treated from three major aspects: the definitive *functional* changes that occur with advancing age, the *anatomical* changes, and the *biochemical* alterations that accompany and underlie the decline in muscle strength and speed of movement as individuals grow old.

Functional Changes

The most conspicuous manifestation of aging is the slower and less vigorous movement seen in all old animals and humans (Simonson, 1965). Thus, even if one's outward facial and body appearance has been surgically rejuvenated, the one outstanding characteristic of advanced age is the marked diminution in strength, speed of movement, and, especially, physical endurance. This is not only true of striated skeletal muscle and, therefore, movement of the limbs and their appendages, but also of the striated heart muscle (myocardium). Reports by Birren (1960) and Welford (1960) point out that there is a linear decrease in muscle strength, particularly in human males, from age 30 onward. This includes strength measurements such as right hand grip, biceps, wrist, or back strength.

Original studies reported in this chapter were supported in part by funds from Grants No. HD00142 and AG00013 from the National Institutes of Health, Grant No. M-74-AG-F from the Heart Association of Greater Miami, Grant No. AG205 from the Florida Heart Association, and a generous personal gift from Mr. Paul F. Glenn of New York City.

The author gratefully acknowledges the technical assistance of Mr. Thomas Lopez in connection with all studies on the biochemical aging of the rat myocardium. The author also acknowledges with deep appreciation the assistance of Dr. Marvin Sussman in the preparation of this chapter.

These age related changes also apply to the striated muscle of lower animals. For example, flight ability in the male house fly, as measured by duration of flight, shows a marked falling off from the first day of adult life (table 2-1). This decline continues steadily to a low of 15 percent of the first day maximum by the ninth postemergence day (Rockstein and Bhatnagar, 1966). For cardiac muscle there are, likewise, a number of reports of senescence. The cardiac output of the male Fischer rate, for example, shows an 18 percent loss in stroke index from 12 to 24 months of age (Rothbaum et al., 1973). Comparable changes in the aging human heart have been reported by Brandfonbrener, Landowne, and Shock (1955). Cardiac output fell by 40 percent and the cardiac index by 37 percent from the third to ninth decade for sixty-seven male subjects ranging from 19 to 86 years. These changes resulted from a fall both in stroke volume and heart rate.

At the cellular level, there are concomitant aging changes in the biophysical properties of skeletal muscle in lower vertebrates. These include an increase in latency and contraction and relaxation times of both fast and slow fibers (Syrový and Gutmann, 1970; Gutmann and Syrový, 1974). Comparable changes in these biophysical properties have been reported for the myocardium of aging rats by Alpert, Gale, and Taylor (1967), Heller and Whitehorn (1972), and Lakatta et al. (1975).

Two additional factors are involved in the aging of muscle. They are the aging of neuromotor function, as shown by reduced conductivity or increased synaptic or motor end plate delay (the motor nerve supply to such muscle), and the reduction in cardiovascular effectiveness in deliverying oxygen to contracting muscle because of reduced cardiac output. (Brandfonbrener, Landowne, and Shock, 1955).

Anatomical Changes

As a postmitotic tissue, muscle fibers are incapable of self replacement upon destruction. Accordingly, the most conspicuous manifestation of muscle atrophy is the progressive loss in muscle mass with age. This is due to diminution both in diameter and in number of muscle fibers (Gutmann and Hanzlíková, 1972; Gutmann, 1977). In humans, this has been shown to occur in a number of different muscles, such changes occurring to different degrees with advancing age, depending on the muscle (Gutmann and Hanzlíková, 1972).

In what is reportedly the first detailed study of change in striated muscle mass with age, Rockstein and Brandt (1961) compared the weights of the left and right gastrocnemius muscle to body weights of male Sprague-Dawley and longer-lived Carworth Farm Nelson (CFN) rats, from weaning through old age.

Table 2-1
Flight Ability of the Male House Fly as a Function of Age

Age (Days)	*No.*	*Duration of Flight (Minutes)*
1	19	420
2	21	365
4	28	265
5	23	220
6	26	180
7	17	135
8	9	125
9	8	63

(The Sprague-Dawley rat has a considerably shorter constant weight age span of 350 to 600 days, in contrast to the 300 to 800 day maximum middle age body weight for the longer-lived CFN strain. Maximum life span for male Sprague-Dawley rats is about eight hundred days versus one thousand days for CFN males.) The median mass for the right and left gastrocnemius muscle declines drastically, to about 45 percent, by the end of 2 years (table 2-2). Moreover, very old male Sprague-Dawley rats characteristically exhibit a muscular-dystrophy-like syndrome of the hind limbs. Extremely old males are reduced to a creeping motion, dragging these limbs behind them. In the longer-lived CFN rat, there is no significant change in gastrocnemius muscle mass with old age, neither on an absolute nor on a muscle weight to body weight basis. Gutmann (1977) reported similar findings in more recent studies of rat and mouse skeletal muscle. The combination of progressively increasing disuse of skeletal muscle by

Table 2-2
Changes in Muscle Mass and Mg-Activated ATPase Activity of the Gastrocnemius Muscle in the Male White Rat

Strain	*Age (Mo)*	*Muscle Weight (Gm)*	*ATPase Activity*
Sprague-Dawley	10	4.6	0.69
	17	4.6	0.51
	26	2.5	0.24
CFN	8	4.1	0.79
	18	4.9	0.58
	26	4.6	0.37

ATPase activity is expressed as μgm P released in 15 min per gm of fresh muscle mass.

the aging individual, and senescence of the neural supply and neuromotor mechanism must contribute to this muscular atrophy.

With diminished muscle mass there is an observable concomitant increase in collagen content and, more significantly, the replacement of some muscle fibers with adipose cells. A great deal of the increased fat content in older skeletal muscle is in the form of cholesterol (Korenchevsky, 1961). Hrachovec and Rockstein (1962) similarly reported a 100 percent increase in the cholesterol content of the gastrocnemius muscle from young to very old age for male Sprague-Dawley and male CFN rats.

One other microanatomical change in muscle is the development and increase of lipofuscin. This golden-brown "aging" pigment is particularly prominent in striated and smooth muscle as well as nerve cells (Gutmann, 1977) in older animals and humans. In humans Strehler et al. (1959) reported a 100 mg per heart per year increase in the lipofuscin content of the human in autopsy tissues from 156 individuals.

Biochemical Changes

Invertebrate Striated Muscle

It is always difficult to establish a cause and effect relationship for concomitant events. In the case of aging muscle, the decline, with age, in the effectiveness of muscle contraction is accompanied by comparable changes in the biochemical components (Gutmann, 1977). What is especially significant, however, is the known changes in enzyme systems that supply the energy for contraction. In an early study, Rockstein and Brandt (1961) reported a drop in activity of the Mg^{++}-activated adenosine triphosphatase (ATPase) by 65 percent for very old male Sprague-Dawley rats (table 2-2). Comparative biochemical studies were made in our laboratory to determine what biochemical events accompany aging of striated muscle. The studies involved two enzyme systems concerned with the delivery of energy for contraction in such muscle; Ca^{++}-activated actomyosin ATPase, the enzyme responsible for the instant release of energy in the contraction process, and ATP-regenerating (arginine or creatine) phosphokinase is responsible for the rapid restoration of the ATP split during muscle contraction. As the peak of flight ability (duration of flight) occurs at one day post emergence, so does the peak activity level of the actomyosin ATPase in the flight muscle (figure 2-1) (Rockstein and Chesky, 1973). As flight ability declines (table 2-1), the activity of this enzyme decline in a steady progressive fashion.

The activity of arginine phosphokinase in the thorax shows a virtually parallel age-related distribution, falling precipitously from its peak level at two days through the fourth day, and more slowly thereafter (Baker, 1975). There is

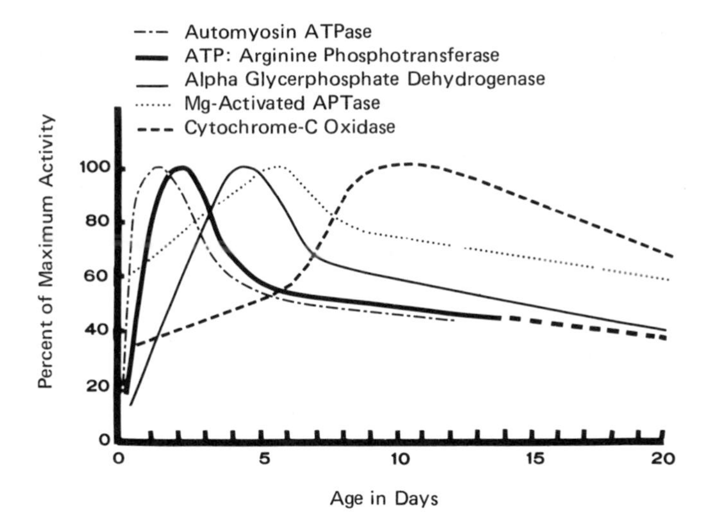

Figure 2-1. Sequence of age-related changes in enzyme activity in the thoracic flight muscle of the male house fly *Musca domestica L.* (Rockstein, Brandt, Baker, and Chesky, unpublished).

a similar pattern of age-related sequential biochemical events involving the extramitrochondrial alpha-glycerophosphate dehydrogenase, and the mitochondrial Mg++-ATPase, and cytochrome *c* oxidase. This is related to failing flight ability, wing loss, and known changes in mitochondrial size and number in the flight muscle of the male fly (Rockstein, 1972).

Vertebrate Striated Muscle

Bárány (1967) reported that the speed of skeletal muscle contraction is directly related to the level of Ca++-activated actomyosin ATPase. This relation was further substantiated by Gutmann and Syrový as regards lower levels of this enzyme in skeletal muscle fibers (1974) and different muscles of aged Wistar rats (1970). In humans, Taylor, Essén and Saltin (1974) found that the activity of this enzyme was directly proportional to the percentage of fast fibers for three different kinds of leg muscle in several male athletes and nonathletes.

Heart Muscle

Like any other organ, normal heart function depends on an ordered sequence of linked biochemical processes concerned with contraction of the myocardium.

Harris (1975), a prominent cardiologist and clinical gerontologist, has suggested that the basis for heart failure in aged persons should be sought in biochemical defects of the aged heart. Accordingly, one might expect that the reduced cardiac output in lower animals and humans, discussed earlier, would be accompanied by comparable lower levels of myocardial actomyosin ATPase activity. Alpert, Gale, and Taylor (1967) reported a 15 percent drop in right ventricular myocardial actomyosin ATPase activity in male Simonson rats from 200 to 1100 days. Moreover, they found a significant correlation between the lowered enzyme activity and (diminished) velocity of shortening (at all loads) of the same heart muscle. In our ongoing studies on biochemical aging of the male Fischer rat heart, we found that the ventricular actomyosin ATPase activity is at its peak level 1 month after weaning (figure 2-2). Its activity then falls steadily to a minimum level (representing a 25 percent reduction from the peak level) by 16 months (Chesky and Rockstein, 1977). At the same time the extractable actomyosin protein content (50 mg per gram) of heart muscle remains constant

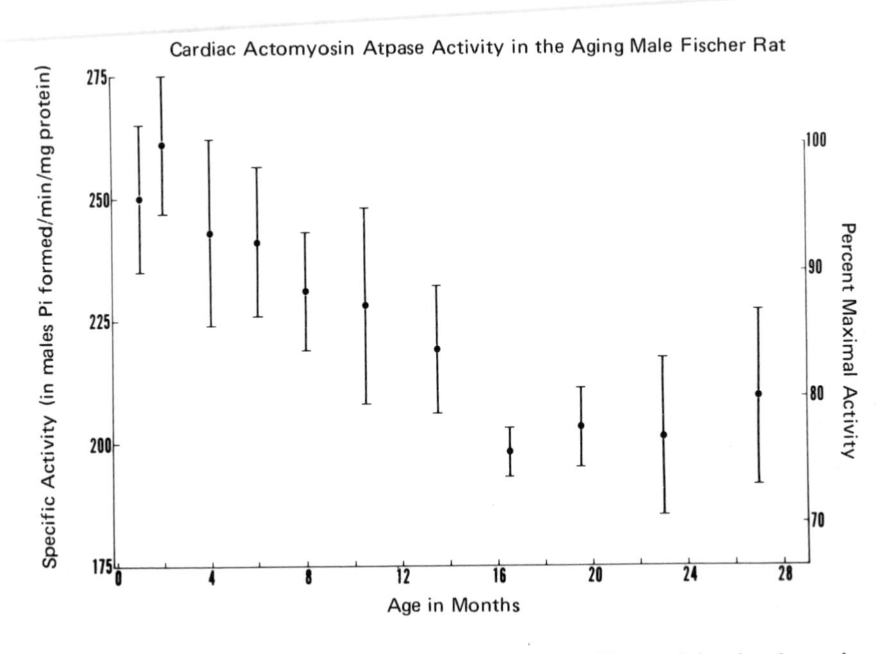

Figure 2-2. Myocardial actomyosin ATPase specific activity in the aging male Fischer rat. Results are shown as mean values ± SD. (Chesky, J.A. and Rockstein, M. Reduced myocardial actomyosin adenosine triphosphatase activity in the aging male Fischer rat. *Cardiovascular Research*, Vol. 11, 1977, pp. 242-246. Reprinted with permission.)

throughout (figure 2-3). An explanation was sought for lowered actomyosin ATPase activity in older animals in the face of a constant extractable actomyosin protein. Actomyosin from the myocardium of 2-month old versus 12-month old male Fischer rats was assayed for ATPase activity for varying concentrations of Ca++. At all concentrations above 2×10^{-4} (figure 2-4) the specific activity of this enzyme is not only higher for the heart of the young rat, but becomes increasingly higher as the Ca++ concentration is increased. Calcium is known to participate in muscle contraction by binding the troponin, thus suppressing the normal inhibition of the contractile protein ATPase in resting muscle by native tropomyosin (the troponin-tropomyosin complex). These data therefore suggest that our previously observed lower myocardial actomyosin ATPase activity in older Fischer rats is due to the diminished capability of older animals to overcome tropomyosin inhibition of the contractile protein ATPase (Rockstein, Chesky, and Lopez, 1978).

We have just completed our most recent study on the enzyme creatine phosphokinase (CPK) which is responsible for the resynthesis of the ATP hydrolyzed by the ATPase during contraction. As actomyosin ATPase, the myocardial CPK of the male Fischer rat falls steadily from its peak at 1 month

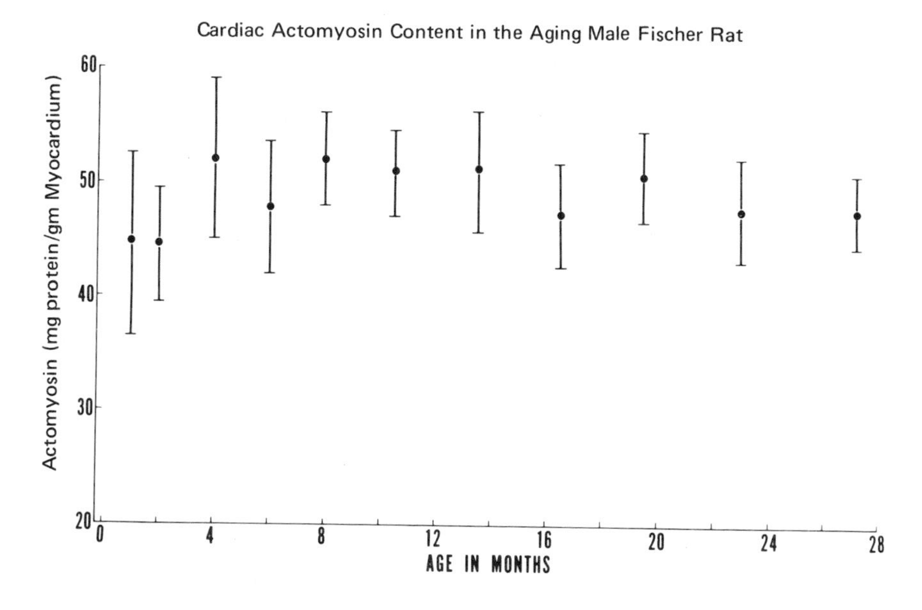

Figure 2-3. Extractable myocardial actomyosin content in the aging male Fischer rat. Results are shown as mean values ± SD. (Rockstein and Chesky, unpublished.)

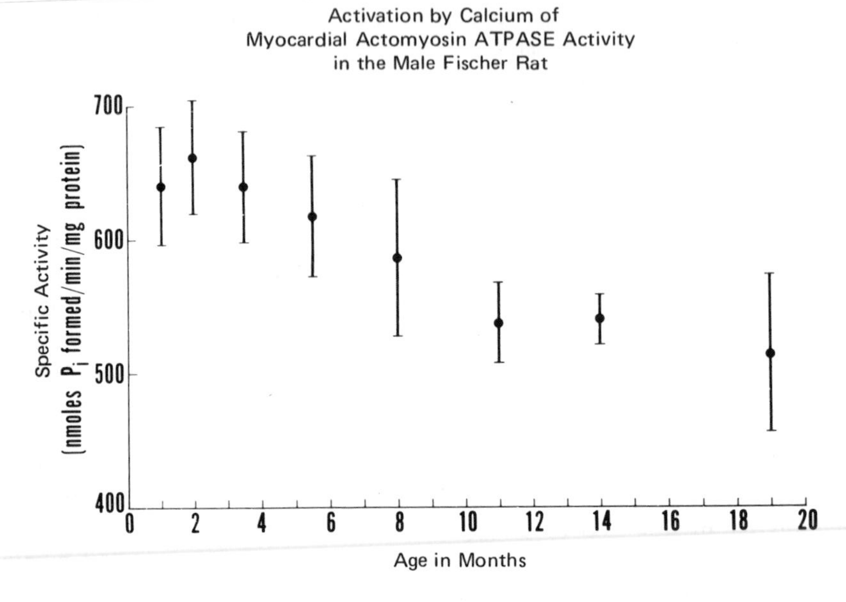

Figure 2-4. The effect of varying calcium concentrations on myocardial actomyosin ATPase specific activity. (Rockstein, M., Chesky, J., and Lopez, T. Calcium sensitivity of myocardial actomyosin ATPase activity in young and mature male Fischer rats. *Mechanisms of Aging and Development*, Vol. 8, 1978, pp. 413-416. Reprinted with permission.)

Table 2-3
Myocardial Creatine Phosphokinase Specific Activity in the Aging Male Fischer Rat (Rockstein and Chesky unpublished)

Age (Mo)	*No. of Experiments*	*Heart Wt (Mg)*	*Body Wt (Gm)*	*Heart Wt / Body Wt*	*Enzyme Activity*[a]
1	6	0.28	86	3.26	653
2	9	0.49	174	2.82	671
3-4	11	0.67	268	2.50	643
5-6	7	0.73	295	2.47	623
7-9	10	0.78	320	2.43	578
10-15	16	0.80	321	2.49	537
16-24	11	0.81	315	2.57	506

[a]*n* moles of Pi/min/mg extracted protein.

post weaning to a low (25 percent less than its original peak) by 12 months of age (table 2-3) (Rockstein, Chesky, and Lopez, 1978).

As a postmitotic tissue, muscle represents an excellent model for the study of normal aging of organisms and their parts. Functionally, there is an overall decline in force, vigor and speed of contraction. At the fiber or cellular level, such failing functional effectiveness with age is reflected anatomically in an increasingly reduced muscle mass due to both loss in number and loss in size of its component fibers. Comparable biophysical changes are likewise observable in increased latency and in longer contraction and relaxation times. Biochemically, in a number of studies the enzyme system responsible primarily for the energy metabolism of muscle contraction, Ca^{++}-activated actomyosin ATPase, has been shown to experience a progressive fall in activity both in striated skeletal and heart muscle with advancing age and failing function. In more limited comparative studies the corresponding ATP-regenerating phosphokinase has been shown to follow a parallel course of decline with age.

References

Alpert, N.R., Gale, H.H., and Taylor, N. The Effect of Age on Contractile Protein ATPase Activity and Velocity of Shortening. In R.D. Tanz, F. Kavaler, and J. Roberts, (Eds.), *Factors Influencing Myocardial Contractility* (New York: Academic, 1967), pp. 127-133.

Baker, G.T. Age-related Activity Changes in Arginine Phosphokinase in the House Fly, *Musca domestica L. J. Gerontol* 30:163-169, 1975.

Bárány, M. ATPase Activity of Myosin Correlated with Speed of Muscle Shortening. *J Gen Physiol* (Suppl) 50:197-218, 1967.

Birren, J.E. Principles of Research on Aging. In J.E. Birren (Ed.), *Handbook of Aging and the Individual* (Chicago: University of Chicago, 1960), pp. 13-14.

Brandfonbrener, M., Landowne, M., and Shock, N.W. Changes in Cardiac Output with Age. *Circulation* 12:557-566, 1955.

Chesky, J.A., and Rockstein, M. Reduced Myocardial Actomyosin Adenosine Triphosphatase Activity in the Aging Male Fischer Rat. *Cardiovasc Res* 11:242-246, 1977.

Gutmann, E. Muscle. In C.E. Finch and L. Hayflick (Eds.), *Handbook of the Biology of Aging* (New York: Van Nostrand, 1977), pp. 445-469.

Gutmann, E. and Hanzlíková, V. *Age Changes in the Neuromuscular System.* (Bristol, England: Scientechnica Ltd, 1972).

Gutmann, E. and Syrový, I. Contraction Properties and Myosin-ATPase Activity of Fast and Slow Senile Muscles of the Rat. *Gerontologia*: 20:239-244, 1974.

Harris, R. Cardiac Changes with Age. In R. Goldman and M. Rockstein (Eds.), *Symposium on the Physiology and Pathology of Human Aging* (New York: Academic, 1975), pp. 109-122.

Heller, L.J., and Whitehorn, W.V. Age-associated Alterations in Myocardial Contractile Properties. *Am J Physiol* 222:1613-1619, 1972.

Hrachovec, J.P., and Rockstein, M. Biochemical Criteria for Senescence in Mammalian Structures. I. Age Changes of the Cholesterol to Phospholipid Ratio in the Rat Liver and Skeletal Muscle. *Gerontologia* (Basel) 6:237-248, 1962.

Korenchevsky, V. *Physiological and Pathological Aging* (New York: Hafner, 1961), pp. 118-119.

Lakatta, E.G., Gerstenblith, G., Angell, C.S., Shock, N.W., and Weisfeldt, M.L. Prolonged Contraction Duration in Aged Myocardium. *J Clin Invest* 55:61-68, 1975.

Rockstein, M. The Role of Molecular Genetic Mechanisms in the Aging Process. In M. Rockstein and G.T. Baker (Eds.), *Molecular Genetic Mechanisms in Aging and Development* (New York: Academic, 1972), pp. 1-10.

Rockstein, M., and Bhatnagar, P.L. Duration and Frequency of Wing Beat in the Aging House Fly, *Musca domestica L. Biol Bull* 131:479-486, 1966.

Rockstein, M. and Brandt, K. Changes in Phosphorus Metabolism of the Gastrocnemius Muscle in Aging White Rats. *Proc Soc Exp Biol Med* 107:377-380, 1961.

Rockstein, M. and Chesky, J. Age-related Changes in Natural Actomyosin in the Male House Fly *Musca domestica L. J Gerontol* 28:455-459, 1973.

Rockstein, M., Chesky, J., and Lopez, T. Calcium Sensitivity of Myocardial Actomyosin ATPase Activity in Young and Mature Male Fischer Rats. *Mech Aging Dev* 8:413-416, 1978.

Rothbaum, D.A., Shaw, D.J., Angell, C.S., and Shock, N.W. Cardiac Performance in the Unanesthetized Senescent Male Rat. *J. Gerontol* 28:287-292, 1973.

Simonson, E. Physical Capacities. In J.T. Freeman (Ed.), *Clinical Features of the Older Patient* (Springfield: Charles C. Thomas, 1965), pp. 76-79.

Strehler, B.L., Mark, D.D., Mildvan, A.S., and Gee, M.V. Rate and Magnitude of Age Pigment Accumulation in the Human Myocardium. *J Gerontol* 14:430-439, 1959.

Syrový, I. and Gutmann, E. Changes in Speed of Contraction and ATPase Activity in Striated Muscle During Old Age. *Exp Geront* 5:31-35, 1970.

Taylor, A.W., Essen, B., and Saltin, B. Myosin ATPase in Skeletal Muscle of Healthy Men. *Acta Physio Scand* 91:568-570, 1974.

Welford, A.T. Psychomotor Performance. In J.E. Birren (Ed.), *Handbook of Aging and the Individual* (Chicago: University of Chicago, 1960), pp. 565-566.

3 Explorations into the Aging of Skeletal-Dental Tissues: An Ultrastructural Study of Aging Cementum

Edgar A. Tonna

Cementum formation is a continuous process that occurs throughout the life of an organism (Zander and Hurzeler, 1958; Louridis, Kyrkanidou, and Demetriou, 1972). This process is essential to mouse and human alike to compensate for eruptive events in response to occlusal attrition. Cementum is accreted to a point where, in older individuals, hypercementosis, excementosis, and cementicle formation become prevalent. Ankylosis of cementum with alveolar bone can also be found (Tonna, 1973a, 1976). Current knowledge reveals that, compared with cells of other parodontal tissues, cementocytes normally exhibit the lowest proliferative capacity (Stahl, Tonna, and Weiss, 1969; Tonna, Weiss, and Stahl, 1972). This low capacity is also exhibited in response to trauma at all ages (Stahl, Tonna, and Weiss, 1968, 1969, 1970; Tonna, Stahl, and Weiss, 1969; Tonna and Stahl, 1973, 1974). Once cementocytes are formed, as in the case of osteocytes, no cellular division occurs. Cementum is generally acellular everywhere it occurs, except at root apexes. Published autoradiographic studies indicate that with increasing age the process of cementum formation at root apexes becomes essentially acellular, whereas acellular cementum may become cellular in response to trauma (Tonna, 1976).

In an electron microscopic study of the teeth of young rats, Jande and Bélanger (1970) reported that cementocytes were observed to go through a complete series of degenerative changes and death. An ultrastructural investigation was undertaken to study changes that take place in cementocytes concomitant with aging in the short-lived mouse model, as well as the aging of cementoblasts and their relationship with the surface of cementum. Investigation of the aging cemental surface was encouraged by the results of a recent study (Tonna, 1978) that showed that the membrane-like arrangement of osteoblasts on the surface of aging bone breaks down. This break-down resulted in the loss of cellular control and biofeedback essential to bone accretion, resorption and, in part, mineral homeostasis. As a consequence, irregular mineralization occurred at the bone surfaces. A similar situation was observed at the perilacunar surfaces of osteocytes (Tonna, 1978). Cementum represents a mineralized tissue that

---

Research was supported by NIA grant No. AG-00314 of the National Institutes of Health, Bethesda, MD.

grows continuously throughout the life of an individual in an irregular manner reminiscent of old bone surfaces. Could it be that cemental surfaces, as well as the perilacunar surfaces of cementocytes, operate under the absence of full cellular control and that cellular biofeedback is largely insufficient to account for a normal mineralization pattern? The ultrastructural studies described here were undertaken to explore this question.

Materials and Methods

Thirty-six short-lived Brookhaven National Laboratory (BNL) inbred strain of Swiss albino mice, aged 5 to 130 weeks, were used in the study. This animal model has a mean life span of less than 1 year. The mice were bred and maintained on Purina rat and mouse pellets, unrestricted water, at a room temperature of $70 \pm 3^{\circ}$ F throughout their life span.

The animals were perfused with 6.25 percent glutaraldehyde fixative (diluted 1:4 with Millonig's phosphate buffer). The maxillas were removed and primary fixation was continued for 1.5 hours in cold (4°C) 6.25 percent glutaraldehyde (pH 7.4). The samples were washed several times in Millonig's buffer and subsequently decalcified for 8 hours in 10 percent ethylenediamine tetraacetic acid-Millonig's buffer (pH 7.4) at room temperature. Roots of the maxillary first molars were selected for study, but longitudinally in a mesial to distal plane and trimmed. Postfixation was carried out in 0.35 OsM 1 percent osmium tetroxide-Millonig's buffer (pH 7.4) for 1.5 hours. This was followed by alcohol dehydration, Epon 812 embedding, and sectioning with a diamond knife at about 700 to 750° A. Sections were placed on Formvar-coated grids and double stained with a saturated solution of uranyl acetate for 20 minutes, followed by lead citrate for 7 minutes. One-micrometer survey sections were also cut and stained with 1 percent methylene blue prepared in 1 percent sodium borate solution. Electron microscopic sections were examined and photographed with a Siemens Elmiskop IA electron microscope at 80 kilovolt peak (kvp). In addition, whole sagittal sections of teeth were prepared via routine histological techniques. Five-micrometer sections were cut from paraffin blocks and stained with hematoxylin and eosin for bright field microscopy.

Results

The histological survey of sections from progressively older animals exhibited typical age concomitant changes as reported in an earlier study (Tonna, 1973a). These changes included hypercementosis, excementosis, cementicle formation and ankylosis, each becoming more severe with increasing age. Cemental accretion also became more irregular. Cementocytes revealed pyknosis and hyperchromasia of nuclei, degeneration, and death, even in young mice. Empty lacunae were also seen. The process became more severe with age. Since turnover of cementoblasts to cementocytes was low in young mice, and nonexistent in older mice, together with cementocyte death in progress at all times, the accretion of large amounts of cementum in older animals was acellular. The arrangement of cementoblasts at the cemental surface was perpendicular to oblique along the periodontium. At the root apexes only a few cementoblasts were in parallel position with the cemental surface.

Electron Microscopy of Osteocytes

The ultrastructural survey of osteocytes revealed few viable cells at 5 weeks of age. These cells were active in matrix formation and were characterized by the presence of a functional nucleus and abundant rough endoplasmic reticulum whose cisternae were distended and filled with secretory products. These cells possessed well-formed mitochondria, several lysosomes, and abundant Golgi vesicles and lamellae. The absence of lacunae and discrete osmiophilic laminae are indicative of young, matrix-producing cells (figure 3-1). Pyknotic, hyperchromatic nuclei of small size were observed in a larger proportion of the small total cell number that makes up the cellular cementum. These cells were scattered, but more prevalent in deeper aspects of the root cementum (figure 3-2). Mitochondria were few and swollen, the Golgi complex was reduced to an insignificant structure, rough endoplasmic reticulum was represented by occasional short lengths, and few scattered ribosomes were present. Vacuoles and granular pigment were sometimes observed. Their reduced cytoplasmic size left large lacunae lined by discrete osmiophilic laminae as evidence of past phases of cementoplasis or ongoing cementoplasis evidenced by the absence of the limiting osmiophilic laminae. Empty lacunae were uncommon at this age.

By 52 weeks, the cementum was studded with hyperchromatic, pyknotic nucleic, and abundant empty lacunae were in evidence. The better preserved cells revealed obvious degenerative changes as well (figure 3-3). Some cells exhibited abundant lysosomes and a striking loss of rough endoplasmic reticulum. Prior to total cell destruction, cytoplasmic swelling accompanied cell necrosis (figure 3-4). Eventually, complete lysis of cells occurred, filling the lacunae with a brei consisting of cellular fragments (figure 3-5). Lacunar "scars" became more abundant with age (figure 3-6). Some cells showed from one to several large lipofuscin granules (age pigment) (figure 7A). These cellular events were more abundant with increasing age. The process of cementoclasis is minimal at all ages. Multiple osmiophilic laminae numbering more than two layers were not encountered at any age at the perilacunar surfaces. At the electron microscopic level much of the cementum deposited beyond 52 weeks of age was acellular.

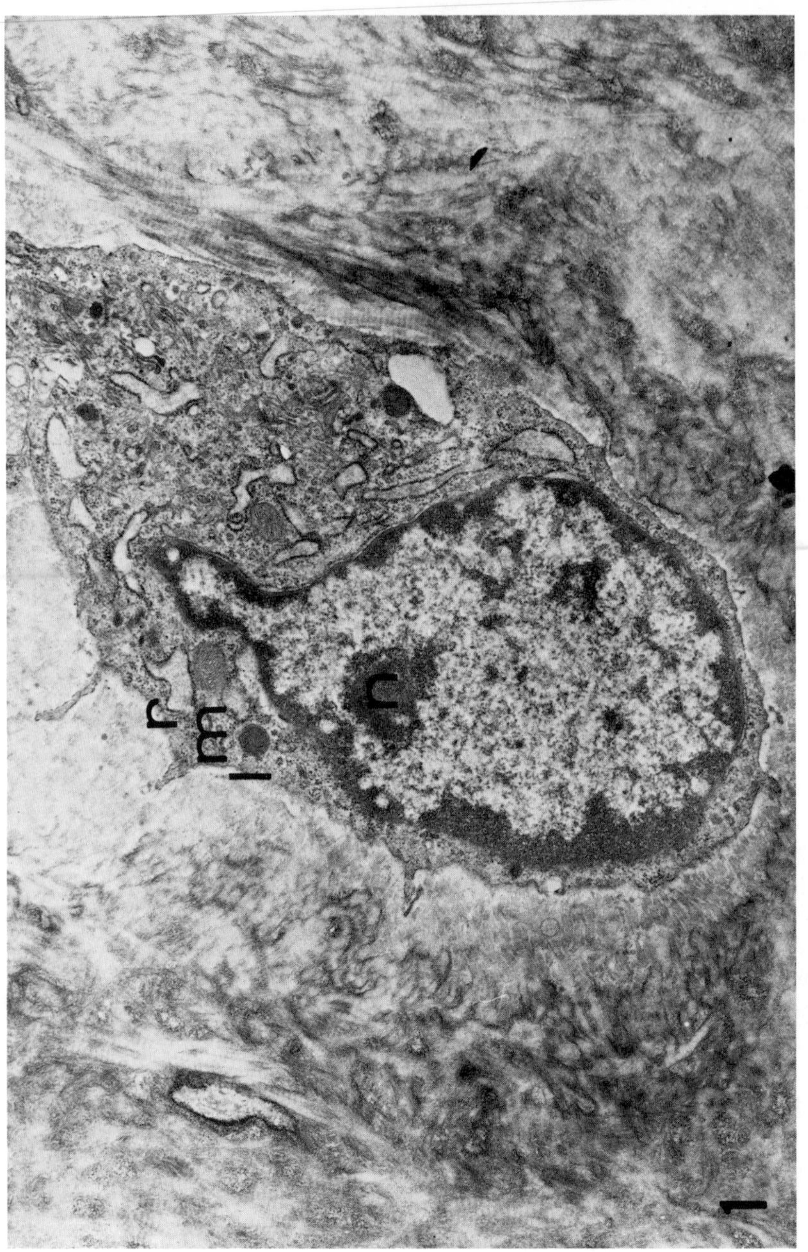

Figure 3-1. Electron micrograph shows a cementocyte from a 5-week-old mouse actively producing cementum matrix. No lacunae are formed. The cell reveals small mitochondria (*m*), lysosomes (*l*), rough endoplasmic reticulum (*r*) with distended cisternae, an abundance of free ribosomes, and an extensive Golgi system (*arrows*). The nucleus is large with peripherally located euchromatin and a prominent nucleolus (*n*). (Original magnification × 5,200.)

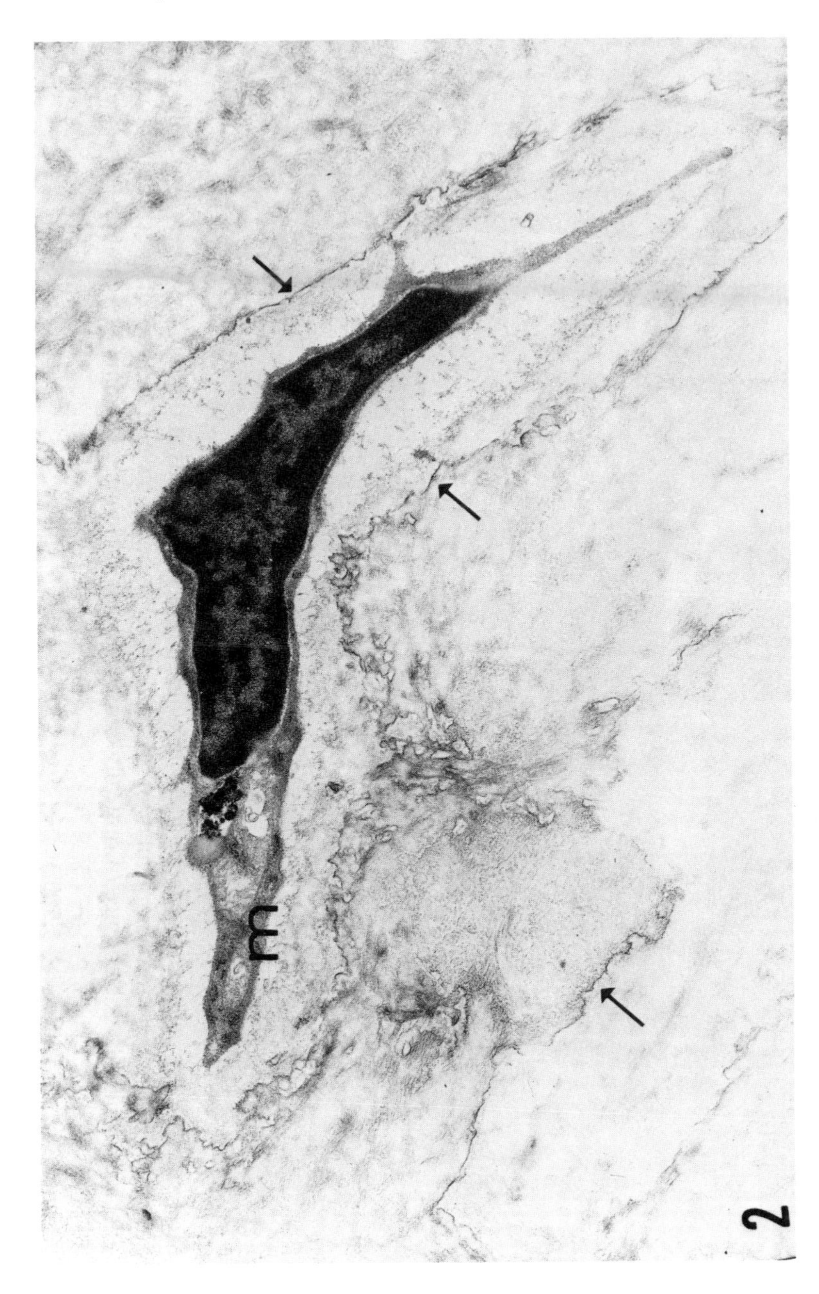

Figure 3-2. Cementocyte from a 5-week-old mouse undergoing degenerative changes. The nucleus is small, pyknotic, and hyperchromatic, while the cytoplasm is significantly reduced. The cell is practically devoid of organelles. Mitochondrial structures are swollen with disrupted cristae (*m*). Vacuoles and granules may be seen. The lacuna was originally wider, but new cementum matrix has narrowed its space. Earlier limits of matrix production are demarcated by electron dense osmiophilic laminae (*arrows*). (Original magnification × 5,200.)

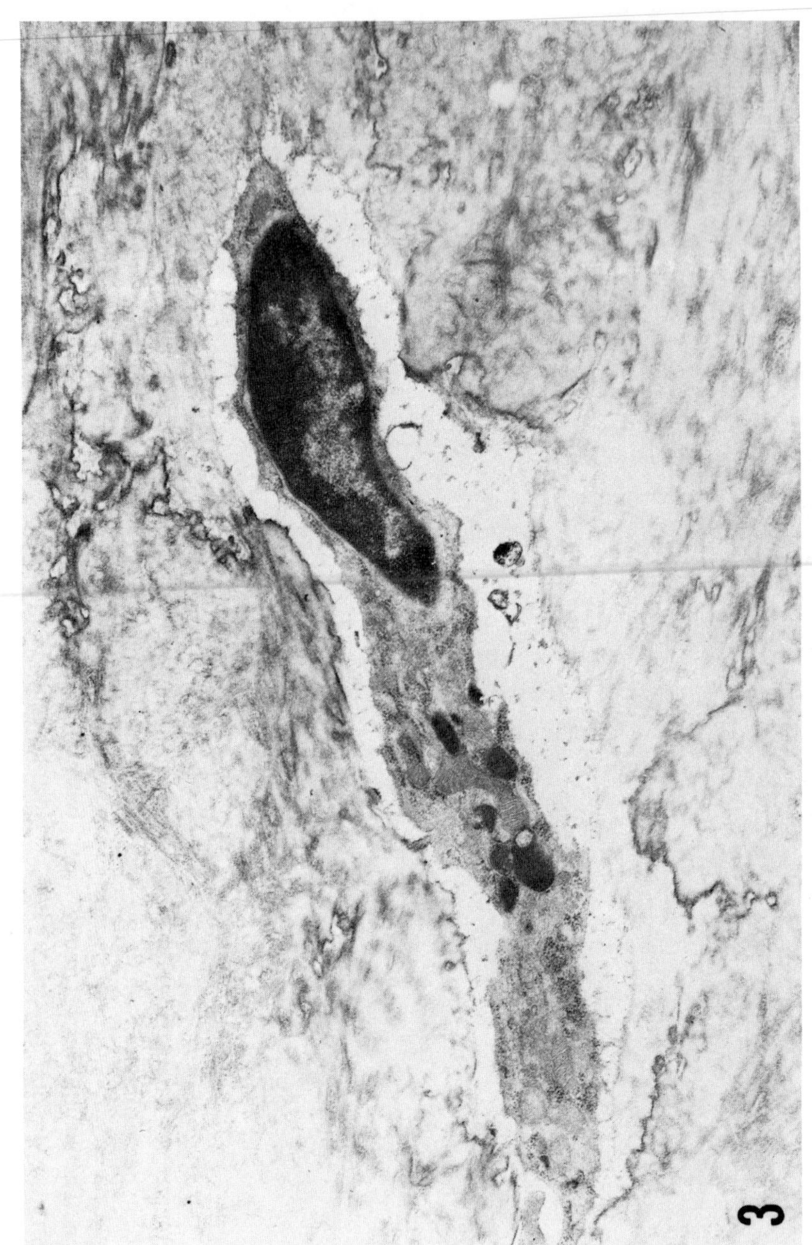

Figure 3-3. Moderately active cementocyte from a 52-week-old mouse. Viable cells at this age are generally smaller than at 5 weeks of age. The full complement of organelles are found. Some matrix production is still in progress. This is evidenced by the absence of optically dense osmiophilic laminae at some stretches of the perilacunar walls.
(Original magnification × 5,200.)

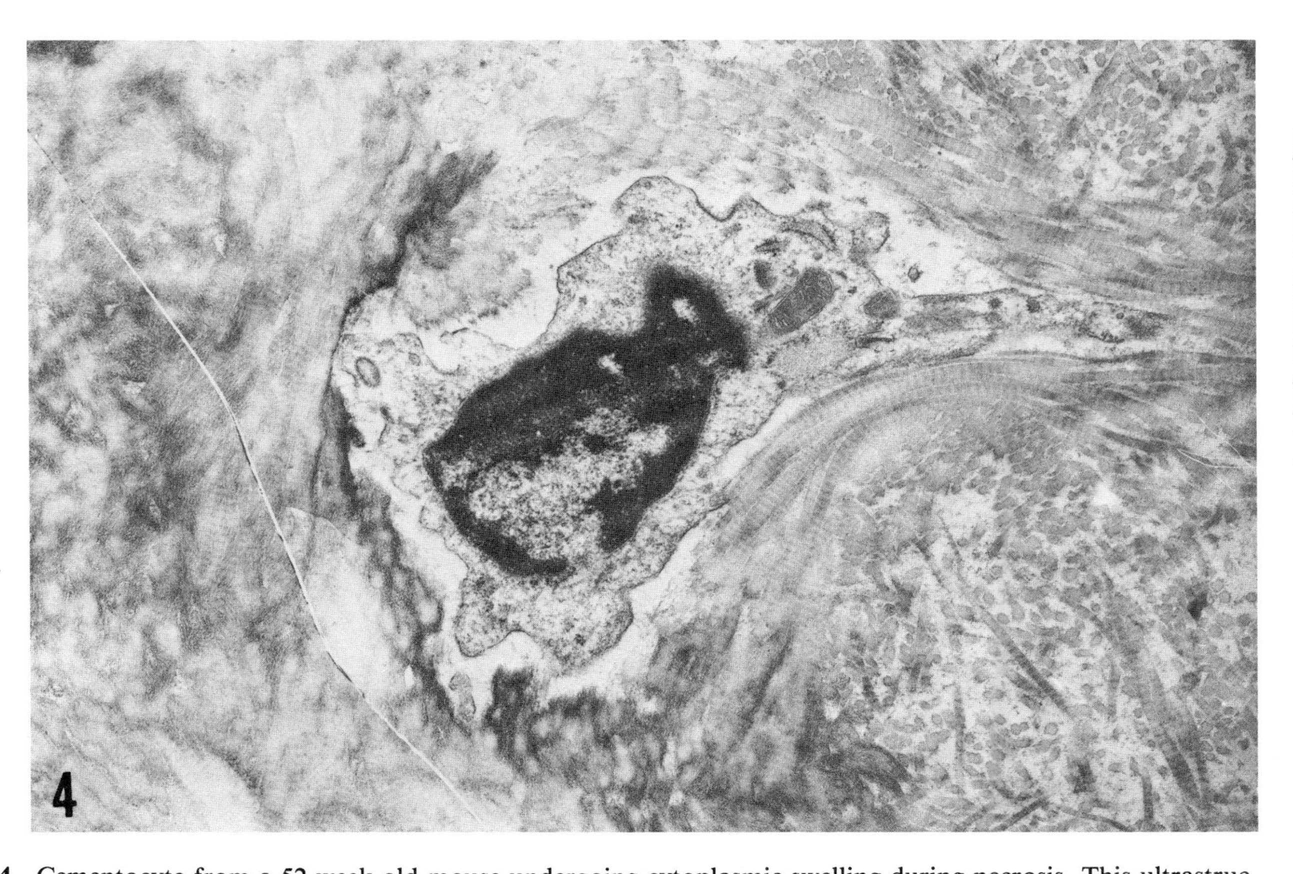

Figure 3-4. Cementocyte from a 52-week-old mouse undergoing cytoplasmic swelling during necrosis. This ultrastructural change preceeds cell lysis and death. (Original magnification × 7,800.)

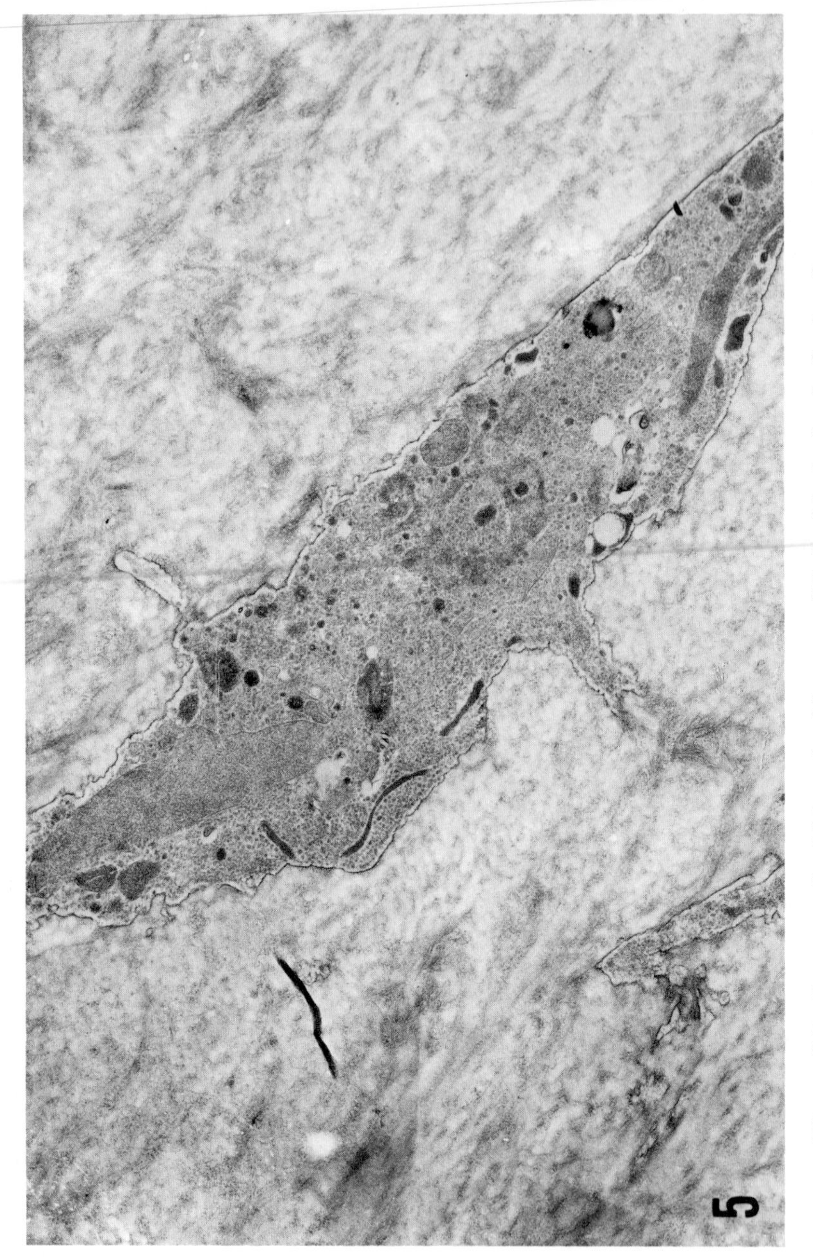

Figure 3-5. Lacuna of a 104-week-old mouse filled with the brei of a lysed cementocyte. (Original magnification × 5,200.)

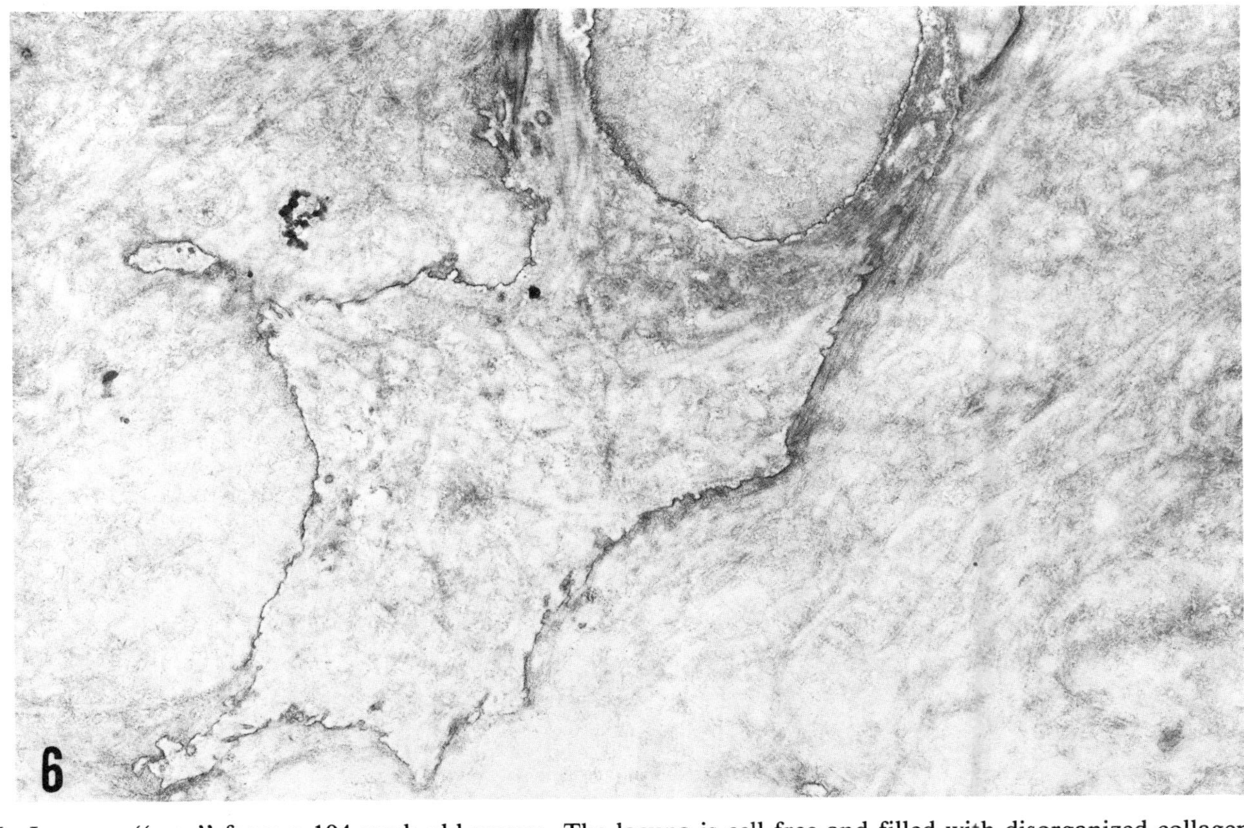

Figure 3-6. Lacunar "scar" from a 104-week-old mouse. The lacuna is cell-free and filled with disorganized collagen fibers and fiber bundles.
(Original magnification × 5,200.)

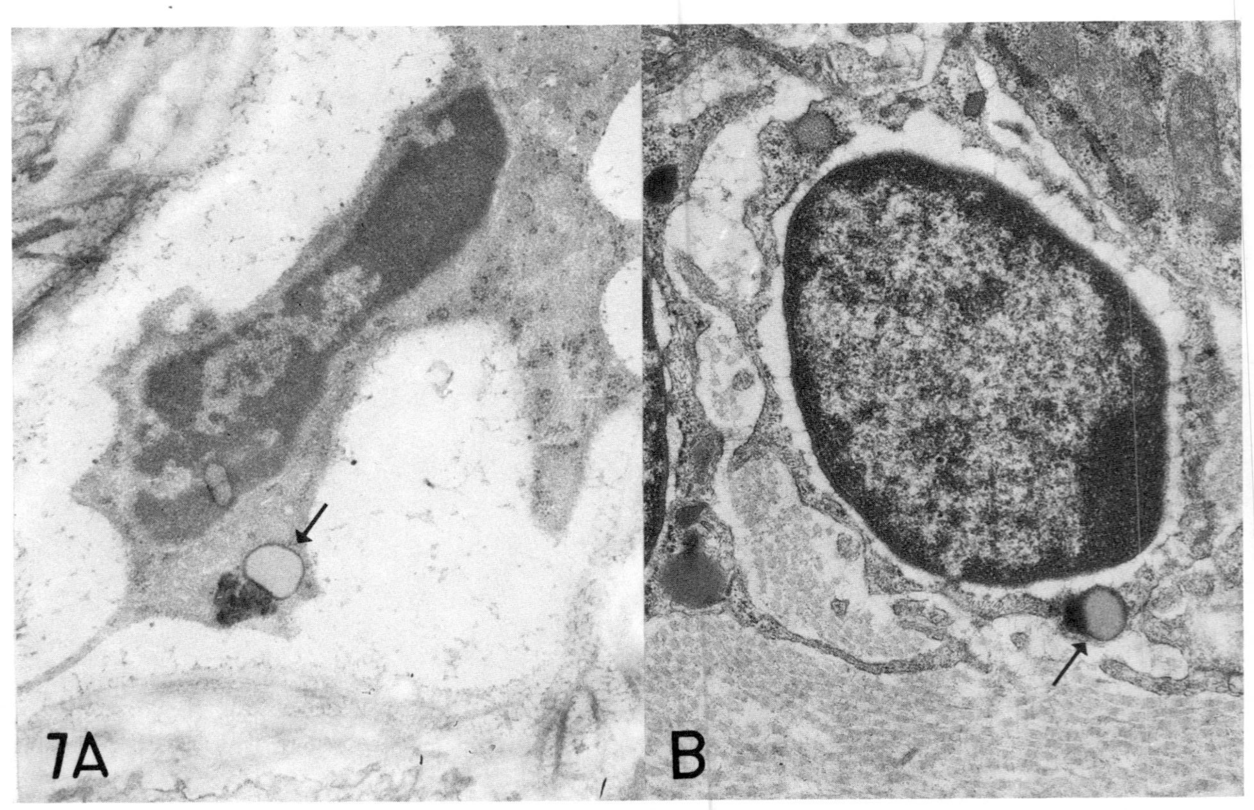

Figure 3-7. Cementocyte (A) from a 104-week-old mouse and cementoblast (B) from a 52-week-old mouse, each with a distinctive lipofuscin granule (*arrows*). (Original magnification × 5,200.)

Electron Microscopy of Cemental Surfaces

The ultrastructural changes associated with aging cementoblasts will be covered in a subsequent publication. In general, however, the cementoblasts of young mice, which are the precursors of cementocytes, were larger. Their cytoplasmic organelles were more abundant. The ground substance was endowed with obvious microfilaments coursing along the plasma membrane and throughout the cytoplasm. Free ribosomes were numerous and widely scattered. The cells were oriented vertically or obliquely and were widely separated by large bundles of periodontal collagen fibers (figure 3-8). Consequently, the cells were generally not in contact with one another. Some cells exhibited several, and sometimes long, cytoplasmic processes. No attempt was made at forming a membrane-like cellular cover over the cemental surface. With increasing age typical changes were observed including reduction in nuclear and cytoplasmic mass, fewer organelles, smaller mitochondria, simplified Golgi complex, minimized free ribosomes and rough endoplasmic reticulum, and reduced matrical collagen synthetic activity, resulting in a greater spacing between cells (figure 3-9). A number of cells exhibited one to several large lipofuscin granules, as well as lysosomes (figure 7B). Cellular degeneration was minimal, but cellular death was not observed. In progressively older animals, fewer very large matrix-producing cells were seen. Active matrix-producing cells, however, were still apparent (figure 3-10).

The nature of the cell-free cemental surface was marked by the continuity of nonmineralized periodontal collagen fiber bundles. The mineralized cementum (in demineralized samples) was characterized by an electron-opaque granular filling surrounding the collagen fibers. Discrete islands of electron-opaque material were seen at the surface. These regions appeared to coalesce, forming the more dense cemental matrix (figure 3-8). This cemental composition was also observed in very old animals, even when the cells lying immediately above exhibited little matrix-forming activity. Elsewhere, especially at the apical foramen, the surface was characterized by an irregular deposition of cementum, producing a highly beaded feature (figure 3-11). On the periodontal side, microcementicle formation was often observed. These structures appeared to form in union with the cemental surface. In many instances a prominent, centrally placed, optically dense structure (round in diameter) was noted (figure 3-12). Cementum formation was in progress throughout the animal's life.

Discussion

Cementum is a specialized, mineralized tissue of mesodermal origin covering the roots of teeth. It can be considered a modified type of bone (Kotanyi, 1966). Aside from its similarities to bone, some significant qualitative and quantitative differences exist. Both intrinsic and concomitant age changes occur. Acellular

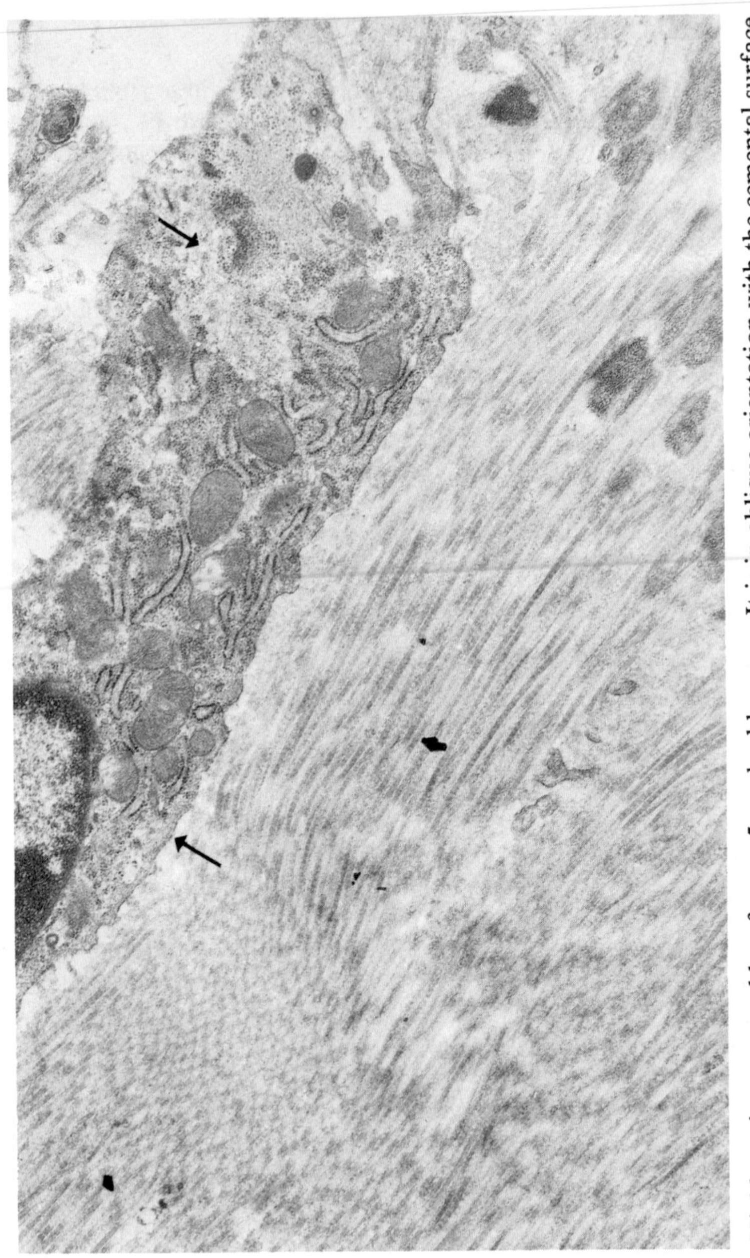

Figure 3-8. Highly active cementoblast from a 5-week-old mouse. It is in oblique orientation with the cemental surface and separated from its neighbors by large bundles of periodontal fibers which are in continuity with the cemental surface. The cell is large, characterized by an abundance of mitochondria and rough endoplasmic reticulum. The cytoplasmic ground substance contains many microfilaments (*arrows*). The mineralized front (this is a demineralized sample) is demarcated by electron dense material associated with the collagen fibers.
(Original magnification × 5,200.)

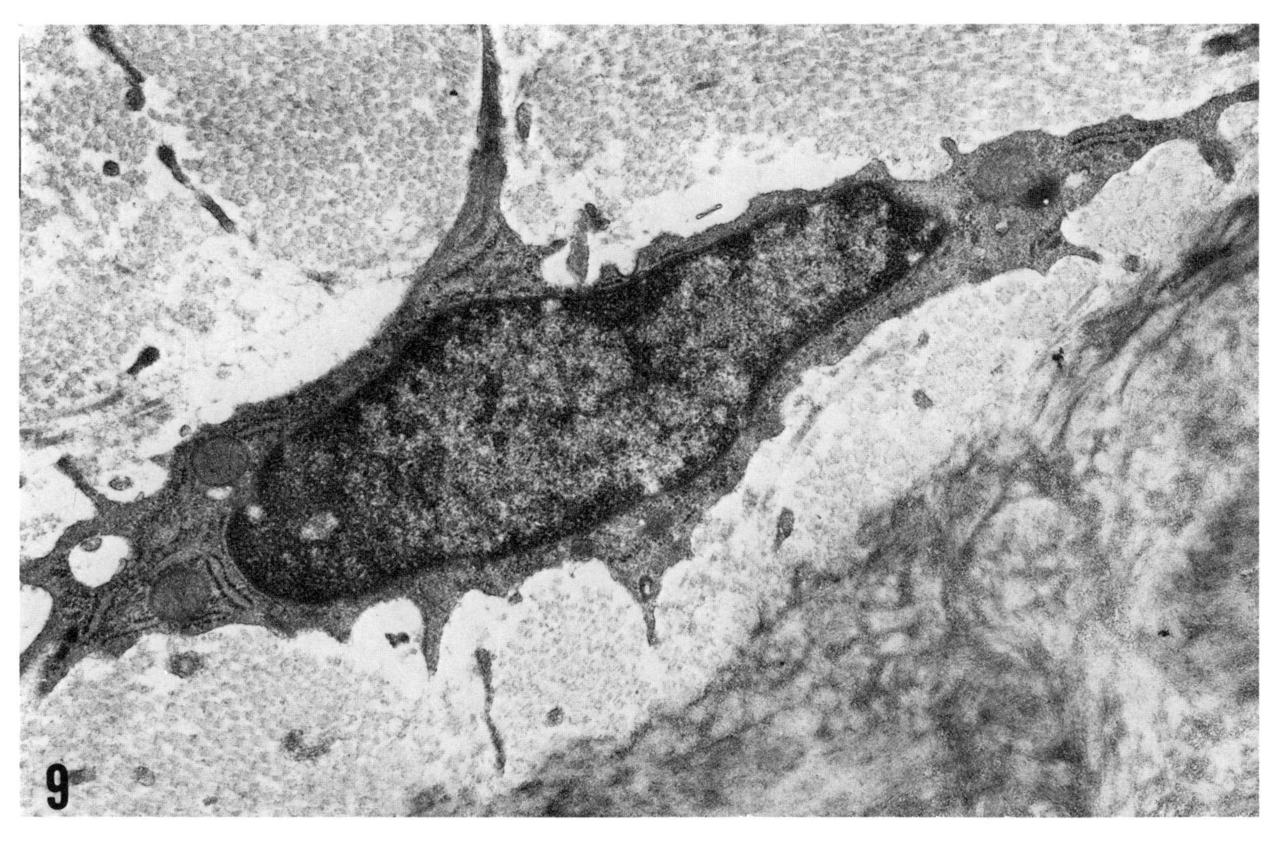

Figure 3-9. A moderately active but aging cementoblast from a 52-week-old mouse (compare with figure 3-8). Nuclear and cytoplasmic reduction is evident, as well as diminished numbers of organelles. (Original magnification × 5,200.)

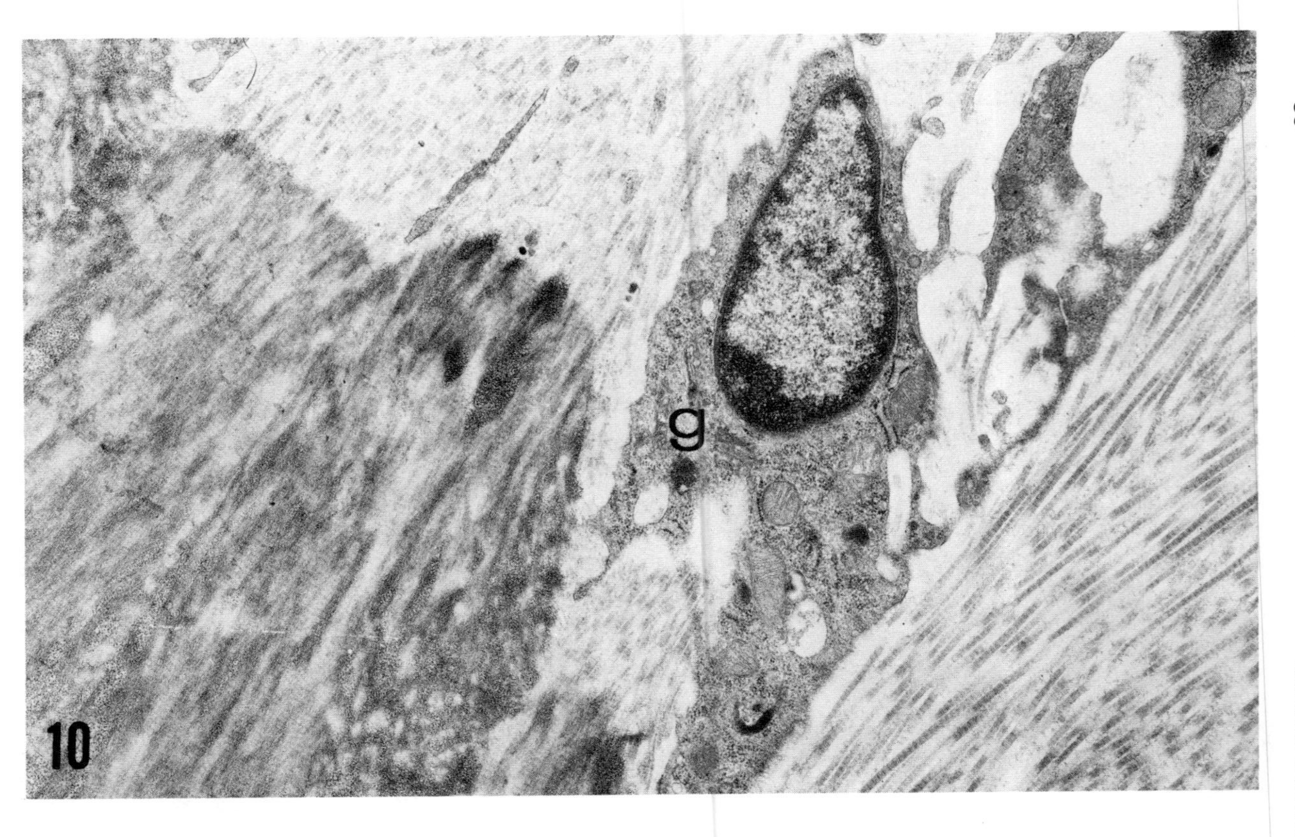

Figure 3-10. Portion of a highly active cementoblast from a 52-week-old mouse. Numerous mitochondria, free ribosomes, and the Golgi complex (*g*) are evident. (Original magnification × 5,200.)

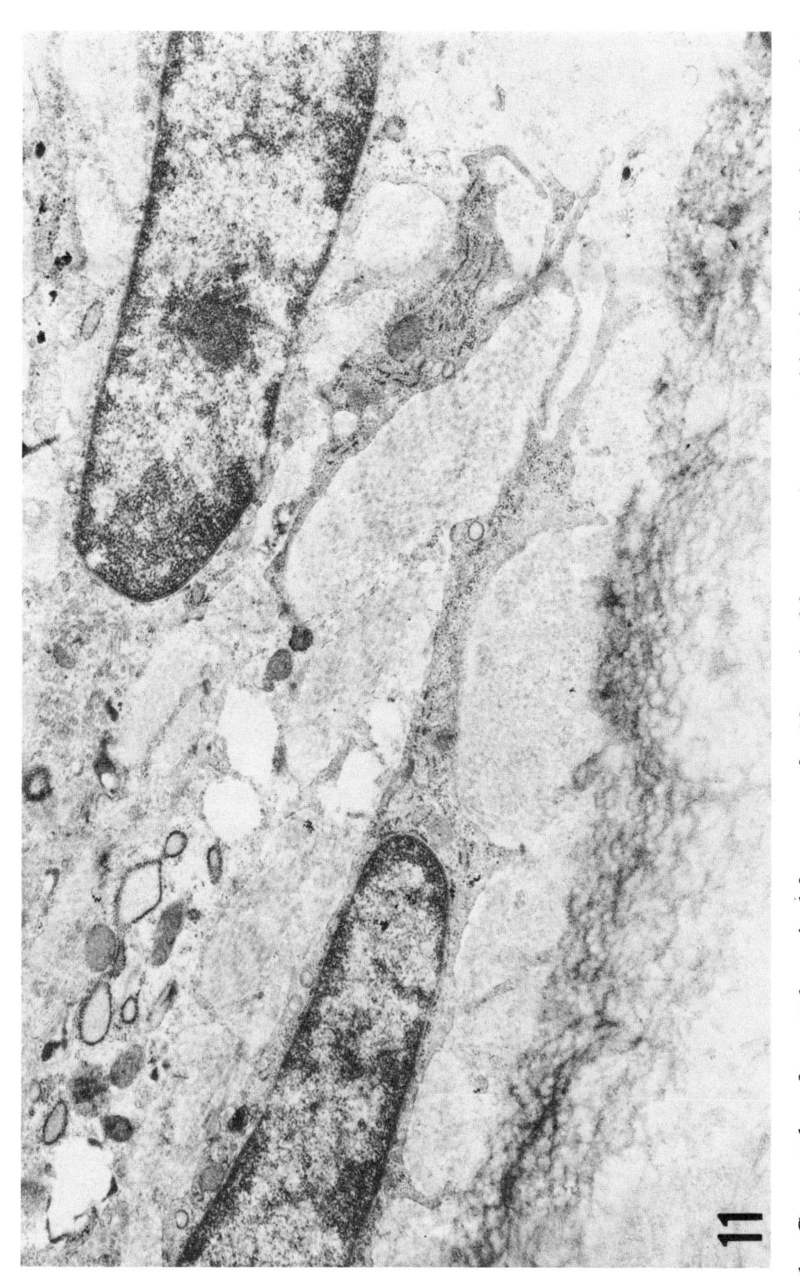

Figure 3-11. Cemental surface at the apical foramen of a 52-week-old mouse. A cementoblast is immediately above, but matrix formation appears to have been completed some time earlier, since the collagen juxtaposition with the surface of the cell is of the large-diameter type, implying maturity. Accretion of cementum at this surface is quite irregular and beaded in appearance. (Original magnification × 5,200.)

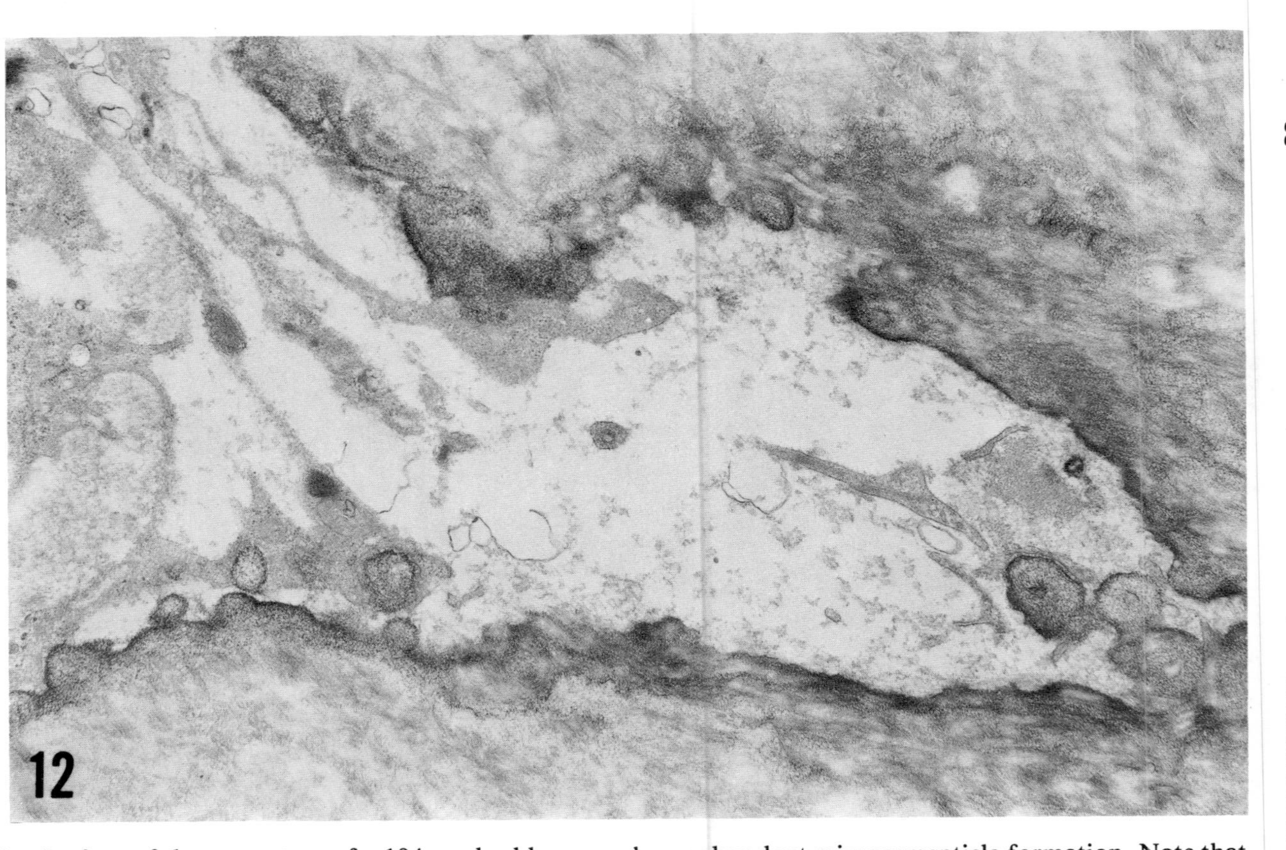

Figure 3-12. Surface of the cementum of a 104-week-old mouse shows abundant microcementicle formation. Note that most structures reveal a centrally positioned, less optically dense component which resembles a fragment of collagen.
(Original magnification × 5,200.)

cementum covers root dentin from the cementoenamel junction to the apexes, but is usually cellular at the apical third. The interradicular surface is covered by acellular cementum in continuity with the cementum elsewhere. Unlike bone, resorption of cementum is not a normal process, yet it is observed often enough in individuals of all ages. Henry and Weinmann (1951) reported that, in a study of 261 human teeth, areas of past and active resorption increased with age. A similar finding was observed in mice with increasing age (Tonna, 1973a). No significant cemental surface resorption was observed in the study described herein. The perilacunar walls of cementocytes exhibited little cemental resorption (cementoclasis), mostly in association with some initial widening of the original lacunar size. On the contrary, ultrastructural evidence clearly showed active cemental accretion (cementoplasis) by cementocytes. In bone, alternate cycles of osteoclasis and osteoplasis are prevalent throughout life at the perilacunar walls of osteocytes. This phenomenon has been observed using various techniques including electron microscopy (Baud, 1968; Vitalli, 1968; Bélanger, 1969; Scherft, 1972; Tonna, 1972a). Cementoplasis, although limited in time, since the cementocyte life span is itself limited, appeared to be the major contribution of cementocytes, and unlike osteocytes, which contribute significantly to mineral homeostasis (Bélanger, 1965; Nichols, 1970), little cyclic activity was observed.

It was observed in the study discussed here that cementocytes underwent extensive degenerative changes, aged, and eventually died as a normal characteristic of their life cycle. In this respect, cementocytes are similar to osteocytes (Jande and Bélanger, 1970; Tonna, 1973b). Once formed, both cementocytes and osteocytes are programmed along a single path leading to death. The process of degeneration appeared to be more rapid in cementocytes than osteocytes. This is perhaps due to a more rapid reduction in the accessibility of nutritive substances and the less successful elimination of waste products of cementocytes. Whatever the reason, cementocyte degeneration and death was often observed in young animals (Jande and Bélanger, 1970). Empty lacunae were also seen in the cementum of 5-week-old mice, but not in bone of that age (Tonna, 1973b). At no time have cementocytes been observed to undergo mitosis or take up ^{3}H-thymidine, a radiotracer used as a marker for cell proliferative capacity (Tonna, Weiss, and Stahl, 1972). Unlike osteocytes which are occasionally released via osteoclasis and destroyed in the process (Tonna, 1972b), cemental resorptive activity was normally insufficient to bring about the release of cementocytes, and these cells remain contained. During aging, they contribute to matrix formation via cementoplasis. This process results in the consolidation of the cementum as a supportive structural unit. Upon completion of this limited contribution, their further presence becomes unessential. The major differences between cementocytes and osteocytes appears to be largely quantitative, but significant qualitative differences also exist, such as the fact that osteocytes contribute significantly to mineral homeostasis, while cementocytes do not.

Ultrastructural age changes in surface cementoblasts were also recognized in this study. These changes were very similar to those recently reported in femoral osteoblasts (Tonna, 1974). With respect to the comparative rate of aging, cementoblasts appeared to remain viable for very long periods of time. Active cells were observed in significant numbers throughout the animal's life span. At femoral bone surfaces the abundance of reasonably active matrix-producing cells is very low in old animals. The surface activity of bone is known to be largely cell mediated and therefore inexorably linked to the functional status of cells and their stage of aging. Inhibition of cellular activity has been shown to be accompanied by the inhibition of calcification (Shipley, Kramer, and Howland, 1926). The successful retainment of viable matrix-producing cells at the cemental surface throughout life is undoubtedly due to the continued functional demands placed on the teeth and the response of cementum to masticatory stress. It has been reported in a number of aging studies of bone, cartilage, and dental tissues that the cellular aging phenomenon is retarded in tissues where functional activity is retained (Tonna, 1971a, 1971b, 1977).

Both cementoblasts and cementocytes revealed occasional to several lipofuscin granules in older animals. Lipofuscin was also observed in old osteoblasts and osteocytes (Tonna, 1975).

The observation made in this study that the presence of viable cells persisted even in the oldest animals is in keeping with the well known fact that the cementum accretion is a life-time process. In a human study of 233 teeth, Zander and Hurzeler (1958) showed a linear relationship between thickness of cementum and age. The rate of cementum apposition in the rat was reported to be greater in young animals (Louridis, Kyrkanidou, and Demetriou, 1972). This was also true for the mouse. The rate decreased very rapidly after 5 weeks of age, and continued to decline more slowly with increasing age. The total mass of cementum, however, increased at the root to a point of reducing the apical foramen, thereby augmenting the age changes to the pulp (Tonna, 1973a).

Cementum was also observed to accumulate in large quantities along the interradicular surface of the tooth. The thickness of the multilayered cementum in old mice was greater than the thickness of tooth dentin (Tonna, 1976). This continued reapposition of new layers of cementum represents aging of the tooth as an organ (Kotanyi, 1966) and maintains the attachment complex intact. The tooth is as old as the youngest layer of cementum. It may, however, be less than its chronologic age. The apposition of cementum appears to occur in response to functional stress, but thick layers of cementum are observed at the roots of unerupted human teeth in aged individuals (Miles, 1961).

A major qualitative difference was found between the surface arrangement of cementoblasts and osteoblasts. In young bone, osteoblasts are largely in intimate relationship with one another via cell body contact, desmosomes, and overlapping protoplasmic extensions, forming a membrane-like cover. The intervening space between the cells and the bone surface form a second compartment that is continuous with the osteocyte lacunae via the canaliculi. This arrangement provides cellular control of bone surface activity important to bone growth, development, aging, repair, and mineral homeostasis. There is increasing evidence that calcium homeostasis is largely a mechanism residing in osteocytes and that the process is separate from that of bone resorption, which may be stimulated when necessary (Frost, 1960; Talmage, Wilmer, and Toft, 1960; Bélanger, 1965; Nichols, 1970).

In an attempt to account for the efforts of parathormone and calcitonin on the movement of calcium ions necessary for plasma level maintenance and bone remodeling, Talmage and associates (1969; 1970; Talmage, Cooper, and Park, 1970) postulated that all bone surfaces are lined by osteoblasts forming a membrane whose purpose is to facilitate the movement of calcium to and from bone surfaces, a mechanism critical to mineral homeostasis and the function of bone in the aged. This hypothesis (Talmage, 1969) postulates that the membrane creates two extracellular fluid compartments. The intercellular space between osteoblasts is sufficient to allow for movement of calcium ions from blood to bone via the normal ion concentration gradient. The concentration of calcium and phosphate ions within the inner compartment depends on the solubility products of ions below those in the outer compartment (on the opposite side of the osteoblasts). These cells are polarized and possess a calcium pump near the outer surface which enables calcium ions to move out of bone against the concentration gradient. The pump eliminates excessive accumulation of cell calcium, which is significantly lower than that of the environmental tissue fluids. The cell is more permeable to calcium ions on the inner compartment side. Calcium ions, therefore, enter the cell in lieu of the concentration gradient between the cell and its environment. Parathyroid hormone mediates the rapid transport of calcium ions from bone across the osteoblast and into the outer compartment by activating the calcium pump in response to increased concentration of intracellular calcium.

In an electron microscopic study of the viability of this membrane structure, it was observed that cell contact and the integrity of the cellular arrangement at bone surfaces was lost during the aging of bone (Tonna, 1978). Older bone, therefore, was exposed to the intracellular fluid compartment without benefit of the two-compartment system and essential cellular control and biofeedback. Reduced cellular metabolism concomitant with aging decreases the local CO_2 tension of the tissue fluids, increasing the pH level and creating an environment favoring the physicochemical deposition of calcium salts. Unusual ultrastructural appearance of irregular mineral deposits and microossicle formation at endosteal surfaces of old animals were observed. These irregularities may have resulted from a combination of reduced cellular metabolism and loss of cellular biofeedback. In the present study, as described in this chapter, the natural arrangement of periodontal fiber bundles continuous with the mineralized cemental surface separates the cementoblasts a sufficient distance to prevent a membrane-like structure from forming, consequently limiting cellular control and the accompanying cellular biofeedback. This being the case, one should expect irregular accretion of cementum very early in the life of the organism as was noted in older bone. Together with prolonged vitality of surface cementoblasts into old age, irregular mineral accretion should be a normal feature of cementum throughout life. The rates at which accretion occurs at cemental surfaces vary with time. Consequently, cementum is laid down in successive layers along all dentinal surfaces. This feature is well recognized in routinely stained histological samples. Bone is also laid down in this manner, resulting in the development of what is called "subperiosteal" or "subendosteal reversal lines," which demarcate one cyclic phase of bone accretion from the next (Tonna, 1959). Such a feature, however, is accountable on the basis of cellular control. This would imply that the cemental surface is not entirely without a cellular contribution, however limited. The continued process, which in large measure appears to be physiochemical, probably accounts for the well recognized irregular features of cemental accretion in young animals, as well as the undesirable development and increased incidence of hypercementosis, excementosis, and cementicle formation in the aged individual. Further investigation into the regulatory features of bone and dental surfaces is in progress. The results of the ultrastructural study of cemental cells and cemental surfaces described here, as well as earlier electron microscopic observations of aging bone provide the following conclusions:

1. Cementocytes and cementoblasts undergo ultrastructural age changes similar to their bone cell counterparts. These include osteocytes and osteoblasts, even to the point of generating lipofuscin granules.
2. Cementocyte degeneration and death is more prevalent and occurs at an earlier age than that observed in osteocytes. During their active life span, cementocytes predominantly exhibit cementoplastic activity, that is, lacunar matrix formation.
3. Cementoblast aging is a slower process than that of osteoblasts. This is believed to be due to the continued functional stress placed on teeth throughout the life of the individual. Consequently, unlike the large surface of old bone, the cemental surface remains formative.
4. Unlike the osteoblasts at young bone surfaces, cementoblasts do not form a membrane-like cellular cover that results in the formation of two distinct extracellular fluid compartments. This difference is due to the separation of cementoblasts by periodontal collagen bundles and the anatomical orientation of these fiber bundles.
5. Old animal bone surfaces lose the integrity of the membrane-like cell layer. With this anatomical change, cellular control and biofeedback of mineral homeostasis is disrupted. The limited cellular control possible at cemental surfaces appears to be retained throughout the animal's life.
6. With the disruption of the bone surface cell cover, irregular mineral

accretion and microossicle formation occurs, generated largely by a physiochemical process. In the absence of an intact cellular cover over cemental surfaces, cementum accretion is irregular in young animals. With increasing age and functional stresses, continued cemental deposition is believed to lead to hypercementosis, excementosis, and cementicle formation in the significant magnitude we observe in the aged.

Cementum, consequently, remains metabolically and proliferatively low-keyed but viable and formative, responding to functional stresses throughout life and should remain responsive to surgical intervention and treatment in the aged.

References

Baud, C.A. Submicroscopic Structure and Functional Aspects of the Osteocyte. *Clinical Orthopaedics* 56:227-236, 1968.

Bélanger, L.F. Osteolysis: An Outlook on Its Mechanism and Causation. In P.J. Gaillard, R.V. Talmage, and A.M. Budy (Eds.), *The Parathyroid Glands Ultrastructure, Secretion and Function* (Chicago: Univ. of Chicago, 1965), p. 137.

Bélanger, L.F. Osteocytic Osteolysis. *Calcified Tissue Res*, 4:1-12, 1969.

Frost, H.M. A New Bone Affliction: Feathering. *J Bone and Joint Surg* 42A:447-456, 1960.

Henry, J.L., and Weinmann, J.P. The Pattern of Resorption and Repair of Human Cementum. *JADA* 42:270-290, 1951.

Jande, S.S., and Bélanger, L.F. The Life-cycle of the Osteocyte. *Clinical Orthopaedics* 94:281-305, 1970.

Kotanyi, E. Cementum. In H. Sicher (Ed.), *Orban's Oral Histology and Embryology* (St. Louis: Mosby, 1966), p. 155-164.

Louridis, O., Kyrkanidou, E.B., and Demetriou, N. Age Effect Upon Cementum Width of Albino Rat: A Histometric Study. *J Periodont* 43:533-536, 1972.

Miles, A.E.W. Ageing in the Teeth and Oral Tissues. In G.H. Bourne (Ed.), *Structural Aspects of Ageing* (New York: Hafner, 1961), p. 352-361.

Nichols, G., Jr. Bone Resorption and Calcium Homeostasis: One Process or Two? *Calcified Tissue Res* 4(Suppl):61-63, 1970.

Scherft, J.P. The Lamina Limitans of the Organic Matrix of Calcified Cartilage and Bone. *J Ultrastructure Res* 38:318-331, 1972.

Shipley, P.G., Kramer, B., and Howland, J.L. Studies Upon Calcification in vitro. *Biochem J* 20:379-387, 1926.

Stahl, S.S., Tonna, E.A., and Weiss, R. Autoradiographic Evaluation of Gingival Response to Injury. I. Surgical Trauma in Young Adult Rats. *Arch of Oral Biol* 13:71-86, 1968.

Stahl, S.S., Tonna, E.A., and Weiss, R. The Effects of Aging on the Proliferative Activity of Rat Periodontal Structures. *J Gerontol* 24:447-450, 1969.

Stahl, S.S., Tonna, E.A., and Weiss, R. Autoradiographic Evaluation of Gingival Response to Injury. III. Surgical Trauma in Mature Rats. *Arch of Oral Biol* 15:537-547, 1970.

Talmage, R.V. The Effects of Parathyroid Hormone on the Movement of Calcium Between Bone and Fluid. *Clinical Orthopaedics* 67:211-223, 1969.

Talmage, R.V. Morphological and Physiological Considerations in a New Concept of Calcium Transport in Bone. *Amer J Anat* 129:467-476, 1970.

Talmage, R.V., Cooper, C.W., and Park, H.Z. Regulation of Calcium Transport in Bone by Parathyroid Hormone. *Vitamins and Hormones* 28:103-140, 1970.

Talmage, R.V., Wilmer, L.T., and Toft, R.J. Additional Evidence in Support of McLean's Feedback Mechanism of Parathyroid Action on Bone. *Clinical Orthopaedics* 17:195-205, 1960.

Tonna, E.A. The Histochemical Nature and Possible Significance of the Subperiosteal Reversal Lines of Aging Rat Femora. *J Gerontol* 14:425-429, 1959.

Tonna, E.A., and Pavelec, M. An Autoradiographic Study of H^3-Proline Utilization by Aging Mouse Skeletal Tissues. I. Bone Cell Compartments. *J Gerontol* 26:310-315, 1971a.

Tonna, E.A. An Autoradiographic Study of H^3-Proline Utilization by Aging Mouse Skeletal Tissues. II. Cartilage Cell Compartments. *Exper Gerontol* 6:405-415, 1971b.

Tonna, E.A. Electron Microscopic Evidence of Alternating Osteocytic-Osteoclastic and Osteoplastic Activity in the Perilacunar Walls of Aging Mice. *Connective Tissue Res* 1:221-230, 1972a.

Tonna, E.A. An Electron Microscopic Study of Osteocyte Release During Osteoclasis in Mice of Different Ages. *Clinical Orthopaedics* 87:311-317, 1972b.

Tonna, E.A. Histological Age Changes Associated with Mouse Parodontal Tissues. *J Gerontol* 28:1-12, 1973a.

Tonna, E.A. An Electron Microscopic Study of Skeletal Cell Aging. II. The Osteocyte. *Exper Gerontol* 8:9-16, 1973b.

Tonna, E.A. Electron Microscopy of Aging Skeletal Cells. III. The Periosteum. *Lab Invest* 31:609-623, 1974.

Tonna, E.A. Accumulation of Lipofuscin (Age Pigment) in Aging Skeletal Connective Tissues as Revealed by Electron Microscopy. *J Gerontol* 30:3-8, 1975.

Tonna, E.A. Factors (Aging) Affecting Bone and Cementum. *J Periodontol* 47:267-280, 1976.

Tonna, E.A. Aging of Skeletal-Dental Systems and Supporting Tissues. In C.E. Finch and L. Hayflick (Eds.), *Handbook of The Biology of Aging*, chapt. 19 (New York: Van Nostrand-Reinhold, 1977), pp. 470-495.

Tonna, E.A. Electron Microscopic Study of Bone Surface Changes During Aging. The Loss of Cellular Control and Biofeedback. *J Gerontol* 33:163-177, 1978.

Tonna, E.A., and Stahl, S.S. A (3H)-Thymidine Autoradiographic Study of Cell Proliferative Activity of Injured Parodontal Tissues of 5-week-old Mice. *Arch Oral Biol* 18:617-627, 1973.

Tonna, E.A., and Stahl, S.S. Comparative Assessment of the Cell Proliferative Activities of Injured Parodontal Tissues in Aging Mouse. *J Dental Res* 53:609-622, 1974.

Tonna, E.A., Stahl, S.S., and Weiss, R. Autoradiographic Evaluation of Gingival Response to Injury. II. Surgical Trauma in Young Rats. *Arch Oral Biol* 14:19-34, 1969.

Tonna, E.A., Weiss, R., and Stahl, S.S. The Cell Proliferative Activity of Parodontal Tissues in Aging Mice. *Arch Oral Biol* 17:969-982, 1972.

Vitalli, P.H. Osteocyte Activity. *Clinical Orthopaedics* 56:213-226, 1968.

Zander, H.A., and Hurzeler, B. Continuous Cementum Apposition. *J Dental Res* 37:1035-1044, 1958.

4 Connective Tissue Change in the Elderly

Jeremiah E. Silbert

Connective tissue comprises the bulk of bone, cartilage, gingiva, and buccal mucosa, where it serves as a matrix of structural elements. It is a major component of the oral cavity. Gross changes in connective tissues throughout the body are a major manifestation of aging, and are reflected in oral tissues as well. However, the specific changes of connective tissue elements with aging are less obvious. Moreover, it is not clear how these specific cellular or biochemical changes relate to gross differences.

Changes with aging have been examined in both cellular and noncellular elements of connective tissue. The cells of the connective tissue include osteocytes, fibroblasts, chondrocytes, and mast cells. Aging of these types of cells has been studied mainly in fibroblasts and to a lesser extent in chondrocytes.

There is an extensive literature on the limitation of the capacity of normal fibroblasts to grow in culture (Hayflick, 1976). Normal human fibroblasts double approximately fifty times before the cultures stop growing and die. This phenomenon is thought to reflect senescence and is in contrast to the growth of malignant cells which have unlimited potential. Not only do the doubling potentials of human fibroblasts decrease as the cultures age, but the doubling potential is less in cells obtained from older donors. It has been suggested that this phenomenon is due to programming of cells at a genetic level and reflects true biological aging.

One suggestion to explain this phenomenon is that cells have a limited facility to undergo repair of their genetic makeup after damage to DNA by random or environmentally produced events. As these normal human fibroblasts age in vitro there are a series of changes that take place in their metabolism (Hayflick, 1976). For example, there is an increase in content of ribonucleic acid (RNA), protein, glycogen, and lipid. The cells also increase in cell size and volume. At the same time there is a decrease in proteoglycan synthesis, DNA content, collagen synthesis, and collagenolytic activity.

Cellular changes in aging are reflected in extracelluar changes, which in turn underlie the visible gross changes. Examination of extracellular matrix is important in considering the aging of connective tissue. The extracellular matrix components of connective tissue consist of collagen, elastin, and proteoglycans, which all show changes with aging. However, as already mentioned, we are only beginning to understand how these changes relate to gross changes.

Collagen is the main protein of connective tissue and provides its characteristic structure. Characterization and synthesis has been studied extensively (Ramachandran and Reddi, 1976). It is synthesized intracellularly as a procollagen molecule which consists of a collagen chain with additional pieces of noncollagenous protein at either end (figure 4-1). The collagen portion is characterized by large amounts of glycine and proline. The proline together with some lysine is hydroxylated to varying degrees within the cell to form hydroxylysine and hydroxyproline. Following hydroxylation, three collagen chains combine with one another to form a triple helix which in turn is stabilized by hydroxyproline. Before excretion of the collagen from the cells, some hydroxylysine is glycosylated with glucose and galactose to form glucosyl-galactosyl-hydroxylysine. Following hydroxylation, the procollagen can then be excreted from the cell. At this time, specific enzymes cleave the pieces of protein at either end to turn the procollagen molecules into collagen molecules. Cross-linking involving lysines within the molecule occurs outside the cell between triple helical collagen molecules. This cross-linking is the last step in collagen fiber formation.

Collagen turnover in the connective tissue is accomplished by means of a collagenase which splits at one specific site on the collagen fibril. This cleavage renders the remainder of the molecule susceptible to degradation by other less specific proteolytic enzymes.

Aging has a number of effects on the collagen molecule in mammalian and avian species.

1. There is a decrease of hydroxyproline content in older collagen (Bornstein, 1976; Barnes et al., 1974). This, in turn, results in a relative obstruction to the excretion of collagen from the cells, since hydroxylation is necessary for excretion to take place. Furthermore, hydroxyproline contributes to thermostability of the collagen helix. Therefore with less hydroxylation there is a decrease in thermostability.

2. There is also an age-related change in hydroxylysine and probably in cross-linking of collagen (Bornstein, 1976). The known cross-links increase to maturity and then decrease with age. Since cross-linking is directly proportional to insolubility, the collagen becomes less soluble with maturity. With later age there is an apparent decrease in cross-linking, but the collagen continues to become more insoluble. It is not known what the functional effect of these changes are.

3. Collagen is known to exist in four or more types. These are described in table 4-1 and vary by virtue of the differences in their amino acid sequences. Type I is the most common collagen found in most connective tissues. Normal cartilage collagen contains only Type II. In addition, there is a Type III collagen which is prominent in fetal skin. Up to maturity there is a decrease in the amount of Type III collagen relative to Type I in skin. Type IV collagen is found in basement membranes. The various types of collagen in other tissues have not been completely identified.

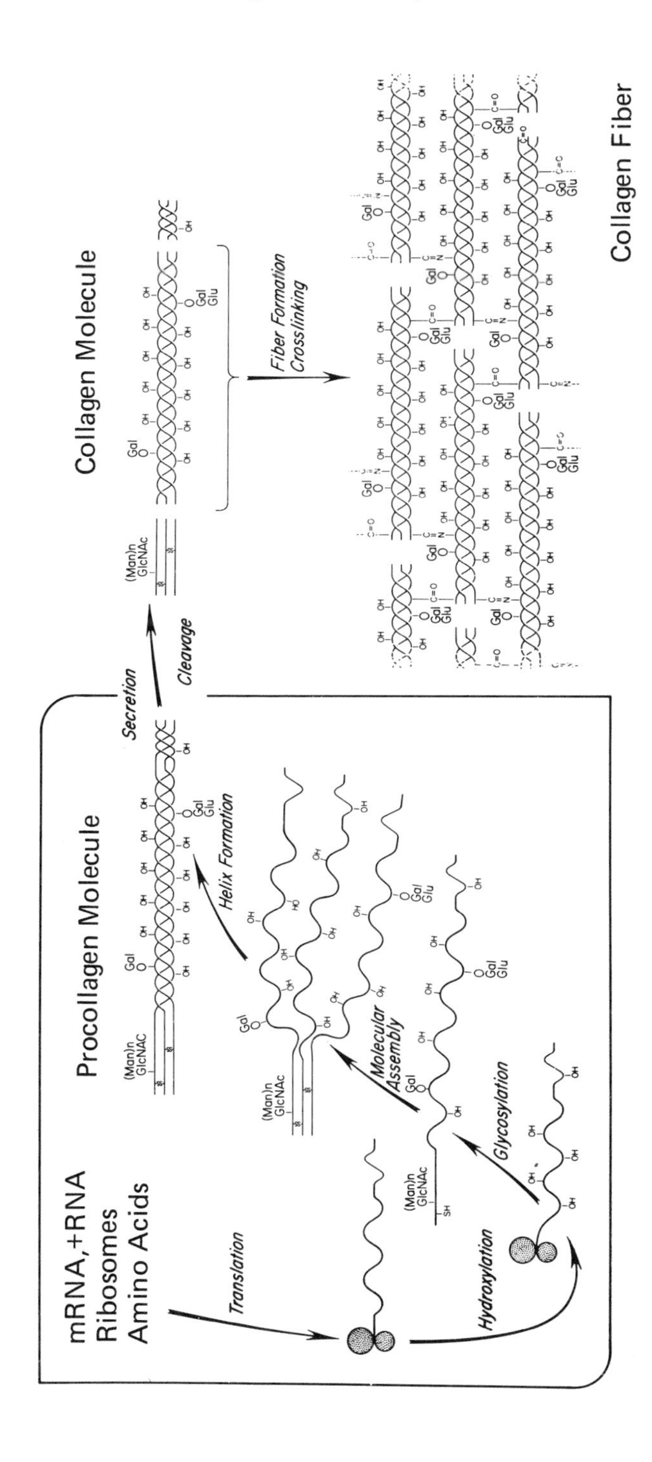

Figure 4-1. Structure and formation of collagen. (Figure courtesy of Dr. Barbara Smith. Reprinted with permission.)

Table 4-1
Collagen Types

Collagen Type	*Chain Composition*	*Tissue Distribution*	*Characteristics*
I	$[\alpha 1(I)]_2 \alpha 2$	Skin, bone, tendon, dentin, gingiva, ligament, fascia, arteries, most abundant	α2 chain Low hydroxylysine and carbohydrate
II	$[\alpha 1(II)]_3$	Cartilage	High hydroxylsine and carbohydrate
III	$[\alpha 1(III)]_3$	Skin, blood vessels, and mesenchymal tissues	Cysteine and disulfide bonds High 4-hydroxyproline Low hydroxylysine and carbohydrate
IV	$[\alpha 1(IV)]_3$	Basement membranes	Highest hydroxylysine and carbohydrate Cysteine and disulfide bonds Highest 3-hydroxyprolin and 4-hydroxyproline Low alanine Largest size

Cartilage has been shown to undergo changes in collagen with aging. When chick chondrocytes are grown in culture, there is a change with aging from production of Type II to Type I (Mayne et al., 1976). Osteoarthritic cartilage also has some Type I collagen as well as Type II (Nimni and Deshmukh, 1973), suggesting that the reversal to Type I collagen is a regeneration phenomenon or a programmed aging phenomenon.

4. There are differences in the susceptibility of collagen to degradation by collagenase and other proteases. Type III collagen is degraded more readily than Type I by nonspecific proteases. A reversal to Type III with age would result in a faster turnover of collagen. It has been suggested that this reversal might take place (Miller et al., 1976).

Elastin is the other major protein component of connective tissues, providing, as its name implies, an elastic component. Little is known about the changes of elastin with aging, but it also undergoes increased cross-linking similar to collagen, making the elastin much less soluble. This lack of solubility has made the study of elastin difficult.

Proteoglycans making up the ground substance are the other major components of connective tissue. The structure of a sample proteoglycan is shown in figure 4-2. These compounds consist of polysaccharide (glycosaminoglycan) chains of varying composition attached to a protein core. The glycosaminoglycan chains always contain disaccharide repeating units consisting of a hexo-

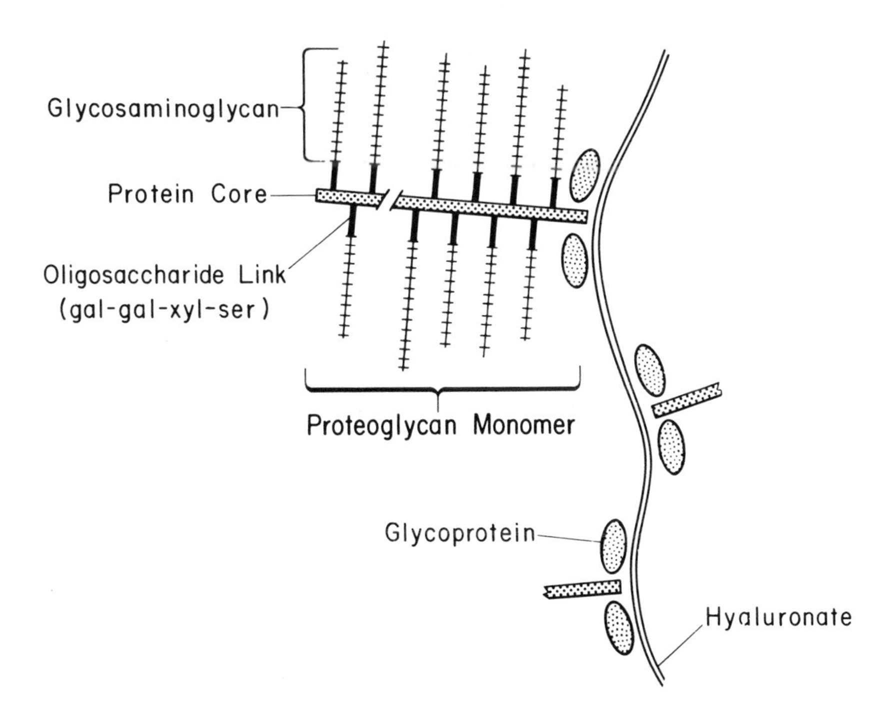

Figure 4-2. Structure of a proteoglycan.

samine alternating with either galactose or a uronic acid. The components and representative disaccharide repeating units of glycosaminoglycans are shown, respectively, in table 4-2 and in figure 4-3. Although an individual chain may have a mixture of uronic acids (some glucuronic acid and some iduronic acid), the hexosamine will always be either all glucosamine or all galactosamine. Heparin and heparan sulfate have a more complicated structure that cannot be entirely represented as disaccharide repeating units. The glycosaminoglycan chains of the various compounds range in size from approximately 15 to 5000 disaccharide units (molecular weight several thousand to several million daltons). They are all linear (unbranched). All hexosamines are substituted on the amino group with either an acetyl or sulfate. In addition, most of the glycosaminoglycans have ester O-sulfate. All of the glycosaminologlycans are highly anionic by virtue of either their uronic acids, their sulfate groups, or both.

The glycosaminoglycan chains are connected through a specific oligosaccharide linkage (xylose-galactose-galactose) to a protein core molecule, thus

Table 4-2
Components of the Glycosaminoglycan Portion of Proteoglycans

Glycosaminoglycan	*Usual MW of Glycosaminoglycan Chain*	*Major Component Sugars*	*Location of Sulfate*	*Linkage*
Hyaluronic acid	$5\text{-}50 \times 10^5$	N-acetylglucosamine	–	β 1, 4
		glucuronic acid		β 1, 3
Chondroitin 4-sulfate (Chondroitin sulfate A)	$2\text{-}5 \times 10^4$	N-acetylgalactosamine	4	β 1, 4
		glucuronic acid		β 1, 3
Chondroitin 6-sulfate (Chondroitin sulfate C)	$2\text{-}5 \times 10^4$	N-acetylgalactosamine	6	β 1, 4
		glucuronic acid		β 1, 3
Dermatan sulfate (Chondroitin sulfate B)	$2\text{-}5 \times 10^4$	N-acetylgalactosamine	4	β 1, 4
		iduronic acid	? 2	α 1, 3*
		glucuronic acid (trace)		β 1, 3
Heparin	$1\text{-}3 \times 10^4$	glucosamine	6, N	α 1, 4
		glucuronic acid		β 1, 4
		iduronic acid	2	α 1, 4*
Heparan Sulfate	$1\text{-}5 \times 10^4$	glucosamine	N	α 1, 4
		N-acetylglucosamine	? 6	α 1, 4
		glucuronic acid		β 1, 4
		iduronic acid	? 2	α 1, 4*
Keratosulfate	$5\text{-}20 \times 10^3$	N-acetylglucosamine	6	β 1, 3
		galactose	6	β 1, 4

*These linkages are identical to the β 1, 3 or β 1, 4 linkages found in hyaluronic acid and chondroitin sulfates or heparin. However, iduronic acid is of the L rather than the D configuration, which results in these bonds, being designated as α rather than β.

forming a proteoglycan unit. Each proteoglycan molecule may have as many as fifty glycosaminoglycan chains attached to this core in a "bottle brush" configuration. The polysaccharide chains may vary in size and sulfate content within a single proteoglycan molecule, so that they are highly heterogeneous. The structures of the various core proteins have not been defined, so it is unknown how much variation there is between different proteoglycan types and between proteoglycans from different tissues. Most of the work on proteoglycan structure has been with proteoglycans obtained from cartilage, and it is not known if the structures in other connective tissues are similar.

In cartilage as many as one hundred of the proteoglycan molecules are in turn attached noncovalently around a core of hyaluronic acid to form aggregates of as much as 100 to 150 million daltons. The attachment of the proteoglycan monomer to the hyaluronic acid core is stabilized by one or more glycoproteins that have not been completely characterized. This aggregate can be dissociated to its proteoglycan monomer by high salt concentration, while lowering of the salt concentration will result in at least a partial reaggregation.

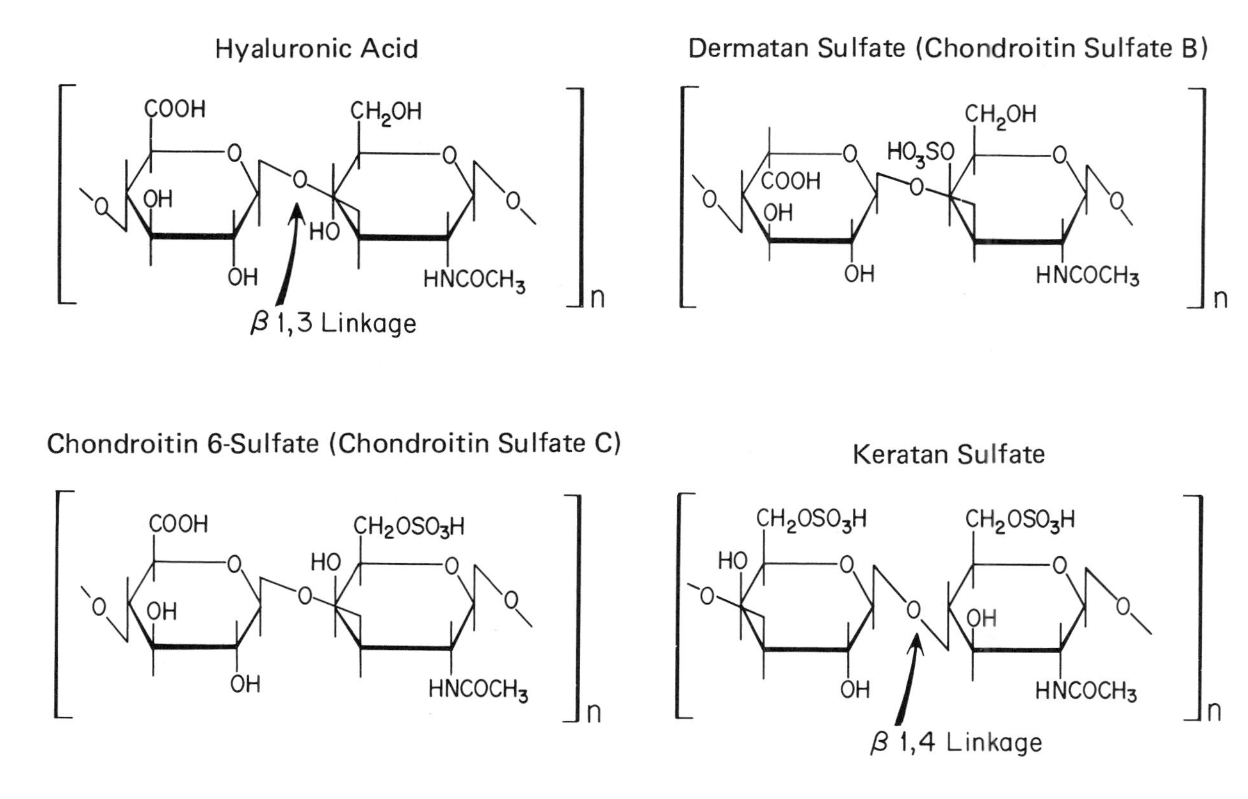

Figure 4-3. Disaccharide repeating units of representative glycosaminoglycans.

Synthesis of the proteoglycan has been examined in some detail (Roden, 1970; Silbert, 1973; Silbert, 1978). The protein core is synthesized first, apparently in a conventional method on the ribosome. Subsequently, it would appear that the sugar chains are built up by addition of individual sugars to this protein core. Intermediates are uridine diphosphate sugars. Following formation of the glycosaminoglycan chains, the sugars are sulfated by specific sulfotransferases. The intermediate for sulfation is 3′phosphoadenosine 5′-phosphosulfate.

The biosynthesis of the proteoglycans takes place in several cell compartments. The enzymes of precursor activation are found in the soluble fraction from cells and, therefore, these reactions appear to take place in the cell cytosol. The ribosome is apparently the site for the protein synthesis of the glycosaminoglycan core protein. The enzymes involved in glycosaminoglycan polymerization and in sulfation appear to be located in the Golgi complex.

Information regarding the control and organization of synthesis within the cell is not well understood. These aspects may prove to be of great importance, since changes in the production of these materials with aging probably relates to aspects of control and metabolic organization rather than simple direct effects of individual steps in the metabolic pathway. An alteration expressed at the cellular level would result in a multiplicity of changes rather than a single specific change.

Much less is known of proteoglycan degradation than is known of synthesis. There are proteases in all tissues that are capable of degrading the protein core of the proteoglycan, and there are enzymes that can degrade some of the glycosaminoglycan chains. However, it is not known if these proteoglycans are totally degraded prior to excretion, whether they are partially degraded, or whether there is some excretion of intact proteoglycans. The relationship of degradation to aging is unknown.

The highly charged polysaccharide chains in the proteoglycans occupy a large volume or domain. In this way the proteoglycans holds as much as one thousand times its own weight in water. Under pressure, this water can be squeezed out with compression of the molecule; on release of the pressure, the molecule reverts to its original domain. Thus proteoglycans act as an elastic component to the connective tissue. The proteoglycans also serve as a filter. The network of polysaccharide chains filters out large molecules while small molecules can penetrate. The negatively charged sulfate ions have the capacity to bind positively charged ions. These in turn can be exchanged for other positively charged ions. The proteoglycans also have an imperfectly understood effect on cell function. It seems clear that they are more than an inert matrix and, through the reactive groups, have an active role to play in connective tissue metabolism.

With aging, several phenomena have been noted.

1. Proteoglycan aggregate formation of cartilage proteoglycan decreases (Perricone, Palmoski, and Brandt, 1977). Since this has also been shown in osteoarthritis (Brandt and Palmoski, 1976), the evidence suggests that osteoarthritis could be considered a direct manifestation of aging.

2. The percentage of keratan sulfate chains in cartilage increases with age, while the percentage of chondroitin sulfate decreases (Kaplan and Meyer, 1959).

3. Sulfation increases with age, so that chondroitin sulfate becomes more highly sulfated. Chondroitin 6-sulfate rises with age relative to the amount of chondroitin 4-sulfate (Mathews and Glagov, 1966). These changes vary widely since there are great differences between individuals.

4. There is considerable evidence that hyaluronic acid is involved in growth and development of connective tissue (Toole, 1976). Fetal tissues such as skin contain high proportions of hyaluronic acid which is lost as the tissues develop and age (Breen et al., 1970). Concomitantly, there is an increase in the amount of sulfated proteoglycans. In regenerating connective tissue there appears to be a general pattern of hyaluronic acid being present, being removed by hyaluronidase, and then being replaced by chondroitin sulfates (Toole, 1976). It is thought that the hyaluronic acid plays a role in directing tissue regeneration, which could be related to the aging process.

Thus there are a series of connective tissue changes that occur with age. These can be considered as isolated observations at present, since they do not define a clear pattern, nor are these changes understandable in terms of their physiological significance.

Changes occurring in collagen include

1. Increased hydroxylation
2. Increased cross-linking resulting in decreased solubility
3. Change of collagen type
4. A related increase in collagen turnover

Elastin shows increased cross-linking and less solubility.

Proteoglycans show

1. Decreased aggregate formation
2. Increased keratan sulfate production
3. Increased 6-sulfation relative to 4-sulfation
4. Loss of hyaluronic acid with a replacement by chondroitin sulfate

References

Barnes, M.J., Constable, B.J., Morton, L.F., and Royce, P.M. Age-Related Variations in Hydroxylation of Lysine and Proline in Collagen. *Biochem J* 139:461-468, 1974.

Bornstein, P. Disorders of Connective Tissue Function and the Aging Process: A Synthesis and Review of Current Concepts and Findings. *Mech Aging and Develop* 5:305-314, 1976.

Brandt, K.D., and Palmoski, M. Organization of Ground Substance Proteoglycans in Normal and Osteoarthritic Knee Cartilage, *Arthritis Rheum* 19:209-215, 1976.

Breen, M., Weinstein, H.G., Johnson, R.L., Veis, A., and Marshall, R.T. Acidic Glycosaminoglycans in Human Skin During Fetal Development and Adult Life. *Biochim Biophys Acta* 201:54-60, 1970.

Hayflict, L. The Cell Biology of Human Aging. *New Eng J Med* 295:1302-1308, 1976.

Kaplan, D. and Meyer, K. Aging of Human Cartilage. *Nature* 183:1267-1268, 1959.

Mathews, M.B. and Glagov, S. Acid Mucopolysaccharide Patterns in Aging Human Cartilage. *J Clin Invest* 45:1103-1111, 1966.

Mayne, R., Vail, M.S., Mayne, P.M., and Miller, E.J. Changes in Type of Collagen Synthesized as Clones of Chick Chondrocytes Grow and Eventually Lose Division Capacity. *Proc Natl Acad Sci USA* 73:1674-1678, 1976.

Miller, E.J., Finch, J.E., Jr., Chung, E., Butler, W.T., and Robertson, P.B. Specific Cleavage of the Native Type III Collagen Molecule with Trypsin: Similarity of the Cleavage Products to Collagenase-Produced Fragments and Primary Structure at the Cleavage Site. *Arch Biochem Biophys* 173:631-637, 1976.

Nimni, M., and Deshmukh, K. Differences in Collagen Metabolism Between Normal and Osteoarthritic Human Articular Cartilage. *Science* 181:751-752, 1973.

Perricone, E., Palmoski, M.J., and Brandt, K.D. Failure of Proteoglycans to Form Aggregates in Morphologically Normal Aged Human Hip Cartilage. *Arthritis Rheum* 20:1372-1380, 1977.

Ramachandran, G.N. and Reddi, A.H. *Biochemistry of Collagen* (New York: Plenum Press, 1976).

Roden, L. Biosynthesis of Acidic Glycosaminoglycans (Mucopolysaccharides). In W.H. Fishman (Ed.), *Metabolic Conjugation and Metabolic Hydrolysis*, vol. 2 (New York: Academic, 1970), pp. 345-442.

Silbert, J.E. Biosynthesis of Mucopolysaccharides and Protein Polysaccharides. In R. Perez-Tamayo and M. Rojkind (Eds.), *Molecular Pathology of Connective Tissues* (New York: Marcel Dekker, 1973), pp. 323-354.

Silbert, J.E. Ground substance. In J.H. Shaw, E.A. Sweeney, C.C. Cappuccino, and S.M. Meller (Eds.), *Textbook of Oral Biology* (Philadelphia: W.B. Saunders, 1978), pp. 453-469.

Toole, B.P. Morphogenetic Role of Glycosaminoglycans (Acid Mucopolysaccharides) in Brain and Other Tissues. In S. Barondes (Ed.), *Neuronal Recognition* (New York: Plenum, 1976), pp. 275-329.

5 Immunologic Changes in Aging and Their Possible Significance to Geriatric Dentistry

Takashi Makinodan and
Marguerite M.B. Kay

Decline in immunologic vigor is one of the characteristics of aging mammals. This phenomenon, commonly referred to as immunologic aging, has been observed not only in humans, but also in all experimental animals examined, including the mouse, rat, hamster, guinea pig, rabbit, and dog (Makinodan and Yunis, 1977). The onset and rate of decline varies with the type of immune response and the species.

The increase in the incidence of infectious, autoimmune, immune complex, and cancerous diseases is associated with immunologic aging. A comparable inverse correlation between immune function and disease incidence has also been observed in immunodeficient newborns and immunosuppressed adults (Fudenberg et al., 1971a; Good and Yunis, 1974; Penn and Starzl, 1972).

What is not clear is whether the diseases compromise normal immune functions, or whether a decline in normal immune functions to threshold levels predisposes individuals to disease. We favor the latter possibility because of the following observations:

1. The onset of decline in thymus-derived T-cell-dependent immune functions can occur as early as sexual maturity when the thymus begins to involute (Makinodan and Peterson, 1962), which is long before immunodeficiency-associated diseases of the elderly are manifested.

2. Immunodeficiency wasting disease, amyloidosis, and autoimmune manifestations can be enhanced in mice by thymectomizing them shortly after birth, and they can be delayed or at times even reversed by reconstituting aging mice with young, but not old, syngeneic thymus or spleen grafts (Yunis et al., 1964; Fabris, Pierpaoli, and Sorkin, 1972).

3. Adult humans subjected to immunosuppressive drug therapy are many times more vulnerable to autoimmunity, amyloidosis, and certain forms of cancer (Cerilli and Hattan, 1974).

4. Patients with primary immunodeficiencies in which the immunity systems fail to develop normal vigor are vulnerable to autoimmunity, amyloidosis, and certain forms of cancer (Good and Yunis, 1974).

5. Cessation of immunosuppressive therapy following inadvertent transplantation of cancer along with renal transplant leads to the prompt rejection of the tumor (Zukoski et all, 1970).

In view of these observations, it is likely that a delay, prevention, or reversal of immunologic aging could delay the onset, minimize the severity, or perhaps even prevent the appearance of certain diseases of the elderly. However, before any attempt is made to intervene with age-associated diseases, an understanding of the mechanism(s) responsible for the decline in immunologic vigor with age would be desirable and essential. Therefore, we first present an overview of this rapidly developing area of research by focusing our attention on the changes that may be responsible for the decline in immunologic vigor with age. Then we consider how autoimmune and immune complex reactions and infection could contribute to the increasing incidence of periodontal lesions among the elderly.

Influence of Age on Immune Functions

Figure 5-1 presents age-associated changes in the relative immunologic activity as reflected in the serum isoantibody concentration in humans. There is a rapid rise in immunologic activity after birth to a peak level at sexual maturity. This is followed by a gradual decline when the thymus begins to involute and atrophy. The figure also presents age-associated changes in the death rate and in the cumulative number of survivors. It can be seen that the changes in these actuarial indexes are preceded by the decline in immunologic activity. Acceleration in the death rate and in the cumulative decrease in the number of survivors occurs when the level of immunologic activity approaches 50 percent of maximum. Such a sequential correlation further strengthens the notion that the immune system plays a major role not only in the survival of individuals, but also in aging, as most postadulthood death is a consequence of aging.

Immunologic aging is due to changes in both the cellular environment and the cells of the immune system. (For a comprehensive review, see Kay and Makinodan, 1976.) At present, we do not know the nature of the responsible factor(s) in the cellular environment. We suspect that two types of factors are involved: deleterious molecular and viral substances and essential nutritional and hormonal substances.

Three types of cellular changes can cause immunologic aging: (a) an absolute decrease in functional cell numbers, (b) a decrease in the functional efficiency of the cells, and (c) a relative decrease in functional cell numbers due to a shift in the proportion of regulatory cells. A recent study of old mice indicates that the number of immune cells in them is comparable to that of young mice, and their reduced antibody response can be explained by the presence of excessive numbers of suppressor cells in about 65 percent of cases, by a reduction in the number of at least one type of cell that exists in excess in young mice in about 25 percent of cases, and by a decrease in the functional efficiency of cells in about 10 percent of cases (Makinodan et al., 1976). These

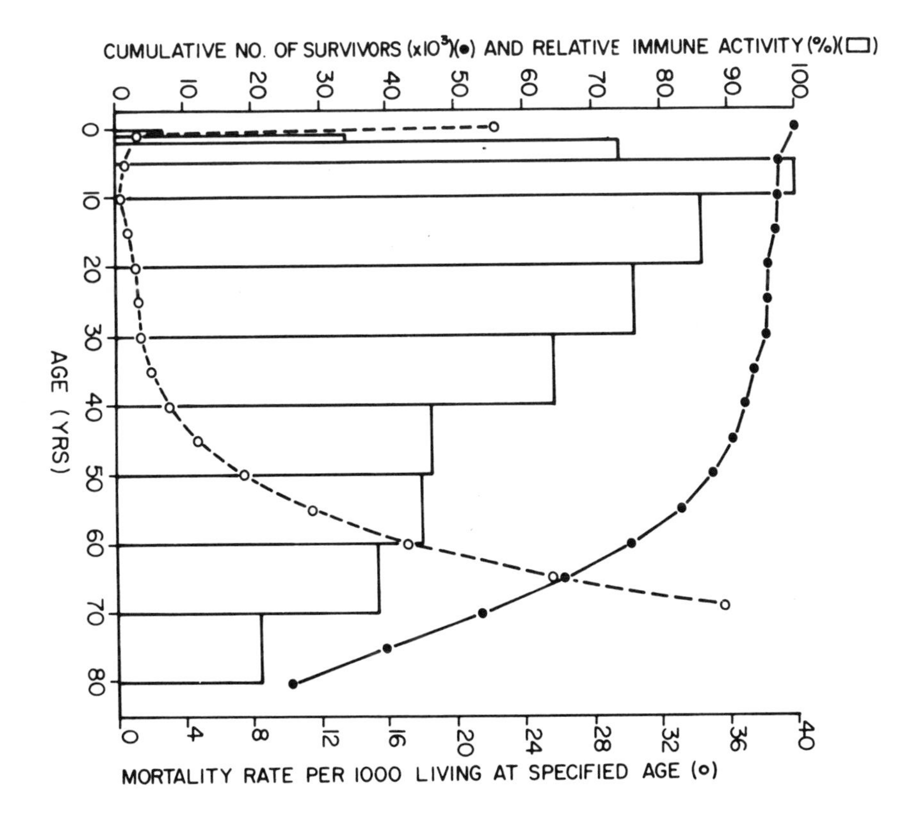

Figure 5-1. Age-related relationship between immunologic activity, mortality rate, and survivors in humans. Histogram represents relative natural serum anti-A isoagglutinin titer (Thomsen and Kettel, 1929); 0 = mortality rate per 1000 living at that specified age (U.S. Bureau of the Census, 1969; 0 = cumulative number of survivors, starting from 100,000 (individuals) (From Kay, M.M.B. and Makinodan, T. Physiologic and Pathologic Autoimmune Manifestations as Influenced by Immunologic Aging. In Natelson, S., Pesce, A.J., Dietz, A.A. (Eds.), *Clinical Immunochemistry*, Washington, D.C.: Am. Assoc. Clin. Chem. Publication, 1978.)

results support our contention that, although there may be a dormant underlying mechanism responsible for the loss of immunologic vigor with age, it is expressed differently between aging individuals, and this fact contributes to the increase in variability of immunologic performance between individuals with age.

Cells of The Immune System

The cells of the immune system can be subdivided into stem cells, thymus-derived T cells, bone-marrow-derived B cells, and macrophages, and each type can be further subdivided (T_1, T_2, T_3 ... T_x). For orientation purpose, the differentiation pathways in an immune response are presented schematically in figure 5-2. All four cell types are being systematically analyzed in relation to age. The results to date indicate that stem cells and T cells show significant age-related changes, while B cells and macrophages show only minimal changes (Makinodan and Yunis, 1977).

Stem Cells

The total number of stem cells in mice generally remains relatively constant throughout the life span of the organism (Chen, 1971). Functionally, they can self replicate in situ throughout the natural life span, unlike stem cell passage in vivo which can be exhausted after about three serial passages (Siminovitch, Till, and McCulloch, 1964). Furthermore, they do not seem to lose their lympho-hematopoietic differentiation ability (Lajtha and Schofield, 1971). However, their clonal expansion rate declines with age (Albright and Makinodan, 1976), as does their ability to generate B cells (Farrar, Loughman, and Nordin, 1974), their ability to "home" into the thymus (Tyan, 1977), and their ability to repair ionizing-radiation-induced DNA damage (Chen, 1974). Regarding their clonal expansion rate, our recent studies indicate that old stem cells remained characteristically old even after they are allowed to self replicate for an extended period of time in genetically compatible young recipients (Albright and Makinodan, 1976). On the other hand, young stem cells can be aged precociously by being allowed to self replicate in genetically compatible old recipients.

T Cells

Present evidence suggests that the total number of T cells does not decrease appreciably with age. However, the proportion of subsets of T cells does change, as reflected in their functions: there is a decline in their mitotic index and a rise in their suppressor index (Makinodan and Yunis, 1977). This suggests that the primary effect of age on T cells is on their differentiation pathway. We tested this hypothesis by assessing the differentiation capacity of aging thymic tissues on stem cells (Hirokawa and Makinodan, 1975). The results revealed that as thymic tissues age, they seem to lose first their capacity to generate T cells with the ability to home into lymph nodes. They then seem to lose their capacity to generate T cells with the ability to respond mitotically to plant lectins and

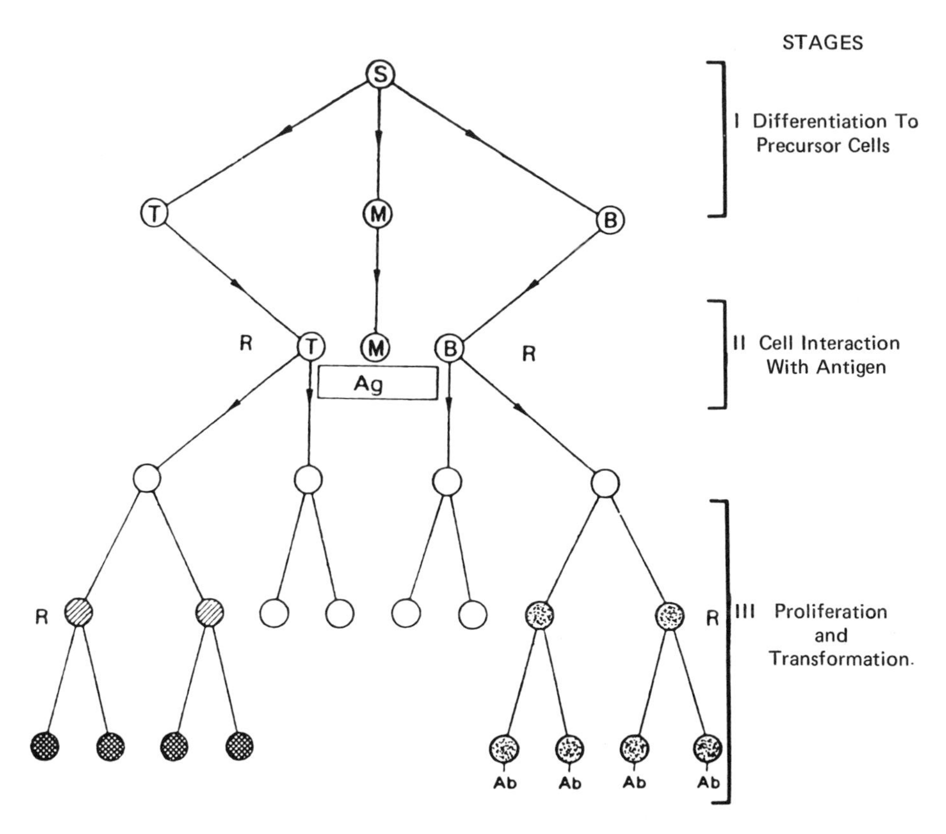

Figure 5-2. Schematic representation of differentiation of immune cells. S = stem cells; T = thymus-derived cells; M = macrophages; B = bone-marrow-derived cells; R = regulatory factors; Ab = antibodies. (From Kay, M.M.B. and Makinodan, T. Physiologic and Pathologic Autoimmune Manifestations as Influenced by Immunologic Aging In Natelson, S., Pesce, A.J., Dietz, A.A. (Eds.), *Clinical Immunochemistry*, Washington, D.C.: Am. Assoc. Clin. Chem. Publication, 1978.)

allogeneic antigens. Their capacity to generate T cells with the ability to home into the spleen, and the ability to enhance antibody response is not lost, but their rate of generating them declines with age. These findings suggest that involution and atrophy of the thymus could be the key to T-cell aging.

In spite of its obvious importance, very little effort has been expended on understanding thymic tissue aging. Hence, we still do not know what mechanisms are responsible for it. Two possibilities can be proposed: a genetically regulated orderly process to self destruct, and an alteration of the DNA of thymus cells in regions with constitutive or regulatory genes. The pacemaker responsible for thymic tissue aging could reside inside or outside the thymus. In the latter case, a very likely site could be in the hypothalamus-pineal-pituitary network.

B Cells

The total number of B cells, as judged by the number of cells with immunoglobulin receptors, does not seem to change appreciably with age, but changes can occur between individuals and between organs within individuals. Thus, for example, Haaijman and Hijmans (1978) reported that the total number of B cells in the spleen and lymph nodes of long-lived CBA mice decreases significantly with age, but the decrease is compensated by a proportional increase in the bone marrow; the bone marrow becomes the major source of B cells in old CBA mice and, perhaps, in other long-lived mice. In humans, studies have been limited primarily to circulating B cells, and the studies indicate that the number of B cells remains relatively constant (Diaz-Jouanen et al., 1975). Unfortunately, we do not know as yet whether the number of circulating B cells corresponds to that in the spleen, lymph nodes, and bone marrow, the last appearing to be the major source of B cells (Haaijman and Hijmans, 1978; Turesson, 1976).

In contrast to the constancy with age in the total B cell population, subpopulations of B cells may fluctuate. For example, in long-lived CBA mice, the number of splenic immunoglobulin (Ig)A-, IgM-, IgG1- and IgG2-positive cells decreases, but the number of splenic IgG3-positive cells remains constant (Haaijman and Hijmans, 1978).

As in the case of total B cell population, the level of serum Ig does not seem to change significantly with age, but the level of individual Ig class does change. In humans the level of serum IgA and IgG tends to increase with age, while that of serum IgM tends to remain constant or decrease slightly (Buckley, Buckley, and Dorsey, 1974; Haferkamp et al., 1966; Lyngbye and Kroll, 1971; Radl et al., 1975).

Although the number of B cells remains relatively stable with age, the response to stimulation with certain T-cell-dependent antigens decreases strikingly (Makinodan and Peterson, 1962). When the responses of young and old mice were systematically evaluated by limiting dilution and dose-response methods, they revealed that the decline is caused by (a) a decrease with age in the number of antigen-sensitive immunocompetent precursor units (IU), which are made up of two or more cell types in various ratios (T_1M, T_2M, ... B_1M_1, B_2M_1 ... $T_1M_1B_1$, $T_2M_1B_3$ ...) (Groves, Lever, and Makinodan, 1970); and (b) a decrease in the average number of functional antibody-forming cells generated by each IU, or the immunologic burst size (IBS) (Price and Makinodan, 1972a, and 1972b). We do not know the cause(s) for the reduction with age in both the relative number of IU and IBS. It could be due to an increase in the number of regulatory T cells which can inhibit the precursor cells making up the IU from interacting with each other, as well as inhibit the proliferation of B cells. The reason for this suspicion is that the total number of Ig-bearing B cells remains relatively constant with age (Diaz-Jouanen et al., 1975; Kay and Makinodan, 1976), and the proliferative capacity of mitogen-sensitive B cells also remains unaltered with age (Hung, Perkins, and Yang, 1975a, 1975b; Makinodan and Adler, 1975). The reduction could also result from an alteration in the ability of certain B cells to interact with other precursor cells making up the IU and in their ability to respond to homeostatic factors during differentiation.

Macrophages

Many of the earlier studies on the mechanism of loss in immunological vigor with age were focused on the macrophages (see review by Teller, 1972). It was thought that because macrophages confront antigens before the T and B cells, any defect in the macrophages could decrease immune functions without appreciable changes in the antigen-specific T and B cells. Studies of this matter showed that macrophages are not adversely affected by aging in their handling of antigens during both the induction of immune responses and phagocytosis. The in vitro phagocytic activity of old mice was equal to or better than that of young mice (Perkins and Makinodan, 1971), and the activity of at least three lysosomal enzymes in macrophages increased rather than decreased with age (Heidrick, 1972). Furthermore, the ability of antigen-laden macrophages of old mice to initiate primary and secondary antibody response in vitro was comparable to that of young mice (Perkins and Makinodan, 1971), and the capacity of splenic macrophages and other adherent cells to cooperate with T and B cells in the initiation of antibody responses in vitro was unaffected by age (Heidrick and Makinodan, 1973). Furthermore, when their in situ antigen-processing ability was indirectly assessed by injecting young and old mice with varying doses of sheep red blood cells, it was found that the slope of the regression line of the antigen dose-antibody response curve and the minimum dose of antigen needed to generate a maximum response were significantly lower and higher, respectively, in old mice (Price and Makinodan, 1972a). Such results could be explained by assuming that the antigen-processing macrophages prevented the antigen-sensitive T and B cells from responding maximally to limiting doses of the antigen (Lloyd and Triger, 1975), perhaps because their number or phagocytic efficiency increased with age (Heidrick, 1972).

Associated with reduced antigen-processing is the failure of antigens to localize in the follicles of lymphoid tissues of antigen-stimulated old mice (Legge and Austin, 1968; Metcalf, Moulds, and Pike, 1966). One clinical implication of these results is that the ability of individuals to detect low doses of antigens, especially weak antigens such as syngeneic tumor antigens, can decline with age, contributing to the age-related poor immune surveillance noted against low doses of certain syngeneic tumor cells in mice (Prehn, 1971). It could also explain why the resistance to allogeneic tumor cell challenge can decline more than one hundred-fold with age in mice manifesting only a four-fold decline in T-cell-mediated cytolytic activity against the same tumor cells (Goodman and Makinodan, 1975).

What emerges from these studies on the cause of immunologic aging is that as individuals become old, their normal immune functions wane as a result primarily of changes affecting the normal differentiation pathway of T cells. Consequently, aging individuals could become susceptible to attack by microbial and other naturally occurring intrinsic and extrinsic agents normally destroyed by T cells (for example, mutated cancer cells) which can lead to debilitating diseases.

Influence of Immunologic Aging on Autoimmunity

Characterization

There are two phases in autoimmunity: first there is an immune response leading to the formation of autoantibody-producing cells, autocytolytic effector cells, or both. This is followed by autoimmune reaction between the target host cell and the autoantibody or between the target host cell and the autocytolytic effector cell, or both. An autoimmune reaction can lead to a disease, commonly called autoimmune disease (AID), but this is not obligatory, nor does it need to play a causative role. It is not surprising that, as emphasized by Fudenberg (1971b), there have been only a few cases of AID in which autoimmune reactions have been demonstrated to play a causative role. The reasons for this are not known. Because AID has been reviewed extensively (Kay, 1976), we need only to reemphasize its two prerequisites: (a) individuals susceptible to AID tend to be genetically predisposed, and (b) AID is most prevalent among individuals with immunologic deficiencies.

With improvement in immunoassays we are detecting more normal individuals with autoantibodies against a variety of cellular components, but not more individuals with AID. Several explanations of this phenomenon can be offered.

1. The concentration of autoantibodies is below the threshold level necessary to trigger clinically detectable AID.
2. The type of autoantibody synthesized is inefficient in activating macrophages and antibody-dependent cytolytic cells.

3. Autoantibodies are not normally accessible to target host cells in sufficient concentration.

Considering these explanations together with the evidence that AID is most prevalent among individuals who are genetically predisposed and immunologically hypoactive, it appears that facultatively pathologic manifestations become pathologic following an episode caused by extrinsic or intrinsic factors (such as viral infection) that sustain and elevate an autoimmune response and sequester appropriate host cells.

An autoimmune reaction could be part of an essential homeostatic process designed to help the body eliminate damaged dying and dead host cells. In support of this notion, as emphasized by Grabar (1975), a series of studies was carried out by Kay (1975) of our laboratory using human red blood cells (RBCs) as the model system. She found that as RBC age, new receptors are exposed on their surface membrane. This enables preexisting IgG autoantibodies to attach immunologically to these receptors, which provides the necessary signal for macrophages to selectively phagocytize old effete RBCs. It appears that certain autoantobodies are contributing to the maintenance of immunologic homeostasis.

Based on these considerations, three types of autoimmune phenomena can be envisioned: (a) physiologic, (b) facultatively pathologic, and (c) pathologic (table 5-1). It becomes apparent that there are two fundamental questions that need to be resolved in autoimmunity: What triggers an autoimmune response? What determines whether an autoimmune reaction is essential for the maintenance of homeostasis, and therefore physiologic, or whether it is pathologic, thus leading to AID? Keeping these unresolved questions in mind, we can now address ourselves briefly to the issue of how these phenomena could be influenced by age-associated changes in immunologic activities.

Age-Associated AID

As indicated earlier, we find that associated with immunologic aging, the frequency of AID increases, together with the frequency of cancer and infection, this relationship is only casually related, and the decline in normal immune functions appears to predispose the aging individual to AID (Kay, 1975).

One of the most revealing recent findings is that of Kay et al. (in press) who, for the first time, evaluated the long-term consequence of parainfluenza viral infection in eight different aging strains of mice and their hybrids (six months postinfection, which is equivalent to 0.25 of a mean life span or 18 human years). They found that the magnitude of age-related thymic involution is more pronounced; the capacity of T cells to respond to mitogenic stimulation is reduced to background levels; the cells are highly susceptible to routine handling; and the frequency of individuals with antiRBC autoantibodies is

Table 5-1
Characteristics of Three Types of Autoimmune Phenomena[a]

Characteristic	*Types*		
	Physiologic	*Facultatively Pathologic*	*Pathologic*
I. Autoimmune Response			
Magnitude of effector cell generation	+	++	+++
II. Autoimmune Reaction			
Specificity of target	+	+ or –	+ or –
Life sustenance	+	–	–
Deleterious effect	–	–	+
III. Association			
Age	–	+	+
Genetic	–	– ?	+
Viral and other types of infection	–	+	+

[a]From Kay, M.M.B. and Makinodan, T. Physiologic and pathologic autoimmune manifestations as influenced by immunologic aging. *Clinical Immunochemistry,* Natelson, S., Pesce, A.J., Dietz, A.A. (Eds.), Washington, D.C.: Am. Assoc. Clin. Chem. Publication, 1978. Reprinted with permission.

increased with age among strains of mice that normally do not express such autoantibodies. Moreover, only those exposed to the viral infection at birth or postadulthood manifested anemia.

Based on these considerations, it seems that AID is triggered by either a loss of self-tolerance, or an infection, or both. Various theories have been offered to explain loss of self-tolerance (emergence of mutant immune cells that are unresponsive to factors controlling self-tolerance, or a defect in the control mechanism that normally maintains self-tolerance), but definitive experimental evidence is still lacking.

Although indirect, experimental and clinical evidence implicating microbial agents as inducers of AID are plentiful (Kay, 1976). For example, conventionally reared animals rendered immunologically deficient by surgical, physical, and chemical treatments develop AID with features that are indistinguishable from those of human AID (for example, Coombs hemolytic anemia). In contrast, animals reared in a germ-free environment fail to develop AID symptoms or do so at a much later stage in life. In NZB mice, an autoimmune-susceptible strain of mice that manifest a disease complex resembling systemic lupus erythematosus in humans, the evidence strongly implicates virus as the cause of the disease complex. Viruses have also been implicated in a number of human AIDs (see table 5-2). The lack of viral specificity in AID supports the view that it is the host response, and not the virus, which determines the pattern of infection (Kay, 1976).

Finally, it should be emphasized that indication of AID may require both the loss of self-tolerance and the participation of microbial agents.

Autoimmune phenomena can be physiologic, facultatively pathologic, or pathologic. Presently, we do not know what determines whether an autoimmune reaction is essential for the maintenance of homeostasis and therefore physiologic, or whether it is potentially pathologic and therefore may lead to AID. On the other hand, the evidence strongly support the view that individuals susceptible to AID tend to be genetically predisposed and immunologically deficient; induction of AID requires loss of self-tolerance or the participation of microbial agents, and as immunologic vigor wanes with age, individuals become more susceptible to infection and AID.

Possible Role of Immunologic Aging in Geriatric Dentistry

It is becoming increasingly apparent that the immune system is involved in practically every pathological process in the body. Thus, it is not surprising that periodontal tissue may also be susceptible to autoimmune and immune complex diseases. Support of this contention comes from various studies. For example,

Table 5-2
Viruses Associated with Autoimmune Disorders in Man[a]

Virus	*Autoimmune Symptoms*[b]
Coxsackie virus	ICN, diabetes
Cytomegelovirus	CHA, diabetes
Epstein-Barr (infectious mononucleosis)	Thrombocytopenia; CHA
Influenza	CHA, A-BMA, diabetes
Myxovirus	ICN, demyelination
Rubella	Polyclonal gammopathy; diabetes
Serum hepatitis	Polyarteritis, hepatitis, ICN, diabetes

[a]Kay, M.M.B. and Makinodan, T. Physiologic and pathologic autoimmune manifestations as influenced by immunologic aging. *Clinical Immunochemistry,* Natelson, S., Pesce, A.J., Dietz, A.A. (Eds.), Washington, D.C.: Am. Assoc. Clin. Chem. Publication, 1978. Reprinted with permission.

[b]CHA = Coombs' positive hemolytic anemia; ICN = immune complex nephritis; A-BMA = antibasement membrane antibody in the lungs, kidneys, or both.

large concentrations of IgG have been detected in the periodontal tissue together with complement and antibodies to plaque bacteria, especially when the tissue is inflammed (Berglund, 1971; Brandzaeg, 1973; Evans, Spaeth, and Mergenhagen, 1966; Kraus and Konno, 1963; Willoughby and Ryan, 1970). Furthermore, it has been reported that chronic periodontitis is caused by a chronic inflammatory lesion of the periodontium leading to a delayed type hypersensitivity involving the T cells (Levy, 1973; Levy and Nelms, 1971; Lehner, 1972; Snyderman, 1973). That complement-activating IgG is the dominating Ig found in the inflammed periodontal tissue suggests that Arthus-type reactions may also contribute to periodontal diseases. The triggering process appears to be a bacterial infection or tissue injury involving the antigens of the dental plaque. To test this notion, Schonfeld, Trump, and Slavkin (1977), succeeded in eliciting in a rabbit an autoantibody response by injecting enamel proteins from another rabbit. It appears that enamel proteins can be sequestered from immune surveillance during an infection and serve as autoantigens.

Based on these considerations, it seems reasonable to assume that the frequency of periodontal lesions triggered by autoimmune and immune complex reactions increases with age, as with many other age-related diseases associated with generalized immunodeficiency state. To this end, studies in dental immunology of aging individuals is encouraged. Preventive dentistry is also encouraged, for an understanding of the pathogenesis of periodontal diseases need not be obligatory to preventive dentistry.

Perspective in Immunogerontology

The field of immunogerontology is still in its scientific infancy, but it has already shown tremendous promise as an experimental model for understanding cellular and molecular aging and as a clinical model to understand AID and other age-associated diseases—diseases that may contribute to periodontal lesions among elderly individuals. Although we do not know what triggers immunologic aging and autoimmune reactions, and what determines whether an autoimmune response is physiologic, facultatively pathologic, or pathologic, we may do so very shortly as judged by the recent increase in research activity in areas such as thymic tissue aging and autoimmune response.

References

Albright, J.W. and Makinodan, T. Decline in the Growth Potential of Spleen-Colonizing Bone Marrow Stem Cells of Long-Lived Aging Mice. *J Exp Med* 144:1204-1213, 1976.

Berglund, S.E. Immunoglobulins in Human Gingiva with Specificity for Oral Bacteria. *J Periodontol* 42:546-551, 1971.

Brandtzaeg, P. Immunology of Inflammatory Periodontal Lesions. *Int Dent J* 23:438-454, 1973.

Buckley, C.E., Buckley, E.G., and Dorsey, F.C. Longitudinal Changes in Serum Immunoglobulin Levels in Older Humans. *Fed Proc* 33:2036-2039, 1974.

Cerilli, J. and Hattan, D. Immunology in Neoplasia Relating to Diagnosis, Therapy, and Transplantation. Immunosuppression and Oncogenesis. *Am J Clin Pathol* 62:218-223, 1974.

Chen, M.G. Age-related Changes in Hematopoietic Stem Cell Populations of a Long-Lived Hybrid Mouse. *J Cell Physiol* 78:225-232, 1971.

Chen, M.G. Impaired Elkind Recovery in Hematopoietic Colony-Forming Cells of Aged Mice. *Proc Soc Exp Biol Med* 145:1181-1186, 1974.

Diaz-Jouanen, E., Williams, R.C., Jr., and Strickland, R.G. Age-Related Changes in T and B cells. *Lancet* 1:688-689, 1975.

Evans, R.T., Spaeth, S., and Mergenhagen, S.E. Bactericidal Antibody in Mammalian Serum to Obligatorily Anaerobic Gram Negative Bacteria. *J Immunol* 97:112-119, 1966.

Fabris, N., Pierpaoli, W., and Sorkin, E. Lymphocytes, Hormones and Aging. *Nature* (London) 240:557-559, 1972.

Farrar, J.J., Loughman, B.E., and Nordin, A.A. Lymphopoietic Potential of Bone Marrow Cells From Aged Mice: Comparison of the Cellular Constituents of Bone Marrow From Young and Aged Mice. *J Immunol* 112:1244-1249, 1974.

Fudenberg, H.H., Good, R.A., Goodman, H.C., Hitzig, W., et al. Primary Immunodeficiencies. Report of a World Health Organization Committee. *Pediatrics* 47:927-946, 1971a.

Fudenberg, H.H. Genetically Determined Immune Deficiency as the Predisposing Cause of "Autoimmunity" and Lymphoid Neoplasia. *Am J Med* 51:295-298, 1971b.

Good, R.A. and Yunis, E.J. Association of Autoimmunity, Immunodeficiency and Aging in Man, Rabbits, and Mice. *Fed Proc* 33:2040-2050, 1974.

Goodman, S.A. and Makinodan, T. Effect of Age on Cell-Mediated Immunity in Long-Lived Mice. *Clin Exp Immunol* 19:533-542, 1975.

Grabar, P. Hypothesis. Auto-Antibodies and Immunological Theories: An Analytical Review. *Clin Exp Immunol* 4:453-466, 1975.

Groves, D.L., Lever, W.E., and Makinodan, T. A Model for the Interaction of Cell Types in the Generation of Hemolytic Plaque-Forming Cells. *J Immunol* 104:148-165, 1970.

Haaijman, J.J. and Hijmans, W. The Influence of Age on the Immunological Activity and Capacity of the CBA Mouse. *Mech Ageing Dev* 7:375-398, 1978.

Haferkamp, O., Schlettwein-Gsell, D., Schwick, H.G., and Storiko, K. Serum Protein in an Aging Population with Particular Reference to Evaluation of Immune Globulins and Antibodies. *Gerontologia* 12:30-36, 1966.

Heidrick, M.L. Age-Related Changes in Hydrolase Activity of Peritoneal Macrophages. *Gerontologist* 12:28, 1972.

Heidrick, M.L. and Makinodan, T. Presence of Impairment of Humoral Immunity in Nonadherent Spleen Cells of Old Mice. *J Immunol* 111:1502-1506, 1973.

Hirokawa, K. and Makinodan, T. Thymic Involution: Effect on T Cell Differentiation. *J Immunol* 114:1659-1664, 1975.

Hung, C-Y., Perkins, E.H., and Yang, W-K. Age-Related Refractoriness of PHA-Induced Lymphocyte Transformation. I. Comparable Sensitivity of Spleen Cells From Young and Old Mice to Culture Conditions. *Mech Ageing Dev* 4:29-39, 1975a.

Hung, C-Y., Perkins, E.H., and Yang, W-K. Age-Related Refractoriness of PHA-Induced Lymphocyte Transformation. II. ^{125}I-PHA Binding to Spleen Cells From Young and Old Mice. *Mech Ageing Dev* 4:103-112, 1975b.

Kay, M.M.B. Mechanism of Removal of Senescent Cells by Human Macrophages in situ. *Proc Natl Acad Sci USA* 72:3521-3525, 1975.

Kay, M.M.B. Autoimmune Disease: The Consequence of Deficient T-Cell Function? *J Am Geriatr Soc* 24:253-257, 1976.

Kay, M.M.B. and Makinodan, T. Immunobiology of Aging: Evaluation of Current Status. *Clin Immunol Immunopathol* 6:394-413, 1976.

Kay, M.M.B. and Makinodan, T. Physiologic and Pathologic Autoimmune Manifestations as Influenced by Immunologic Aging. In Natelson, S., Pesce, A.J., Dietz, A.A. (Eds.), *Clinical Immunochemistry* (Washington, D.C.: Am. Assoc. Clin. Chem., 1978).

Kay, M.M.B., Mendoza, J., Hausman, S., and Dorsey, B. Age-Related Changes in the Immune System of Mice of 8 Medium and Long-Lived Strains and Hybrids. II. Effect of Natural Infection with Parainfluenza Type I Virus (Sendai). *Mech Ageing Dev* (in press).

Kraus, F.W. and Konno, J. Antibodies in Saliva. *Ann NY Acad Sci* 106:311-329, 1963.

Lajtha, L.J. and Schofield, R. Regulation of Stem Cell Renewal and Differentiation: Possible Significance in Aging *Advances Gerontol Res* 3:131-146, 1971.

Legge, J.S. and Austin, C.M. Antigen Localization and the Immune Response as a Function of Age. *Australian J Exp Biol Med Sci* 46:361-365, 1968.

Lehner, T. Cell-Mediated Immune Responses in Oral Disease: A Review. *J Oral Pathol* 1:39-58, 1972.

Levy, B.M. and Nelms, D.C. Migratory Inhibition Factor Associated With Chronic Destructive Periodontitis. *J Dent Res* 50:505, 1971.

Levy, B.M. Prevention of Periodontal Disease—A Pathologist's View. *Int Dent J* 23:476-480, 1973.

Lloyd, R.S. and Triger, D.R. Studies on Hepatic Uptake of Antigen. III. Studies of Liver Macophage Function of Normal Rats and Following Carbon Tetrachloride Administration. *Immunology* 29:253-263, 1975.

Lyngbye, J. and Kroll, J. Quantitative Immunoelectrophoresis of Proteins in Serum From Normal Population: Season-, Age-, and Sex-Related Variations. *Clin Chem* 17:495-500, 1971.

Makinodan, T. and Peterson, W.J. Relative Antibody-Forming Capacity of Spleen Cells as a Function of Age. *Proc Natl Acad Sci USA* 48:234-238, 1962.

Makinodan, T. and Adler, W. Effects of Aging on the Differentiation and Proliferation Potentials of Cells of the Immune System. *Fed Proc* 34:153-158, 1975.

Makinodan, T., Albright, J.W., Good, P.I., Peter, C.P., and Heidrick, M.L. Reduced Humoral Immune Activity in Long-Lived Old Mice: An Approach to Elucidating Its Mechanisms. *Immunology* 31:903-911, 1976.

Makinodan, T. and Yunis, E. *Immunology and Aging* (New York: Plenum, 1977).

Metcalf, D., Moulds, R., and Pike, B. Influence of the Spleen and Thymus on Immune Responses in Aging Mice. *Clin Exp Immunol* 2:109-120, 1966.

Penn, I. and Starzl, T.E. Malignant Tumors Arising de novo in Immunosuppressed Organ Transplant Recipients. *Transplantation* 14:407-417, 1972.

Perkins, E.H. and Makinodan, T. Nature of Humoral Immunologic Deficiencies of the Aged. *In Proceedings of the 1st Rocky Mountain Symposium on Aging* (Fort Collins, Colorado: Colorado State University, 1971), pp. 80-103.

Prehn, R.T. Evaluation of the Evidence for Immune Surveillance. In R.T. Smith and M. Landy (Eds.), *Immune Surveillance* (New York: Academic, 1971), pp. 451-462.

Price, G.B. and Makinodan, T. Immunologic Deficiencies in Senescence. I. Characterization of Intrinsic Deficiencies. *J Immunol* 108:403-412, 1972a.

Price, G.B. and Makinodan, T. Immunologic Deficiencies in Senescence. II. Characterization of Extrinsic Deficiencies. *J Immunol* 108:413-417, 1972b.

Radl, J., Sepers, J.M., Skvaril, F., Morell, A., and Hijmans, W. Immunoglobulin Pattern in Humans Over 95 Yeras of Age. *Clin Exp Immunol* 22:84-90, 1975.

Schonfeld, S.E., Trump, G.N., and Slavkin, H.C. Immunogenicity of Two Naturally Occurring Solid-Phase Enamel Proteins. *Proc Soc Exp Biol Med* 155:111-114, 1977.

Siminovitch, L., Till, J.E., and McCulloch, E.A. Decline in Colony-Forming Ability of Marrow Cells Subjected to Serial Transplantation Into Irradiated Mice. *J Cell Physiol* 64:23-31, 1964.

Snyderman, R. The Role of the Immune Response in the Development of Periodontal Diseases. *Int Dent J* 23:310-316, 1973.

Teller, M.N. Age Changes and Immune Resistance to Cancer. *Adv Gerontol Res* 4:25-43, 1972.

Thomsen, O. and Kettel, K. Die Starke der Menschlichen Isoagglutinine und Entsprechende Blutkörperchenrezeptoren in Verschiedenen Lebensaltern. *Atschr f Immunitatsforsch u Exper Therap* 63:67-93, 1929.

Turesson, I. Distribution of Immunoglobulin-Containing Cells in Human Bone Marrow and Lymphoid Tissues. *Acta Med Scand* 199:293-304, 1976.

Tyan, M.L. Age-Related Decrease in Mouse T-Cell Progenitors. *J Immunol* 118:846-851, 1977.

U.S. Bureau of the Census. *Statistical Abstracts of the United States*, 1969. 90th ed. (Washington: Government Printing Office, 1969).

Willoughby, D.A. and Ryan, G.B. Evidence for a Possible Endogenous Antigen in Chronic Inflammation. *J Pathol* 101:233-239, 1970.

Yunis, E.J., Hilgard, H., Sjodin, K., Martinez, C., and Good, R.A. Immunological Reconstitution of Thymectomized Mice by Injections of Isolated Thymocytes. *Nature* (London) 201:784-786, 1964.

Zukoski, C.I., Killen, D.A., Ginn, E., Matler, B., Lucas, D.O., and Siegler, H.F. Transplant Carcinoma in an Immunosuppressed Patient. *Transplantation* 9:71-74, 1970.

Neuroendocrine Changes in Aging

Paola S. Timiras

A theory on aging attracting considerable interest among gerontologists combines both cellular and organismic aspects. It postulates that a "program for aging" genetically encoded in the brain (Everitt and Burgess, 1976; Finch, 1973; Kanungo, 1975) may be expressed by a precisely defined timetable of growth, development, and aging (Segall and Timiras, 1976). From specific centers in the brain, the controlling signal relays to the peripheral tissues and organs by neural (somatic and autonomic) and hormonal stimulation or inhibition. Evidence for this program, perhaps analogous to similar programs regulating other timed physiologic interactions, is still very tentative. Its nature and localization remain to be clearly identified.

Nevertheless, because of the central role of the brain and endocrines in the control of all bodily functions and the synchronization of several rhythmic functions, it is reasonable to suggest as a working hypothesis that a clock exists located in some discrete area of the brain and influenced by environmental factors. Data supporting this theory derive primarily from observations of the aging nervous and endocrine systems and from experiments where alterations in neuroendocrine interrelations lead to disturbances not only of growth and maturation but of aging as well. Experimental manipulations of these interrelations by varying conditions and agents—dietary, pharmacologic, environmental—provide animal models in which to test the competence of neuroendocrine integrations regulating a timetable of major events and length of the life span. This chapter highlights some of the changes that occur with aging in the brain and endocrines and presents animal models in which prolongation of the life span and of physiologic competence is achieved through modification of neuroendocrine activity.

Aging of the Brain

Brain aging has been subject to numerous reviews and publications in recent years, both clinical and experimental (Birren and Schaie, 1977; Everitt and Burgess, 1976; Finch and Hayflick, 1977; Timiras and Bignami, 1976; Timiras and Vernadakis, 1972). Although a number of studies have demonstrated a decrease in brain size and loss of neurons, in several animal species, including humans, aging patterns remain equivocal. On the other hand, an increase in glial cell population was observed in some brain areas, and this was interpreted as a compensatory reaction to the declining functional capacity of the neurons (Brizzee, Sherwood, and Timiras, 1968). Other changes in neurons include accumulation of lipofuscin, loss of Nissl substance, presence of neurofibrillar tangles, and a striking loss of dendrites. The loss of dendrites, and consequently, of synaptic connections may be related to concomitant alterations in neurotransmission (Timiras and Bignami, 1976).

Furthermore, alterations in cholinergic systems and the concentrations of certain amino acids considered to act as neurotransmitters have been described in the brain of senescent rats (Valcana and Timiras, 1969; Timiras, Hudson, and Oklund, 1973), and changes with aging in levels and metabolism of monoamine neurotransmitters have been reported in the brains of mice (Finch, 1973) and chickens (Vernadakis, 1973, 1975), and also, in plasma, platelets, and human brains (Robinson, 1975). These studies show that the overall picture of the aging brain is one of neurotransmission imbalance—preferential decrements may occur in some neurotransmitters in some specific regions while others remain unaffected. In some cases, excess or deficit of a certain neurotransmitter results in functional alterations ascribable to a single loss (such as the decrease in dopamine in the corpus striatum in patients affected with Parkinson's disease), and, in other cases, it results in imbalances among several neurotransmitters. For example, preliminary studies have shown that the ratio of serotonin (inhibitory) to dopamine (excitatory) in the cerebrum of rats markedly increases from adulthood to old age, suggesting a progressive preponderance of inhibition with aging (Segall, Miller, and Timiras, 1975; Timiras, 1975).

Normal brain function depends on the delicate tuning of inhibitory and excitatory impulses. A disequilibrium of this balance has severe and widespread functional repercussions involving somatic, visceral, and endocrinologic functions. This balance can become so unstable with old age that deviations are induced even by minor shifts in neurotransmission (Timiras, 1975). Thus, loss and impairment of synapses in the cerebral cortex may be responsible for the progressive removal of the more subtle modulatory aspects of cortical activity and the consequent fuctional decrements of senility, such as decreasing muscular strength, lack of dexterity and agility, failing cognitive performance, and deficits in association, retrieval, and recall of information (Scheibel and Scheibel, 1975).

Disturbances in monoamine metabolism have been linked to age-related phenomena such as graying of the hair (L-DOPA is a melanin precursor), alterations in sleep and speech, increased incidence of extrapyramidal behavioral disorders, and alterations in hypothalamic control of visceral and endocrine functions. These considerations also suggest that the reduction of salivary flow in the mouths of elderly individuals may depend more on alterations in the autonomic control of salivary secretion than in the sporadic changes reported in the secretory cells. In turn, failure of local functions (regulation of oral microflora, protection of oral mucosae) and systemic functions (regulation of iodine and calcium metabolism, excretion of drugs) of the salivary glands would have significant consequences for oral biology and metabolic (digestive and excretory) competence of the aged.

Aging of Endocrines

As for the brain, numerous studies have attempted to delineate changes in endocrine function identifiable as having a causative role in aging (Everitt and Burgess, 1976; Finch and Hayflick, 1977; Timiras, 1972). The resulting information has been, for the most part circumstantial inasmuch as cessation of endocrine function or clearcut alterations in hormone levels and metabolism could not be detected except for the arrest of ovarian function at menopause.

A typical example of the dichotomy between signs of endocrine insufficiency and unaltered hormone levels is represented by the case of the thyroid gland. Whereas its crucial role during early development in body growth and brain maturation and its influence during adulthood on basal metabolic rate are undisputed, its involvement in aging processes remains controversial. Several investigators have related some of the features of senescence (decreased metabolic rate, diminished motor activity, impaired muscular strength, dryness of skin, sparseness of hair) to those of the hypothyroid state, even though comparison of thyroid activity as a function of age in adults and old individuals has not revealed profound differences, nor has the administration of thyroid hormones rejuvenated older persons (Gregerman, 1967). Therefore, the hypothesis of hypothyroidism as a concomitant of aging was discarded for some time. More recent work, however, seems to indicate that even if thyroid function is unchanged, the sensitivity of the target tissues, including the brain, to thyroid hormones decreases with old age (Frolkis, Verzhikovskaya, and Valueva, 1973). According to evidence based on age-related observations of thyroid and hypophyseal interrelations, responsiveness of the thyroid gland to thyrotropic hormone also decreases with age (Ooka, Segall, and Timiras, 1978). In addition, other studies have suggested the existence of a pituitary factor, the release of which increases with aging and is responsible for the decreased responsiveness to thyroid hormones of tissues from old rats (Denckla, 1974).

As for thyroid hormones, the secretion and metabolism of adrenocortical hormones remain unaffected by aging, at least under steady state conditions. On the other hand, changes in number or affinity of steroid hormone receptors during development and aging support the hypothesis that aging induces alterations in the ability of animals and tissues to respond to hormonal signals rather than in the secretory activity of the endocrine glands themselves (Roth, 1974, 1975). With respect to the brain, a 55 to 65 percent reduction in the concentration of glucocorticoid binding sites has been described in cortical neurons of senescent rats relative to their mature counterparts (Roth, 1976).

This reduction, particularly striking in neurons, also involves glial cells and other brain constituents, but to a much lesser degree; it is not affected by adrenalectomy, nor does it show differential partitioning of sites between nucleus and cytoplasm (Roth, 1976). Receptors for sex steroids in the rat brain also seem to decrease in number and, possibly, affinity with old age (Kanungo, 1975).

Changes comparable to osteoarthritis and osteoporosis occur frequently at the mandibular condyle and in the mandibular and maxillary bones, respectively, with aging. These changes, like the corresponding skeletal changes, are influenced by a number of factors. Declining hormonal levels or declining sensitivity of bone tissues to hormones–particularly sex and adrenocortical steroids–play an important role in their pathogenesis. Similarly, gingival tissue is extremely sensitive to systemic stress (hormonal, nutritional) as well as to local insults (mechanical, bacterial, fungal). Therefore, hormonal changes with aging may be responsible for the marked gingival recession associated with old age, either by directly affecting the gingival tissue itself or by indirectly increasing the incidence of infections through alterations in immunologic competence.

Neuroendocrine Interrelations

From what we know of the neuroendocrine relations in the adult and the changes in the nervous and endocrine systems with aging, the following sequence of events relating neurotransmission to neuroendocrine balance may be postulated (figure 6-1). During development, neurotransmitters in several cortical and subcortical centers progressively mature (Loizou, 1972) and begin to exert a regulatory action on the neurosecretory cells of the hypothalamus, reaching stability during adulthood (Wurtman, 1970). Coincident with the maturation of these hypothalamic neurosecretory systems, the releasing and inhibiting hormones they produce trigger the anterior pituitary to synthesize and secrete its tropic hormones which, in turn, stimulate the target endocrines to secrete their respective hormones. These hormones, especially thyroid, adrenocortical, and gonadal hormones, reach the target effector cells where they may act as "gene triggers" causing target tissues to undergo developmental changes. The activity of each of the control systems–cerebral cortex, hypothalamus, pituitary, and other endocrines–and the positive and negative feedbacks that regulate them, may be impaired with aging. If, as it has been postulated, the monoaminergic neurons in the higher brain centers represent the pacemakers that regulate the biologic clock governing development and aging (Everitt and Burgess, 1976; Finch, 1973; Segall et al., 1978; Segall and Timiras, 1975, 1976), it follows that any alterations of the activity of these neurons with aging would lead to alterations in neurotransmitter activity; the latter, in turn, would have repercussions on neural, endocrine, muscular, secretory, and motor functions as variously manifested in the aged (involution of reproductive organs; loss of fertility, muscular strength, ability to recover from stress; impairment of secretory, cardiovascular, respiratory activity). Indeed, the possibility that oral and dental tissues may also be affected by alteration of this regulation has already been mentioned.

That programmed changes in the activities of genes are not confined to fertilization but continue to later ages and are triggered by hormonal influences is well documented in several animal species, particularly insects and amphibians (Comfort, 1979, Finch and Hayflick, 1977; Timiras, 1972). If we assume that such a programming is operative in mammals also, and is regulated by neural and endocrine systems, interventions at the level of these systems may influence aging as well as development. Speculative as this hypothesis may appear, it has the advantage of providing a practical handle with which to investigate aging processes. We have today various means of altering monoamine levels and metabolism in the brain and a rationale to expect that these alterations affect several functions throughout the life span. Some experimental approaches illustrating animal models in which the life span has been modified are presented in the next section.

Experimental Animal Models

Several studies by McCay (1952), Berg (1960), and Ross (1976) have shown that rats kept on a diet restricted in calories but having the normal ratio of nutrients remain immature for long periods of time and resume growth when realimented at liberty. In the strain studied by McCay, animals reportedly lived for more than one thousand four hundred days—double the normal life span; in addition, the incidence and severity of the pathologic changes associated with old age (atherosclerosis, neoplasms) were diminished in comparison to control animals of similar chronological age (fed an unrestricted diet). These experiments demonstrating that the life span of a mammal can be significantly extended in the laboratory represent a landmark in gerontology.

Similar results have been obtained by feeding rats from weaning to approximately two years of age a diet restricted in tryptophan, an essential amino acid and precursor of the neurotransmitter serotonin. Under these conditions, growth and maturation were severely retarded, but when the animals were returned to a complete, commercial diet, average and extreme life span was prolonged, and a number of functions, (reproduction, adaptation to stress) remained comparable to those of chronologically younger animals that had been maintained on the standard diet with adequate amounts of tryptophan during the entire life span (Segall and Timiras, 1975, 1976).

Our understanding of the role of essential amino acids in growth suggests that the maturational and functional alterations observed in tryptophan-deficient rats may be mediated at a number of levels. At the cellular level, the

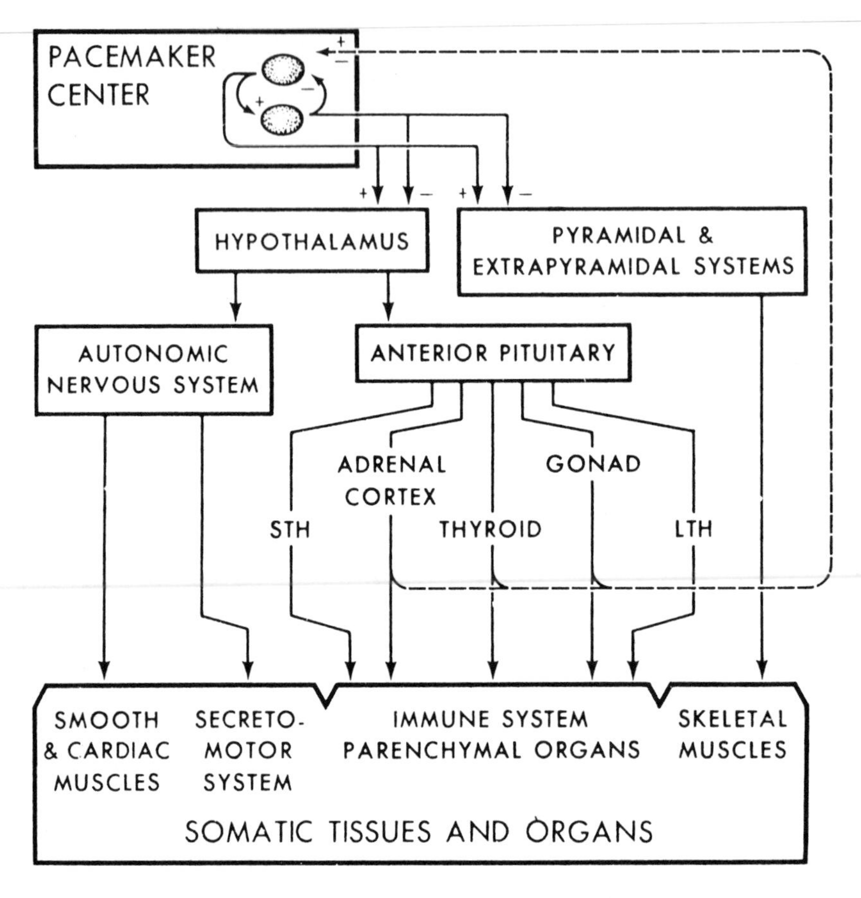

Figure 6-1. Schematic drawing of the brain-endocrine theory of programmed aging. Specific pacemaker centers are comprised of groups of excitatory (+) or inhibitory (−) neurons which feed back to each other by direct or indirect neural processes and create stimulatory (+) or repressive (−) influences on brain areas such as the hypothalamus (which controls the autonomic nervous and neuroendocrine systems) and the pyramidal and extrapyramidal nervous systems (which control skeletal muscle tone and movement). These influences then affect the structure and function of the musculature (smooth, cardiac, and striated), the exocrine glands, the immune system, and the parenchymal organs. With aging, it is hypothesized that inhibitory neural influences are programmed to become predominant, creating a loss in muscle tone and function, alterations or decline in the elaboration of many secretions, cardiovascular impairment, immunologic suppression, paren-

Figure 6-1. *(cont.)*
chymal organs and, therefore, homeostatic performance loss, as well as many other physiologic deficits associated with senescene. The dashed line represents hypothetical feedback influences of the thyroid and steroid hormones on the regulatory centers of the brain.

essential amino acids are necessary to produce the myriad of enzymes and structural proteins involved in growth and development; in addition, the essential amino acids are required for the formation of hypothalamic and pituitary hormones and, furthermore, tryptophan as well as phenylalanine, another essential amino acid, are precursors of serotonin, norepinephrine, and dopamine and, as such, are implicated directly in neurotransmission. Because of the role of monoamines in regulating the production of hypothalamic hormones, it follows that a tryptophan deficiency could impair the production of hypothalamic hormones and, in turn, of pituitary hormones, thereby disturbing neuroendocrine control and, perhaps, the action of the biologic clock purported to govern both growth and aging.

Neurotransmitter levels and metabolism can also be modified by drugs. These modifications can affect the course of aging and the length of the life span. Characteristic among the studies of this group are those showing that administration of L-dopa, a precursor of dopamine, is capable of retarding growth and delaying the onset of aging in mice (Cotzias et al., 1977). These findings agree with other studies in which parachlorophenlalanine (PCPA), a substance that blocks the formation of serotonin by inhibiting one of the steps of its synthesis (tryptophan decarboxylase activity), was used to delay growth and maturation (Segall et al., 1978).

It has further been shown that these dietary and pharmacologic treatments not only affect brain neurotransmitter levels, but also act on the pituitary and target endocrines. Anterior pituitary changes, after tryptophan or caloric restriction or PCPA administration included the following. At the light microscopic level, decreased cell size and decreased basophilia, particularly in the thyrotropes, as well as reduced cell number and basophilia in the gonadotropes were noted. At the electron microscopic level, a decrease in the number of gonadotropes, an increase in the number of vacuoles in both thyrotropes and remaining gonadotropes, and loss of endoplasmic reticulum and Golgi structures, changes in cytoplasmic to nucleus ratio, and increased autophagic activity suggested a decrease in functional activity. This was supported by a marked atrophy of the ovary and alterations in thyroid hormone levels and thyroid-pituitary relations (Segall et al., 1978; Ooka, Segall, and Timiras, 1978). Multiple forms of gonadotropins have been described after castration in rats (Bogdanove, Nolin, and Campbell, 1975), and it has been proposed that pituitary hormones may be modified by proteinase systems after their synthesis at the ribosome (Smith and Van Frank, 1975).

In the preceding section, the hypothesis that with aging, the pituitary gland produces a factor capable of interfering with the effectiveness of endogenous thyroid hormones was presented as an example of altered hormonal interactions with aging (Denckla, 1974). From all these studies, it can be suggested that, with aging, the pituitary may produce hormones that are "incompletely sculptured" by post-translationally active enzymes and alter cellular metabolism (Segall et al., 1978). It may be further postulated that this incomplete sculpturing with aging is related to a change in the interaction between the pituitary and the hypothalamus and, perhaps indirectly, with higher regions of the brain.

Other experimental procedures capable of modifying physiological events throughout the life span include the administration of iproniazid, a monoamine oxidase inhibitor, and hormonal and electrical stimulation; with these interventions it has been possible to reinitiate estrous cyclicity in old rats and to restore some of their physiologic competence (Clemens et al., 1968; Quadri, Kledzik, and Meites, 1973).

Studies on the aging of the brain (alterations in synaptic structure and in levels and metabolism of neurotransmitters) and the endocrines (changes in synthesis and release of hormones and number and properties of hormone receptors) suggest that aging processes, as other critical events throughout the life span, are dependent on integrative neuroendocrine regulations. Accordingly, a "program of aging," genetically encoded in the brain, may regulate a precisely defined timetable of growth, maturation, and aging. Evidence in support of such a program, possibly analogous to similar programs regulating other timed physiologic interactions (biologic clocks) is still tentative. Nevertheless, because of the key role of nervous and endocrine systems in the control of all bodily functions and in the synchronization of several rhythmic functions, and because of our increasing knowledge of the mechanisms by which this role is implemented, it appears useful to postulate that such a clock exists, is located in the brain, and is influenced by endocrine and environmental factors. Based thereupon, experiments have been conducted in which dietary manipulations such as caloric restriction or deficiency in tryptophan (an essential amino acid and precursor of the neurotransmitter serotonin) and administration of pharmacologic agents capable of altering neurotransmission (L-dopa and inhibitors of monoamine enzymes) have resulted in disturbances of growth and development, in prolongation of physiologic competence, and, in some cases, in extension of life span as well. These data may help to explain some of the manifestations of old age, including dental and parodontal aging (decline in autonomic control of salivary secretions, decline in hormonal levels and their relation to osteoporosis, gingival recession and immunologic suppression with increased incidence of oral infections and cancer); more important, these experiments provide useful models with which to test the role of neuroendocrine imbalances in aging and to explore the means for modifying and eventually preventing or minimizing imbalances.

References

Berg, B.N. Nutrition and Longevity in the Rat. I. Food Intake in Relation to Size, Health, and Fertility. *J Nutr* 71:242-254, 1960.

Birren, J.E. and Schaie, K.W., Eds. *The Handbook of the Psychology of Aging.* (New York: Van Nostrand and Reinhold, 1977).

Bogdanove, E.M., Nolin, J.M., and Cambell, G.T. Qualitative and Quantitative Gonad-Pituitary Feedback. *Recent Prog Horm Res* 31:567-626, 1975.

Brizzee, K.R., Sherwood, N., and Timiras, P.S. A Comparison of Cell Populations at Various Depth Levels in Cerebral Cortex of Young Adult and Aged Long-Evans Rats. *J Geront* 23:289-297, 1968.

Clemens, J.A., Amenomori, Y., Jenkins, T., and Meites, J. Effects of Hypothalamic Stimulation, Hormones, and Drugs on Ovarian Function in Old Female Rats. *Prox Soc Exp Biol Med* 132:561-563, 1969.

Comfort, A. *The Biology of Senescence.* 3rd Edition. (New York: Elsevier, 1979).

Cotzias, G.C., Miller, S.T., Tang, L.C., Papavasiliou, P.S., and Wang, Y.Y. Levodopa, Fertility, and Longevity. *Science* 196:549-551, 1977.

Denckla, W.D. Role of the Pituitary and Thyroid Glands in the Decline of Minimal O_2 Consumption With Age. *J Clin Invest* 53:572-581, 1974.

Everitt, A.V. and Burgess, J.A., Eds. *Hypothalamus, Pituitary, and Aging.* (Springfield: Charles C. Thomas, 1976).

Finch, C.E. Monoamine Metabolism in the Aging Male Mouse. In Rockstein, M. and Sussman, M.L. (Eds.), *Development and Aging in the Nervous System* (New York: Academic, 1973), pp. 199-218.

Finch, C.E. and Hayflick, L., Eds. *The Handbook of the Biology of Aging* (New York: Van Nostrand Reinhold, 1977).

Frolkis, V.V., Verzhikovskaya, N.V., and Valueva, G.V. The Thyroid and Age. *Exp Geront* 8:285-296, 1973.

Gregerman, R.I. The Age-Related Alteration of Thyroid Function and Thyroid Hormone Metabolism in Man. In Gitman, L. (Ed.), *Endocrines and Aging* (Springfield: Charles C. Thomas, 1967), pp. 161-173.

Kanungo, M.S. A Model for Aging. *J. Theoret Biol* 53:253-261, 1975.

Loizou, L.A. The Postnatal Ontogeny of Monamine-Containing Neurons in the Central Nervous System of the Albino Rat. *Brain Res* 40:395-418, 1972.

McCay, C.M. Chemical Aspects of Aging and the Effect of Diet Upon Aging. In Lansing, A.I. (Ed.), *Cowdry's Problems of Aging* (Baltimore: Williams and Wilkins, 1952), pp. 139-202.

Ooka, H., Segall, P.E., and Timiras, P.S. Neural and Endocrine Development After Chronic Tryptophan Deficiency in Rats: II. Pituitary-Thyroid Axis. *Mech Ageing Dev* 71:19-24, 1978.

Quadri, S.K., Kledzik, G.S., and Meites, J. Reinitiation of Estrous Cycles in Old Constant-Estrous Rats by Central-Acting Drugs. *Neuroendocrinology* 11:248-255, 1973.

Robinson, D.S. Changes in Monoamine Oxidase and Monoamines with Human Development and Aging. *Fed Proc* 34:103-107, 1975.

Ross, M.H. Nutrition and Longevity in Experimental Animals. In Winick, M. (Ed.), *Nutrition and Aging* (New York: John Wiley and Sons, 1976).

Roth, G.S. Age-Related Changes in Specific Glucocorticoid Binding by Steriod-Responsive Tissues of Rats. *Endocrinology* 91:82-90, 1974.

Roth, G.S. Changes in Hormone Binding and Responsiveness in Target Cells and Tissues During Aging. In Cristofalo, V.J., Roberts, J., and Adelman, R.C. (Eds.), *Explorations in Aging* (New York: Plenum, 1975), pp. 195-208.

Roth, G.S. Reduced Glucocorticoid Binding Site Concentration in Cortical Neuronal Perikarya From Senescent Rats. *Brain Res* 107:345-354, 1976.

Scheibel, M.E. and Scheibel, A.B. Structural Changes in the Aging Brain. In Brody, H., Harman, D., and Ordy, J.M., (Eds.), *Aging Series: Clinical, Morphologic, and Neurochemical Aspects in the Aging Central Nervous System* (New York: Raven, 1975), vol. 1, pp. 11-37.

Segall, P.E. and Timiras, P.S. Age-Related Changes in Thermoregulatory Capacity of Tryptophan-Deficient Rats. *Fed Proc* 34:83-85, 1975.

Segall, P.E., Miller, C., and Timiras, P.S. *Aging of CNS Monoamines.* 10th International Congress of Gerontology, vol. II, Jerusalem, 1975, p. 87.

Segall, P.E. and Timiras, P.S. Pathophysiologic Findings After Chronic Tryptophan Deficiency in Rats: A Model for Delayed Growth and Aging. *Mech Aging Dev* 5:109-124, 1976.

Segall, P.E., Ooka, H., Rose, K., and Timiras, P.S. Neural and Endocrine Development After Chronic Tryptophan Deficiency in Rats: I. Brain Monoamine and Pituitary Responses. *Mech Aging Dev* 7:1-17, 1978.

Smith, R.E. and Van Frank, R.M. The Use of Amino Acid Derivatives of 4-Methoxy-Beta-Naphthylamine for the Assay and Subcellular Localization of Tissue Proteinases. In Dingle, J.T. and Dean, R.T., (Eds.), *Lysosomes in Biology and Pathology* (North Holland: Elsevier, 1975), vol. IV, pp. 193-249.

Timiras, P.S. *Developmental Physiology and Aging.* (New York: Macmillan, 1972).

Timiras, P.S. *Neurophysiological Factors in Aging, Recent Advances.* 10th International Congress of Gerontology, vol. 1, Jerusalem, 1975, p. 50.

Timiras, P.S. and Bignami, A. Pathophysiology of the Aging Brain. In Elias, M.F., Eleftheriou, B.E., and Elias, P.K. (Eds.), *Special Review of Experimental Aging Research* Progress in Biology. (Bar Harbor: EAR, Inc., 1976), pp. 351-378.

Timiras, P.S., Hudson, D.B., and Oklund, S. Changes in Central Nervous System Free Amino Acids with Development and Aging. *Prog Brain Res* 40:267-275, 1973.

Timiras, P.S. and Vernadakis, A. Structural, Biochemical and Functional Aging of the Nervous System. In Timiras, P.S. (Ed.), *Developmental Physiology and Aging* (New York: Macmillan, 1972), pp. 502-526.

Valcana, T. and Timiras, P.S. *Choline Acetyltransferase Activity in Various Brain Areas of Aging Rats.* 8th International Congress of Gerontology, Vienna, 1969, vol. II, p. 24.

Vernadakis, A. Neuronal-Glial Interactions During Development and Aging. In Thorbecke, G.J. (Ed.), *Biology of Aging and Development:* FASEB Monographs, vol. 3 (New York: Plenum, 1975), pp. 173-188.

Vernadakis, A. Comparative Studies of Neurotransmitter Substances in the Maturing and Aging Central Nervous System of the Chicken. *Prog Brain Res* 40:231-243, 1973.

Wurtman, R.J. Brain Catecholamines and the Control of Secretion From the Anterior Pituitary Gland. In Meites, J. (Ed.), *Hypophysiotropic Hormones of the Hypothalamus: Assay and Chemistry* (New York: Krieger, 1970).

7 The Neuropathology of Aging and Dementia

Kalidas Nandy

There are currently about twenty-one million people over 65 years of age in the United States and this number has been projected to double by the turn of the century. Mean life expectancy has increased significantly during the past decades, and this trend is expected to continue. According to recent hospital and nursing home statistics, nearly three million people over the age of 65 are suffering from clinical senile dementia.

Deteriorations of mental functions, sensory processes, and motor coordination are commonly associated with aging. Since the brain exerts a controlling influence over the entire body as well as mediating the environmental input and behavioral adaptation, its deterioration may lead to various deficits in other systems. The deterioration of mental functions is of particular concern to practicing dentists, as affected patients are unable to take proper care of their oral structures. A number of neuropathologic changes occur in the brains of aged mammals. Some of these are markedly accelerated in senile dementia. This chapter provides an overview of the state of the art on this subject with some discussion of the underlying etiological factors.

Neurological Changes

Gross Changes

The human brain increases rapidly in weight from 493 gm at 3 months of age to a peak of about 1400 gm by the age of 20 years. There is a progressive loss of brain weight after maturity, and this reduction is more marked in patients with senile dementia than in healthy subjects (Himwich, 1959; Appel and Appel, 1942; Tomlinson, 1972; Minckler and Boyd, 1968; Arendt, 1972). Associated with the reduction in the weight is shrinkage of the brain volume (Böning, 1925; Himwich, 1959; Blinkov and Glezer, 1968), increase in the size of the ventricular cavities (Morel and Wildi, 1955; Heinrich, 1939; Himwich, 1959), and a reduction of the cortical thickness and subcortical white matter (Morel and Wildi, 1955).

Microscopic Changes

Major microscopic changes associated with aging and dementia include neuronal loss, lipofuscin pigment formation, loss of dendritic spines, amyloid deposition and formation of neuritic (senile) plaques, neurofibrillary tangles, granulovacuolar degeneration, and Hirano bodies and Lewy bodies (Wisniewski and Terry, 1976).

Neuronal Loss. One of the most conspicuous changes in the brain of aging mammals is the consistent and progressive loss of nerve cells in the CNS, although there is considerable controversy in the literature on the methods of study, the degree of loss, and the regional differences in the brain (Brody and Vijayashankar, 1977). Most investigators tend to agree that age-related loss in the neurons is more pronounced in the cerebral cortex, cerebellum, and hippocampus than in the brainstem and spinal cord. The studies on cerebellar cortex in both animals and humans revealed a consistent decrease in number of Purkinje cells with age (Ellis, 1919; Inukai, 1928; Corsellis, 1976). On the other hand, Brody (1955) studied the number of neurons in the human cerebral cortex ranging from newborn to 95 years of age and found the greatest loss in the superior temporal, precentral, and superior frontal gyri and hippocampus. Colon (1972) found a substantial random loss of neurons in the different areas of the cerebral cortex by the ninth decade. Later on he found a more profound loss of neurons in the brains of patients with senile dementia (Colon, 1973). The absolute number of neurons and the thickness of the cortex were studied by Shefer (1972) in the different areas of the cerebral cortex of mentally healthy old people as well as in patients with senile dementia, Alzheimer's disease, vascular dementia, and Pick's disease. According to this study, the absolute number of neurons was reduced by about 20 percent in the mentally healthy aged and about 40 percent in the case of senile dementia. Tomlinson and Henderson (1976) studied the question of cell loss using an automated counting device (Quantimet) and confirmed the earlier observations of a progressive neuronal loss in the cerebral cortex. Although the loss of neurons associated with aging and senile dementia is fairly well documented, there is no clear understanding of the underlying pathology (table 7-1).

Autoantibodies against CNS structures in humans and other animals have been detected in a number of pathological conditions as possible factors in brain damage. Incidence of antibodies to neuronal structures have been reported in cases of multiple sclerosis and schizophrenia using immunofluorescence methods (Heath and Krupp, 1967). Antibodies against brain tissue were also observed in patients with cerebrovascular accidents, and the extent of damage was correlated with the severity of the ischemia of the cerebral structures involved (Motycka and Jezkova, 1975). Using a complement-dependent ^{51}Cr cytotoxicity assay with neuroblastoma cells, sera from 75 percent of the patients with systemic lupus erythematosus exhibited antineuronal activity mediated by IgM antibody (Bluestein, 1978). Antibodies against nerve cells have also been reported in healthy men and rhesus monkeys, and an increasing number yielded positive results with advancing age (Felsenfeld and Wolf, 1972; Eddington and Dalessio, 1970).

Table 7-1
Neuropathological Changes in Aging and Dementia
Cell Loss and Autoimmunity

Characteristic Features	*Pathological Conditions*	*Etiological Factors*	*References Cited*
Mostly seen as distorted or shrunken cell bodies with lobulated or broken nuclei and pale nucleoli. Prominent in cerebral and cerebellar cortices and hippocampus	Aging Alzheimer's disease Senile dementia Pick's disease Huntington's disease Creutzfeldt-Jacob's disease	Unknown Autoimmune reaction (?) Virus (?) Circulatory disturbances (?)	Bluestein, 1978 Brody, 1955 Brody and Vijayashanker, 1977 Burch, 1968 Chaffee et al., 1978 Colon, 1972 and 1973 Corsellis, 1976 Eddington and Dalessio, 1970 Ellis, 1919 Felsenfeld and Wolf, 1972 Heath and Krupp, 1967 Ingram et al., 1974 Inukai, 1928 Makinodan, 1976 Motycka and Jezkova, 1975 Nandy, 1972a, 1972b, 1972c, 1975, and 1977 Nandy, 1978a, 1978b Nandy et al., 1975 Shefer, 1972 Threatt et al., 1971 Tomlinson and Henderson, 1976

Recent studies on the possible role of autoimmune reactions in neuronal degeneration in aging have thrown further light on the subject (Threatt, Nandy, and Fritz, 1971; Nandy, 1977, 1978b; Chaffee, Nassef, and Stephen, 1978). Ingram, Phegan, and Blumenthal (1974) studied the age-related frequency of gamma globulin fraction of human sera, which binds specifically with neurons in sections of human brain tissue, and found an increased frequency and intensity with advancing age. Brain-reactive antibodies (BRA) have been demonstrated in sera of old mice but not of young mice in both C57BL/6 and NZB mice using indirect immunofluorescence and ^{51}Cr cytotoxicity tests (Threatt, Nandy, and Fritz, 1971). The antibodies are specific against brain tissues and these increase progressively as a function of age (Nandy, 1972a; Nandy, Fritz, and Threatt, 1975). BRA were detected equally in sera of germ-free and control old mice and appeared to be caused by autostimulation of the animals' immune systems (Nandy, 1972c). Blood-brain barrier appeared to play an important role in separating these circulating antibodies from the brain antigen, and a large number of neurons showed immunological reactions and morphological damage when the barrier was damaged in old mice (Nandy, 1972b, 1975). A study on the sera of clinically diagnosed cases of senile dementia demonstrated a significantly higher level of BRA than their age-matched controls. The precise relation of BRA to neuronal degeneration and dementia is not clearly understood (Nandy, 1978b).

The mechanism of formation of BRA is also a matter of considerable speculation. Makinodan (1976) reported the age-related deterioration of the immune functions in normal individuals. This deterioration was also associated with increased incidence of autoimmune disorders. Autoimmune diseases of old persons are numerous and include rheumatoid arthritis, systemic lupus erythematosus, chronic thyroiditis (Hashimoto's disease), amyloidosis, and autoimmune hemolytic anemia (Burch, 1968). The formation of BRA could be more evidence of autoimmune reactions in old animals, and this might play a significant role in the neuronal degeneration associated with aging and senile dementia. Further studies are necessary to acquire a better understanding of this problem.

Lipofuscin Pigment. One of the most consistent changes in the brain of aging mammals is the intracytoplasmic deposition of lipofuscin pigment. The pigment in nerve cells of vertebrates was probably first reported by Hannover (1842), although the term "lipofuscin" was first introduced in the literature by Borst (1922). The pigment has been variously named a chromolipid, a ceroid, a lipochrome, an age pigment, a "wear and tear" pigment, and a cytolipochrome. The pigment is easily demonstrated by its histochemical, fluorescent, and ultrastructural characteristics. Pigment formation appears to be a continuous process starting at 2 to 3 months in mice and increasing progressively as a function of age. Lipofuscin appears to develop in early and late stages, which differ in their histochemical, fluorescent, and ultrastructural properties. The early form, predominantly found in young animals, is more easily stained by periodic acid-Schiff (PAS) and Sudan black B methods and has a greenish-yellow fluorescence. The late stage, frequently encountered in older animals, is more easily stained with Nile blue and ferric-ferricyanide methods and has an orange-yellow fluorescence. The latter form is also more resistant to treatment with enzyme and lipid solvents (Nandy, 1971).

Lipofuscin has also been found in the neurons in a number of pathological conditions of the brain that shorten life span, such as progeria, Warner's syndrome, Batten-Vogt syndrome, and ceroid-lipofuscinosis in dogs. Siakotos et al., (1970) analyzed the pigment in dogs and found this syndrome to be somewhat different from the typical lipofuscin of normal aging. It was noted that ceroid has a higher concentration of acidic lipid polymer, iron, calcium, and copper.

Despite numerous reports on the lipofuscin pigment in the literature, our knowledge of its mode of origin and physiopathologic significance is surprisingly lacking. There is a great deal of difference of opinion among the investigators on the genesis of the pigment. Lipofuscin might be derived from lysosomes, mitochondria, and other organelles within the cell. The more accepted notion has been in favor of lysosomal origin. The strong acid phosphatase activity and the striking ultrastructural similarity between lipofuscin and lysosomes are the major evidences for this hypothesis (Nandy, 1971; Samorajski, Keefe, and Ordy, 1964; Nandy, 1978a). Biochemical isolation of the pigment from brain samples followed by electron microscopy provides further evidence in support of this hypothesis (Siakotos et al., 1972). Arguments have also been made in favor of the possible origin of the pigment from the mitochondria (Hess, 1955; Roizin, 1964). The areas of pigment formation in the neurons of the mesencephalic nucleus of the trigeminal nerve have been correlated with high concentration of the mitochondria (Hasan and Glees, 1972). It has been suggested that pigment formation may be preceded by an increased concentration and clumping of mitochondria, resulting in the disturbance of normal metabolic activity. This condition might lead to the accumulation of insoluble fatty acids that are introduced in pigment formation (Glees and Gopinath, 1973). Glees and Gopinath have extended the work on lipofuscin formation in tissue culture with similar observations.

Numerous reports in the literature indicate that lipofuscin is found in the nondividing cells that are more likely to show the effects of aging (Nandy, 1971; Samorajski, Keefe, and Ordy, 1964; Hasan and Glees, 1972; Samorajski, Ordy, and Keefe, 1965; Brody, 1960). Recent studies in our laboratory using neuroblastoma cells in culture have provided further evidence along this line. The tumor cells are capable of dividing indefinitely in tissue culture, but exhibit properties of normal neurons if division is arrested by chemicals such as papaverine, cyclic AMP, or prostaglandin E_1. However, when these agents were omitted from the culture media, the cells resumed their division. This resumption of cell division was associated with a marked reduction in the pigment formation (Nandy and Schneider, 1976; Schneider and Nandy, 1977; Nandy, Baste, and Schneider, 1978). Repetition of the experiment provided further confirmation of the positive correlation between cell differentiation and lipofuscin formation.

Several intriguing questions remain to be answered. Why do nondividing cells accumulate the pigment unlike the mitotic cells? Why does lipofuscin pigment accumulate in the neurons of older animals but not in the young? It may be speculated that the cells in the young animals have the special ability to metabolize or reutilize the products of intracellular wear and tear, which might be lost during the aging process. For example, a change or loss of certain lysosomal enzymes might take place during the lifetime of animals and account for the accumulation in the old neurons of partially digested or undigested residue or "cellular garbage" as lipofuscin pigment.

The understanding of the functional significance of the pigment in the neurons is even more lacking. While some investigators think that the pigment might be harmful to the cells, others favor its beneficial effects. This confusion may be due partly to the lack of direct evidence of the functions of the cells with and without the pigment. Ideally, studies should be carried out on the functional properties of the cells before and after the formation of pigment as well as following the removal of the pigment by drugs.

Studies by Nandy (1978) and Nandy and Lal (1978) showed a significant improvement of learning and memory in mice following centrophenoxine treatment, and this was also associated with a reduction in lipofuscin in the neurons of cerebral cortex and hippocampus. A detrimental effect on learning and memory with increased lipofuscin in the neurons was seen in rats on a vitamin E deficient diet (Lal et al., 1973). Therefore, it may be argued that a relation between lipofuscin formation and neuronal function might exist. Although there is no direct evidence to indicate that lipofuscin is harmful or toxic to the cell, the process of wear and tear underlying pigmentogenesis might still be detrimental to cellular functions. Lipofuscin may represent the product of the damage rather than be a causative factor. On the other hand, the accumulation of large amounts of the pigment occupying a substantial part of the cell soma might also be detrimental to smooth functional operations within the cell. Much more work is needed to obtain a clearer understanding of the mode of formation and the significance of the pigment (table 7-2).

Dendritic Spine Loss. Another age-related change in the brain is the progressive loss of spines from the dendritic arbor of pyramidal cells in the rat cerebral cortex using the Golgi impregnation method (Feldman and Dowd, 1975). Ultrastructural examination of the neuropil within the dendritic clusters at the layer IV pyramidal cells also revealed a decrease in the number of synapses (Feldman, 1977). The application of the Golgi method to brain tissue from aged and senile subjects has thrown further light on the possible physiologic significance of the loss of spines (Mehraein, Yamada, and Tarmowska-Dzidusko, 1975; Scheibel and Scheibel, 1975; Scheibel et al., 1974). A progressive attrition of the dendritic arborization has been detected in the neocortex, entorhinal cortex, and the archicortex including the hippocampus in both aged individuals and in those afflicted with dementia. While both the apical and basilar dendrites are involved, the latter, developing latest in the course of ontogeny, are also first to be lost (Scheibel and Scheibel, 1975). Scheibel and Scheibel described another distinctive change in the dendritic morphology in the entorhinal cortex and archicortex known as spindle bodies, which are characterized by an early degeneration of the primary dendritic shaft.

Although the precise significance of this geographic clustering is not clear, a relation to circulating factors such as autoimmune bodies has been suggested (Scheibel and Scheibel, 1977). In this connection, the work of Rapport and Karpiak (1976) appears interesting. These authors noted that the antiserum produced in rabbit against rat whole brain and specific brain fractions produced specific behavioral changes such as conditioned and spontaneous alternation,

Table 7-2
Neuropathological Changes in Aging and Dementia

Characteristic Features	*Pathological Conditions*	*Etiological Factors*	*References Cited*
Lipofuscin Formation			
Intracytoplasmic granules mostly in the large neurons in humans and animals; identified by characteristic autofluorescence, stainability with PAS, Sudan black B, Nile blue sulfate and carbol fuchsin. Electron microscopy shows membrane-bound electron dense bodies with vacuoles of varying sizes within the lysosomes	Aging Progeria (?) Warner's syndrome (?) Batten-Vogt syndrome Senile dementia (?) Down's syndrome (?)	Unknown Chronic wear and tear Hypoxia Vitamin E deficiency Intracellular lipid peroxidation (?)	Borst, 1922 Glees and Gopinath, 1973 Hannover, 1842 Hasan and Glees, 1972 Hess, 1955 Lal et al., 1973 Nandy, 1971, 1978a Nandy and Lal, 1978 Nandy and Schneider, 1976 Roizin, 1964; Nandy et al., 1978 Samorajski et al., 1964, 1965 Schneider and Nandy, 1977 Siakotos et al., 1970, 1972
Dendritic Spine Loss			
Demonstrated by Golgi impregnation in humans and animals in cerebral cortex and hippocampus and cerebellum	Aging Senile dementia Alzheimer's disease	Unknown Cell death Disturbances of dendro-plasmic flow Autoimmunity (?)	Feldman, 1977 Feldman and Dowd, 1975 Mehraein et al., 1975 Rapport and Karpiak, 1976, 1978 Scheibel et al., 1974 Scheibel and Scheibel, 1975, 1977

visual discrimination, maze behavior, and passive avoidance associated with alterations in the electroencephalogram (EEG) pattern. Antiserum against the synaptic membrane fraction was most effective in altering EEG patterns and interfering in the retention of acquisition of all behavioral tasks except visual discrimination. When rabbit antiserum to rat synaptic membrane fraction was injected intravenously into pregnant rats on the nineteenth day, behavioral deficits including slow acquisition rates and poor retention in two-month-old male rats were observed (Rapport and Karpiak, 1978). These studies provide evidence in favor of functional alterations caused by antibodies against synaptic membrane fraction. The possibility of spine loss due to autoantibodies requires further investigation.

Neuritic (Senile) Plaques. One of the neuropathological hallmarks in the brain of patients with senile dementia is the formation of neuritic (senile) plaques as first described by Simchowicz (1911). The most classical form of the neuritic plaque is spherical clusters of granular or filamentous materials ranging from 5 to 150 microns in diameter. Those plaques often have a dense argyrophilic core that gives a positive reaction to amyloid and mucopolysaccharides and appear bifringent in polarized light. These are most commonly found in the deep layers of frontal cortex, hippocampus, and parahippocampal gyrus (Ball, 1978). Electron microscopic studies have shown that the classical plaques consist of amyloid cores surrounded by degenerating fibers and reactive cells (microglia or astrocytes).

Other types of plaques may consist of either amyloid alone or without any amyloid core (Wisniewski and Terry, 1973). Although there is no complete agreement as to the chemical nature of amyloid, two types are generally recognized (Benditt and Eriksen, 1973). While amyloid B is composed primarily of light chain immunoglobulin components of a variable molecular weight (8,000 to 25,000 daltons), the amino acid sequence of amyloid A (secondary) has no homology to any immunoglobulin. Based on these observations, it has been suggested that amyloid core probably represents antigen-antibody complexes catabolized by phagocytes and degraded by lysosomes (Glenner et al., 1971, 1973). Other investigators claim that amyloid is a direct toxic cause of neuritic degeneration and senile plaque formation (Schwartz, 1970; Wisniewski, Terry, and Hirano, 1970; Wisniewski and Terry, 1976).

Amyloid fibrils have also been demonstrated in senile plaques in the brains of patients with senile dementia and Alzheimer's disease using immunoperoxide technique (Ishii and Haga, 1976). Despite numerous studies, the origin of the amyloid is rather controversial. It has been postulated that amyloid fibrils may be formed following endocytosis of polypeptide immunoglobulin light chains by phagocytic cells and subsequent intralysosomal proteolysis. Ensuing exocytosis would presumably deposit these aggregates extracellularly as amyloid fibrils (Glenner et al., 1971). Some investigators, on the other hand, believe that leakage of amyloid precursors might occur, resulting in vascular and perivascular deposit of amyloid (Scholz, 1938). This may have some relation to formation of senile plaques. The possible involvement of autoimmune reactions in the genesis of these neuritic plaques is not clearly understood (table 7-3).

Neurofibrillary Tangles. Perhaps the most characteristic neuropathology of senile dementia is the intracytoplasmic formation of the neurofibrillary tangles originally described by Alzheimer (1906). These tangles are also found in smaller numbers in the aged and a number of other pathological conditions of the brain (Hirano, 1970; Wisniewski and Terry, 1970) and occur mostly in the frontal and temporal cerebral cortices and the hippocampus. Although these elements are primarily observed in the perikaryon, they might also occur in the dendritic and synaptic endings (Wisniewski, Ghetti, and Terry, 1973). Ball (1978) analyzed the topographic distribution of neurofibrillary tangles, granulovacuolar degeneration, and rodlike bodies of Hirano in hippocampal cortex of patients with

Table 7-3
Neuropathological Changes in Aging and Dementia

Characteristic Features	*Pathological Conditions*	*Etiological Factors*	*References Cited*
Amyloid Lesions			
Mainly demonstrated by Congo red, green bifrigence in polarized light, cresyl violet metachromesia Chemical types: Secondary (A) type: no similarity with immunoglobulin Primary (B) type: light chain–immunoglobulin	Aging Senile dementia Alzheimer's disease Immune disorders Angiopathy Congophila	Unknown Autoimmunity Foreign protein reactions	Glenner et al., 1971, 1973 Scholz, 1938
Neuritic Plaques			
Found extracellularly in cerebral cortex, hippocampus. Several types are found; commonest form consists of amyloid core surrounded by degenerating fibers and reactive cells. Other forms are made up of amyloid clone or with no amyloid core. Visualized by silver impregnation, H & E, PAS, Congo red	Senile dementia Alzheimer's disease Vascular disorders Aging Down's syndrome	Unknown Autoimmunity (?) Disturbance of axoplasmic flow by N.F. tangles (?)	Ball, 1978; Benditt and Eriksen, 1973 Glenner et al., 1971, 1973 Ishii and Haga, 1976 Schwartz, 1970 Simchowicz, 1911 Wisniewski et al., 1970 Wisniewski and Terry, 1973, 1976

Alzheimer's dementia and mentally healthy subjects using semiautomated scanning stage microscope. The order of predilection for neurofibrillary tangles in decreasing severity were entorhinal cortex, subiculum, and presubiculum. These results were confirmed by a similar study carried out on two most vulnerable zones, the hippocampus and parahippocampal gyrus, in a number of clinically diagnosed cases of senile dementia and normal-aged people (Kemper, 1978). Kemper suggested that the involvement of these areas strategically located to interfere with the orderly flow of information between neocortex, limbic cortices, and subcortical centers might be responsible for the profound symptoms in this disease.

The tangles are compact clusters of neurofibrils producing abnormal neuronal configuration and show bifringency in polarized light. As observed in electron micrographs, the neurofibrillary materials are masses of abnormal microtubules, 200 to 220 Å in width, that display periodic constrictions every 800 Å (Terry and Wisniewski, 1972; Kidd, 1964). Normal microtubules are about 240 Å in diameter with the dense wall of about 60 Å thick, while normal neurofilaments are approximately 100Å thick. The tangles consisting of paired helical filaments are strongly argentophilic and, like normal neurofilaments, are well preserved after direct osmic acid fixation. Normal tubules are generally not observed following osmication and are not argentophilic (Wisniewski and Terry, 1973). As regards the chemical composition, the microtubules are composed of tubulin protein subunits (molecular weight 110,000 daltons) and the neurofilaments contain acid fibrous protein (molecular weight approximately 50,000 daltons). The protein composition of "twisted tubule" materials is not clearly understood, but the average molecular weight of the protein subfractions is about 50,000 daltons, similar to major neurofilament protein (Iqbal et al., 1977).

The neurofibrillary tangle has been experimentally induced in animal models by intraventricular injection of aluminum salts as well as by addition of the salt in culture in neuroblastoma cells (Crapper, 1976; Crapper and DeBoni, 1977). More recently, it has been observed that rabbit antineurofilamentous serum prepared against antigens isolated from chicken brain or human sciatic nerve reacted strongly with neurofibrillary tangles induced by intracerebral injection of aluminum phosphate in rabbits (Dahl and Bignami, 1978). Jankovic et al. (1977) studied the cytotoxicity of rabbit antisera to rat brain tubulin and S-100 protein. These authors observed that antitubulin serum was both cytotoxic and immunofluorescence positive to rat T lymphocytes (not B cells) and anti-S-100 protein serum was not. These studies raise important questions about the antigenic properties of neurofibrillary tangles, which might share antigenic determinants with normal neurofilaments as well as T lymphocytes. The etiology and pathogenesis of the neurofibrillary degeneration are far from clear at present (table 7-4).

Table 7-4
Neuropathological Changes in Aging and Dementia

Characteristic Features	*Pathological Conditions*	*Etiological Factors*	*References Cited*
Neurofibrillary Tangles			
Thick fibrillary material in the cytoplasm demonstrated by silver impregnation. Electron microscopy shows twisted tubules of 200-220 A° in diameter with periodic construction to 100-150 A° every 800 A°	Alzheimer's disease Senile dementia Aging Postencephalitic parkinsonism; Amyotropic lateral sclerosis Parkinsonian dementia	Unknown Colloidal change (?) Amyloid change (?) Immune reaction (?) Aluminum toxicity (?) Virus (?)	Alzheimer, 1906 Ball, 1978 Crapper, 1976, 1977 Dahl and Bignami, 1978 Hirano, 1970 Iqbal et al., 1977 Jankovic et al., 1977 Kemper, 1978 Kidd, 1964 Terry and Wisniewski, 1972 Wisniewski et al., 1973 Wisniewski and Terry, 1970
Granulovacuolar Degeneration			
Intraneuronal vacuole measuring up to 5μ containing small hemotoxylinophilic granule in the center measuring .5-1.5μ Found mostly in basal ganglia, brainstem, and cerebral cortex Inverse relation with the presence of lipofuscin Electron microscopy shows membrane-bound vacuoles containing collection of electron dense granular material	Senile dementia Presenile dementia Aging	Unknown Autophagic vacuole	Morel and Wildi, 1955 Simchowicz, 1911; Wisniewski and Terry, 1973

Granulovacuolar Degeneration. The presence of granulovacuolar degeneration was initially demonstrated by Simchowicz (1911) in the cytoplasm of hippocampal pyramidal neurons in cases of senile dementia. Less frequently, it is also found in cases of Pick's disease as well as in old people with and without neurofibrillary changes. Granulovacuolar degeneration is characterized by intracytoplasmic argyrophilic and hematoxylinophilic granules (0.5 to 1.5 microns in diameter) within a vacuole up to 5 microns in diameter. Ultrastructurally, the lesions appear to consist of membrane-bound vacuoles containing the electron dense bodies and bear some resemblance to the autophagic vacuoles of lipofuscin pigment (Wisniewski and Terry, 1973). Although vacuolar degeneration might result from the breakdown of lipofuscin pigment (Morel and Wildi, 1955), its precise mode of origin and significance in both aging and dementia is not clear.

Lewy Bodies and Hirano Bodies. Lewy bodies are observed primarily in the neurons of substantia nigra and locus ceruleus in patients with postencephalitic Parkinsonism. These structures are also seen in old people without Parkinsonism or other neurological problems (Beheim-Schwarzback, 1957; Lipkin, 1959; Greenfield and Bosanquet, 1953). They are rounded hyaline bodies, 5 to 25 microns in diameter, and appear under the electron microscope to consist of densely packed filaments. Lewy bodies and neurofibrillary tangles tend to have an inverse relation with each other (table 7-5).

Hirano bodies, originally described by Hirano (1965), are eosinophilic structures found in the neurons of patients with amyotrophic lateral sclerosis, Parkinsonism, dementia complex, Guam-Parkinsonism-dementia complex, Pick's disease (Schochet, Lampert, and Lindenberg, 1968), kuru (Field, Mathews, and Raine, 1969), Alzheimer's disease and senile dementia as well as normal aging (Wisniewski, Terry and Hirano, 1970). Ultrastructurally, these bodies consist of filaments (60 to 100 Å wide) often arranged in parallel arrays that alternate perpendicularly with sheets of similar thickness, giving the structure a beaded appearance in some tissue sections. There is no known relationship of this structure to neurofibrillary tangles. The mode of origin and the significance of these bodies in both normal aging and senile dementia are not clearly understood (table 7-5).

Various neuropathological changes in the brain of aged persons as well as in senile dementia have been reviewed. The gross changes include reduction of weight and volume of the brain, with thinning of the cortex. The microscopic changes described are neuronal loss, lipofuscin formation, loss of dendritic spines, granulovacuolar degeneration, formation of neuritic (senile) plaques, neurofibrillary tangles, Lewy bodies and Hirano bodies. The pathogenesis of these changes and their significance in aging and dementia are not clearly understood. Since aging is associated with deterioration of the immune system and increased incidence of autoimmune disorders, the possible involvements of autoimmune reactions in these neuropathological changes have been discussed. It

Table 7-5
Neuropathological Changes in Aging and Dementia

Characteristic Features	*Pathological Conditions*	*Etiological Factors*	*References Cited*
Lewy Bodies			
Commonly found in pigmented cells of the locus ceruleus and substantia nigra. Electron microscopy shows packed filaments often with a homogeneous granular mass at the center	Postencephalitic parkinsonism Aging Senile dementia	Unknown	Beheim-Schwarzback, 1957 Greenfield and Bosanquet, 1953
Hirano Bodies			
Intracytoplasmic eosinophilic rod-like structures; Electron microscopy shows aggregates of filamentous (sheet-like) structures; the filaments are 60-100 A° wide and often arranged in parallel arrays alternating perpendicularly with the sheets	ALS-P.D. complex Pick's disease Kuru, ALS, senile and presenile dementia Aging	Unknown	Field et al., 1969 Hirano et al., 1965 Schochet et al., 1968 Wisniewski et al., 1970

is hoped that the information provided in this chapter will permit a better understanding of the neuropathology of the aging and those affiliated with senile dementia.

References

Alzheimer, A. Uber Eine Eigenartige Erkrankung der Hirnrinde. *Zbl Nervenh Psychiatr* 18:177-179, 1906.

Appel, R.W. and Appel, E.M. Intracranial Variation in the Weight of Human Brain. *Human Biol* 14:48-68, 1942.

Arendt, A. In *Handbuch der Allegemeinen Pathologie,* H. Gottfried (Ed.) (New York: Springer, 1972).

Ball, M.J. Histotopography of Cellular Changes in Alzheimer's disease. In Nandy, K. (Ed.), *Senile Dementia: A Biomedical Approach* (New York: Elsevier, 1978).

Beheim-Schwarzback, D. Weitere Beobachtungen an Nervenzellkernen. *J Hirnforsch* 3:105-148, 1957.

Benditt, E.P. and Eriksen, N. In *Peptides of the Biological Chemistry*. H. Peeter (Ed.), (New York: Pergamon, 1973).

Blinkov, S.M. and Glezer, I.I. *The Human Brain in Figures and Tables* (New York: Plenum, 1968).

Bluestein, H.G. Neurocytotoxic Antibodies in Serum of Patients with Systemic Lupus Erythematosus. *Proc Natl Acad Sci* 75:3965-3969, 1978.

Boning, A. *Zschr Neurol* 94:72-84, 1925.

Borst, M. *Pathogische Histologie* (Leipzig: Vogel, 1922), p. 210.

Brody, H. Organization Cerebral Cortex. III. A Study in the Human Cerebral Cortex. *J Comp Neurol* 102:511-556, 1955.

Brody, H. The Deposition of Aging Pigment in the Human Cerebral Cortex. *J Gerontol* 16:258-261, 1960.

Brody, H. and Vijayashankar, N. Anatomical Changes in the Nervous System. In C.E. Finch and L. Hayflick (Eds.), *Handbook of the Biology of Aging* (New York: Van Nostrand Reinhold Co., 1977).

Burch, P.R. *An Enquiry Concerning Growth, Disease and Aging* (Edinburgh: Oliver and Boyd, Ltd., 1968).

Chaffee, J., Nassef, M., and Stephen, R. Cytotoxic Autoantibody to the Brain. In Nandy, K. (Ed.), *Senile Dementia: A Biomedical Approach* (New York: Elsevier, 1978).

Colon, E.J. The Elderly Brain. A Quantitative Analysis of Cerebral Cortex in Two Cases. *Psychiat Neurol Neurochir* (Amsterdam) 75:261-270, 1972.

Colon, E.G. The Cerebral Cortex in Presenile Dementia, Some Observations on the Purkinje Cell Population and on Brain Volume in Human Aging. *Acta Neuropath* (Berlin) 23:281-290, 1973.

Corsellis, J.A.N. Some Observations on the Purkinje Cell Population and on Brain Volume in Human Aging. In Terry, R.D. and Gershon, S. (Eds.), *Neurobiology of Aging* (New York: Raven, 1976).

Crapper, D.R. Functional Consequences of Neurofibrillary Degeneration. In Terry, R. and Gershon, S. (Eds.), *Neurobiology of Aging* (New York: Raven, 1976).

Crapper, D.R. and DeBoni, U. Aluminum and the Genetic Apparatus in Alzheimer's Disease. In Nandy, K. and Sherwin, I. (Eds.), *The Aging Brain and Senile Dementia* (New York: Plenum, 1977).

Dahl, D. and Bignami, A. Immunochemical Cross-Reactivity of Normal Neurofibrils and Aluminum Induced Neurofibrillary Tangles. *Exp Neurol* 58:74-80, 1978.

Eddington, J.S. and Dalessio, D.J. The Assessment of Immunofluorescence Methods of Humoral and Antimyelin Antibodies in Man. *J Immunol* 105:248-255, 1970.

Ellis, R.S. A Preliminary Quantitative Study of Purkinje Cells in Normal, Subnormal and Senescent Human Cerebella. *J Comp Neurol* 30:229-252, 1919.

Feldman, M.L. and Dowd, C. Loss of Dendritic Spines in Aging Cerebellar Cortex. *Anat Embryol* 148:279-289, 1975.

Feldman, M. Dendritic Changes in Aging Rat Brain: Pyramidal Cell Dendritic Length and Ultra-Structure. In Nandy, K. and Sherwin, I. (Eds.), *The Aging Brain and Senile Dementia* (New York: Plenum, 1977).

Felsenfeld, G. and Wolf, R.F. Relationship of Age and Serum Immunoglobulins to Autoantibodies Against Brain Constituents in Primates. 1-A Study of Apparently Healthy Men, Macaca Mullata and Erythrocibus Pates. *J Med Primatol* 1:287-296, 1972.

Field, E.J., Mathews, J.D., and Raine, C.S. Electron Microscopic Observations on the Cerebellar Cortex in Kuru. *J Neurol Sci* 8:209-224, 1969.

Glees, P. and Gopinath, G. Age Changes in the Centrally and Periapically Located Sensory Neurons in Rat. *Z Zellforsch* 141:285-298, 1973.

Glenner, G.G., Terry, R.D., Harada, M., Isersky, C., and Page, D. Amyloid Fibril Protein. *Science* 172:1150-1151, 1971.

Glenner, G.G., Terry, R.D., Isersky, C. Amyloidosis, Its Nature and Pathogenesis. *Semin Hematol* 10:65-82, 1973.

Greenfield, J.G. and Bosanquet, F.D. *J Neurol Neurosurg Psychiatr* 16:213-222, 1953.

Hannover, A. Videnskapsselsk. *Naturvidensk Math Afh* (Copenhagen) 10, 1842.

Hasan, M. and Glees, P. Genesis and Possible Dissolution of Neuronal Lipofuscin. *Gerontologia* 18:217-236, 1972.

Heath, R.G. and Krupp, I.M. Schizophrenia as an Immunologic Disorder. *Arch Gen Psychiatr* 16:1-9, 1967.

Heinrich, A. *Z Alternsforsch* 1:345-354, 1939.

Hess, A. The Fine Structure of Young and Old Spinal Ganglia. *Anat Record* 123:399-424, 1955.

Himwich, H.E. In *The Process of Aging in the Nervous System,* J.E. Birren, H.A. Imus and Eindle, W.F. (Eds.), (Springfield: Charles C. Thomas, 1959).

Hirano, A. *Ciba Foundation Symposium on Alzheimer's Disease and Related Conditions.* Wolstenholme, G.E.W. and O'Connor, M. (Eds.), (London: Churchill, 1970).

Hirano, A. Slow, Latent and Temperate Virus Infections. In Gajdusek, D.C., Gibbs, C.J., and Alpers, M. (Eds.), *National Institute of Neurological Diseases and Blindness Monograph No. 2* (Bethesda, MD: National Institutes of Health, 1965), pp. 23-37.

Ingram, C.R., Phegan, K.J., and Blumenthal, H.T. Significance of an Aging-Linked Neuron Binding Gamma-Globulin Fraction of Human Sera. *J Geront* 29:20-72, 1974.

Inukai, T. On the Loss of Purkinje Cells with Advancing Age from Cerebellar Cortex of Albino Rat. *J Comp Neurol* 45:1-31, 1928.

Iqbal, K., Wisniewski, H., Grunde-Iqbal, I., and Terry, R.D. Neurofibrillary Pathology: An Update. In Nandy, K. and Sherwin, I. (Eds.), *The Aging Brain and Senile Dementia* (New York: Plenum, 1977).

Ishii, T. and Haga, S. Immuno-Electron Microscopic Localization of Immunoglobulins in Amyloid Fibrils of Senile Plaques. *Acta Neuropath* (Berlin) 36:243-249, 1976.

Jankovic, B.D., Horvat, J., Mitrovic, K., and Mostarica, M. Rat Brain Lymphocyte Antigen. *Immunochem* 14:75-78, 1977.

Kemper, T. Senile Dementia: A Focal Disease of the Temporal Lobe. In Nandy, K. (Ed.), *Senile Dementia: A Biomedical Approach* (New York: Elsevier 1978).

Kidd, M. Alzheimer's Disease, an Electron Microscopic Study. *Brain* 87:303-320, 1964.

Lal, H., Pogacar, S., Kaly, P.R., and Puri, S.K. Behavioral and Neuropathological Manifestations of Nutritionally Induced Central Nervous System Aging in the Rat. In Ford, D. (Ed.), *Neurobiological Aspects of Maturation and Aging* (New York: Elsevier, 1973), pp. 129-140.

Lipkin, L.E. Cytoplasmic Inclusions in Ganglion Cells Associated with Parkinsonian States. *Am J Pathol* 35:1117-1134, 1959.

Makinodan, T. Immunobiology of Aging. *J Am Geriatr Soc* 24:249-252, 1976.

Mehraein, P., Yamada, M., and Tarmowska-Dzidusko, F. Quantitative Study on Dendrites and Dendritic Spines in Alzheimer's Disease and Senile Dementia. In Krelibirg, G.W. (Ed.), *Psychology and Pathology of Dendrites* (New York: Raven, 1975), pp. 453-458.

Minckler, T.M. and Boyd, E. In *Pathology of the Nervous System,* vol. I. Minckler, T.M. (Ed.), (New York: McGraw-Hill, 1968).

Morel, F. and Wildi, E. General Cellular Pathochemistry of Senile Presenile Alterations of the Brain. *Schweiz Arch Neurol Psychiatr* 76:348-360, 1955.

Motycka, A. and Jezkova, Z. Autoantibodies and Brain Ischemia Topography. *Cas Lek Ces* 114:1455-1457, 1975.

Nandy, K. Properties of Neuronal Lipofuscin Pigment in Mice. *Acta Neuropathol* 19:25-32, 1971.

Nandy, K. Brain-Reactive Antibodies in Mouse Serum as a Function of Age. *J Geront* 27:173-177, 1972a.

Nandy, K. Neuronal Degeneration in Aging and After Experimental Injury. *Exp Geront* 7:303-311, 1972b.

Nandy, K. Brain-Reactive Antibodies in Serum of Germ-Free Mice. *Mech Aging Dev* 1:133-138, 1972c.

Nancy, K., Fritz, R.B., and Threatt, J. Specificity of Brain-Reactive Antibodies in Serum in Old Mice. *J Geront* 30:269-274, 1975.

Nancy, K. Significance of Brain-Reactive Antibodies in Serum of Aged Mice. *J Geront* 30:412-416, 1975.

Nandy, K. and Schneider, F.H. Lipofuscin Pigment Formation in Neuroblastoma Cells in Culture. In Terry, R.D. and Gershon, S. (Eds.), *Neurobiology of Aging* (New York: Raven, 1976).

Nandy, K. Immune Reactions in Aging Brain and Senile Dementia. In Nandy, K. and Sherwin, I. (Eds.), *The Aging Brain and Senile Dementia* (New York: Plenum, 1977).

Nandy, K. Morphological Changes in the Aging Brain. In Nandy, K. (Ed.), *Senile Dementia: A Biomedical Approach* (New York: Elsevier, 1978a).

Nandy, K. Brain-reactive Antibodies in Aging and Senile Dementia. In Terry, R.D., Katzman, R., and Bick, K. (Eds.), *Alzheimer's Disease–Senile Dementia and Related Disorders,* (New York: Raven, 1978b).

Nandy, K. and Lal, H. Neuronal Lipofuscin and Learning Deficits in Aging Mammals. In Deniker, P. et al. (Eds.), *Neuropsychopharmacology* (New York: Pergamon, 1978).

Nandy, K., Baste, C., and Schneider, F.H. Further Studies on the Effects of Centrophenoxine on Lipofuscin Pigment in Neuroblastoma Cells in Culture: An Electron Microscopic Study. *Exp Geront* 13:311-322, 1978.

Rapport, M.M. and Karpiak, S.E. Discriminative Effects of Antisera to Brain Constituents on Behavior and EEG Activity in the Rat. *Res Commun Psych Psychiatr Behav* 1:115-124, 1976.

Rapport, M.M. and Karpiak, S.E. Immunological Perturbation of Neurological Functions. In Nandy, K. (Ed.), *Senile Dementia: A Biomedical Approach* (New York: Elsevier, 1978).

Roizin, L. Some Basic Principles of Molecular Pathology: Ultrastructural Organelles as Structural-Metabolic and Pathogenetic Gradients. *J Neuropathol Exp Neurol* 23:209-252, 1964.

Samorajski, T., Keefe, J.R., and Ordy, J.M. Intracellular Localization of Lipofuscin Age Pigment in the Nervous System of Aged Mice. *J Geront* 19:261-276, 1964.

Samorajski, T., Ordy, J.M., and Keefe, J.R. The Fine Structure of Lipofuscin Age Pigment in the Nervous System of Aged Mice. *J Cell Biol* 26:779-795, 1965.

Scheibel, M.E., Davies, T.L., Lindsay, R.D., and Scheibel, A.B. Basilar Dendrite Bundles of Giant Pyramidal Cells. *Exp Neurol* 42:307-319, 1974.

Scheibel, M.E. and Scheibel, A.B. Structural Changes in the Aging Brain. In Brody, H., Ordy, M., and Herman, D. (Eds.), *Aging,* vol. 1 (New York: Raven, 1975).

Scheibel, M.E. and Scheibel, A.B. Differential Changes with Aging in Old and New Cortices. In Nandy, K. and Sherwin, I. (Eds.), *The Aging Brain and Senile Dementia* (New York: Plenum, 1977).

Schneider, F.H. and Nandy, K. Effects of Centrophenoxine on Lipofuscin Formation in Neuroblastoma Cells in Culture. *J Geront* 32:132-139, 1977.

Schochet, S.S., Lampert, P.W., and Lindenberg, R. Fine Structure of the Pick and Hirano Bodies in a Case of Pick's Disease. *Acta Neuropathol* 11:330-337, 1968.

Scholz, W. *Ztrschr Ges Neurol Psychiatr* 162:694-704, 1938.

Schwartz, P. *Amyloidosis: Cause and Manifestations of Senile Deterioration.* (Springfield: Charles C. Thomas, 1970).

Shefer, V.P. Absolute Number of Neurons and Thickness of the Cerebral Cortex During Aging, Senile and Vascular Dementia, and Pick's and Alzheimer's Diseases. *Zh Neuropath Psikhiat Korsakkole* 72:1024-1029, 1972.

Siakotos, A.N., Watanabe, I., Siato, A., and Flesicher, S. Procedures for Isolation of Two Distinct Lipo-Pigments From Human Brain, Liposfuscin and Ceroid. *Biochem Med* 4:361-375, 1970.

Siakotos, A.N., Goebel, H.H., Patel, V., Watanabe, I., and Zeman, W. The Morphogenesis and Biochemical Characteristics of Ceroid Isolated From Cases of Neuronal-Ceroid-Lipofuscinosis. In Volk, B.W. and Aronson, S.M. (Eds.), *Sphingolipid, Sphingolipidosis and Allied Disorders* (New York: Plenum, 1972), pp. 53-61.

Simchowicz, T. *Hist Histopath Arb* 4:267-277, 1911.

Terry, R.D. and Wisniewski, H.M. Ultrastructure of Senile Dementia and of Experimental Analog. In Gatiz, C.M. (Ed.), *Aging and the Brain* (New York: Plenum, 1972).

Threatt, J., Nandy, K., and Fritz, R. Brain-Reactive Antibodies in Serum of Old Mice Demonstrated by Immunofluorescence. *J. Geront* 25:316-323, 1971.

Tomlinson, B.E. Morphological Brain Changes in Non-Demented Old People. In VanPraag, H.M. and Kalverborz, A.F. (Eds.), *Aging of the Central Nervous System, Biological and Psychological Aspects* (Haarlem: DeErven F. Bohn, N.V., 1972).

Tomlinson, B.E. and Henderson, G. Some Quantitative Cerebral Findings in Normal and Demented Old People. In Terry, R.D. and Gershon, S. (Eds.), *Neurobiology of Aging* (New York: Raven, 1976).

Wisniewski, H. and Terry, R.D. In Wolstenholme, G.E.W. and O'Connor, M. (Eds.), *Ciba Foundation Symposium on Alzheimer's Disease and Related Conditions,* (London: Churchill, 1970).

Wisniewski, H., Terry, R.D., and Hirano, A. Neurofibrillary Pathology. *J Neuropathol Exp Neurol* 29:163-176, 1970.

Wisniewski, H.M. and Terry, R.D. Morphology of the Aging Brain, Human and Animal. In Ford, D.H. (Ed.), *Progress in Brain Research,* vol. 40 (Amsterdam: Elsevier, 1973).

Wisniewski, H., Ghetti, B., and Terry, R.D. Neuritic (Senile) Plaques and Filamentous Changes in Aged Rhesus Monkeys. *J Neuropathol Exp Neurol* 32:566-584, 1973.

Wisniewski, H.M. and Terry, R.D. Neuropathology of Aging Brain. In Terry, R.D. and Gershon, S. (Eds.), *Neurobiology of Aging,* (New York: Raven, 1976).

8 Stroke in the Geriatric Population

Thomas D. Sabin

Practicing dentists inevitably encounter cerebrovascular disease in many phases of their practice, for stroke is now the third most common cause of death in the United States. Approximately a half million people in this country will suffer their first stroke in the next twelve months; of these, 75 percent will be over the age of 65 and another 35 percent will die within the first thirty days following their stroke. Of those who survive, half will retain a significant residual disability.

Cerebral Ischemia and Infarction

The term "stroke" is a general term that implies the sudden onset of a neurological deficit. The abrupt appearance of neurologic syndromes suggests a vascular cause even though there is a 5 percent error rate in the diagnosis of a stroke. There are two broad categories of strokes—focal cerebral ischemia or infarction and intracranial hemorrhage.

If an area of brain tissue is rendered temporarily ischemic, the patient may have transient symptoms because of a dysfunction of an affected portion of brain. These attacks are known as transient ischemic attacks or TIAs. If the decrease in blood flow is sufficiently prolonged, the tissues die, resulting in cerebral infarction with irreversible damage to the nerve cells. In both of these circumstances, the clinical symptoms often point to a definite anatomical localization within the brain, aiding the diagnosis. For example, the middle cerebral artery supplies the speech areas in the left hemisphere and the motor control of the opposite face and arm. If a patient suddenly develops aphasia and paralysis of the right arm and face, this clustering of deficits resembles infarction of the brain in the left middle cerebral artery distribution. There are many constellations of signs and symptoms for the various arteries that supply the cerebral hemispheres and the brainstem.

Syndromes associated with disease of the carotid arteries attract special attention because they are accessible to the vascular surgeon. Acute occlusive disease of the carotid in the neck may result in destruction of brain tissue with both anterior and middle cerebral artery distribution. When the occlusive process advances slowly, collateral blood vessels develop over the surface of the brain, supplementing the alternate channels of the circle of Willis. Then, if stroke occurs, the amount of infarcted brain tissue will be less, limited to the cortical region between the central supply of the anterior and middle cerebral artery, resulting in a so-called "border zone" stroke (Romanul and Abramowicz, 1964).

Hypertensive patients are likely candidates for lacunar strokes. These strokes consist of small 3 to 20 mm rounded infarcts occurring in the distribution of the end arteries that penetrate to the core of the hemispheres from the base of the brain. Certain syndromes such as pure motor hemisplegia, pure hemisensory loss, and clumsy-hand dysarthria have been associated with lacunar infarcts (Fisher, 1965). When an individual suffers multiple lacunar infarcts, dementia and widespread symmetric motor disorders may give the appearance of a degenerative disease.

After a brain infarction has been diagnosed, the next step is to search for an abnormality in the wall of the artery of supply, a disturbance of the general circulation, or an abnormality of blood constituents.

Artherosclerosis is the leading cause of stroke in the elderly. This slowly progressive degenerative disease of blood vessels causes ulceration of arterial linings followed by stenosis and thrombosis of the arteries. There is no known cause for artherosclerosis, but certain risk factors have been identified. Genetic determinants, diabetes, abnormalities of lipid metabolism, and hypertension all markedly increase the rate of development of the disease. Modifiable risk factors such as dietary intake of lipids, obesity, cigarette smoking, and physical inactivity have been subject to large-scale public education efforts to reduce the prevalence of artherosclerosis. Other diseases may damage the walls of arteries, and certain inflammatory diseases such as systemic lupus erythematosis often lead to arterial occlusion. Severe neck injury can damage the endothelial lining of the carotid artery and result in the formation of a clot which may occlude the carotid artery or be thrown off as an embolism to the brain.

Emboli can arise from scarred heart valves, a sequela to rheumatic fever. Dentists are now well aware that the bacteremia resulting from various dental manipulations can initiate infective endocarditis in the individual with rheumatic heart disease. The endocardial scar at the site of a myocardial infarction can also give rise to cerebral emboli. Ulcerated artherosclerotic plaques in the carotid or vertebral arterial systems may give rise to cholesterol or thrombotic emboli which pass into the cerebral circulation.

Abnormalities of the blood constituents such as hypercoagulability (thrombocytosis), hyperviscosity (polycythemia), or simply severe anemia may also produce focal cerebral syndromes. Dynamic circulatory events should always be considered in the evaluation of a patient with a cerebral infarct or TIA. Transient periods of arrhythmia, postural hypotension, or other factors that lower the entire cerebral blood flow may cause focal syndromes because the ischemia may be most pronounced in the distribution of a stenotic artery.

Hemorrhages

Intracranial hemorrhage is often a more devastating event than cerebral infarction. Bleeding into the brain substance or into the spaces surrounding the brain (subarachnoid space) must be short-lived; otherwise, the rapid accumulation of volume in the nonexpandible cranial vault results in rapid death.

Primary intracerebral hemorrhage is nontraumatic bleeding into the brain substance, and is another complication of hypertension. Occasional cases do occur in normotensive individuals with bleeding diatheses such as chronic liver disease, anticoagulant therapy, and blood dyscrasias. The four most common sites for primary hypertensive hemorrhages are the core of the brain in the region just lateral to the basal ganglia, the thalamus, the pons, and the cerebellum. Cerebellar hemorrhage is characterized by an explosive onset of severe headache, especially in the occipital region, nausea, vomiting, and severe walking difficulty (ataxia). It is important to recognize cerebellar hemorrhage early, since it is possible to successfully remove the hemorrhage by neurosurgical intervention; deeply situated hemorrhages are not accessible enough for surgical treatment. In progressive stages, the patient may lose consciousness and develop ocular signs.

Intracerebral hemorrhage may also be caused by a vascular malformation. The most common site for these tangles of abnormal vessels is at the junction between the occipital and parietal lobes. This malformation may extend from the surface of the brain down to the ventricular wall. Affected persons usually have a preexisting history of headache disorder or focal seizures. Since the bleeding occurs from vessels at venous pressure, the episodes are apt to be less severe than hypertensive intracerebral hemorrhages.

Spontaneous bleeding into the subarachnoid space is often caused by rapture of a small arterial aneurysm. These originate in an embryologic arterial wall defect, especially common at branching sites. With aging, and especially if hypertension is present, a ballooning occurs at these sites where thin-walled saccular aneurysms develop. These aneurysms tend to be clustered about the circle of Willis. A brief bout of bleeding into the subarachnoid space causes severe headache, stiff neck, and obtundation. The major therapeutic effort is directed toward prevention of further episodes of aneurysmal bleeding, as spontaneous bleeding is associated with high morbidity and mortality.

Diagnostic Procedures

Because the treatment of these diverse stroke syndromes varies with each individual, accurate diagnosis is essential. A detailed general medical and neurological evaluation is mandatory. The bedside examination must include listening over the arteries of the neck for the presence of bruits that might point to a focal area of arterial narrowing. In addition, it is important to perform a complete blood count, certain blood chemistries, urinalysis, electrocardiograms, and skull and chest roentgenograms on all stroke patients. Palpation of facial, temporal, and carotid arteries can indicate the location of vascular obstruction.

Arteries can be visualized by injecting radiopaque solution into the artery and taking a rapid sequence of x-rays of the neck and head. This provides a dynamic view of the entire cerebral arterial and venous supply. Focal areas of stenosis because of artherosclerosis, characteristic features of vasculitis, or arterial aneurysms are well delineated by this technique. Arteriography outlines precisely the structure of vascular malformations including the origin of arteries supplying any abnormal as well as the draining veins.

Another valuable study in evaluating the stroke patient is computerized tomography (CT) of the brain (New, 1975). This relatively recent development permits a noninvasive visualization of the brain by a computer-constructed display of tissue densities which represents the anatomy of brain in horizontal "slices". The technique is especially well suited to the evaluation of the stroke patient. Using a minicomputer, the method combines x-ray tomography and mathematical image reconstruction. A narrow beam of x-rays passes through the head into a carefully aligned scintillation detector; the x-ray tube and detectors are mounted on a gantry and the whole system moved 225 degrees around the head in one degree increments. At each degree, tissue absorption data is obtained from the amount of x-ray energy that reaches the scintillation counter. An image of the skull and intracranial contents is produced by mathematical analysis of this energy absorption data. This image is composed of points representing density values of the tissues. High density bone is displayed as white on the cathode ray tube and the various shades of gray represent brain tissue. Gray matter is slightly denser than white matter and spinal fluid is less dense than brain tissue and appears black in the illustrations. When brain tissue is infarcted, the density of the damaged tissue begins to decrease during the first day. Over subsequent weeks there is a steady decline in density until it reaches that of spinal fluid at the end of several weeks. The CT picture is characterized by a region of low density, often triangular in shape and conforming to the distribution of one of the cerebral arteries. Figure 8-1 shows the appearance of a middle cerebral artery infarction. The characteristic distribution of a posterior cerebral artery infarct is illustrated in figure 8-2.

Although circulating blood is about the same density as brain tissue, when blood is extravasated there is a rapid rise in density. Therefore, blood in the subarachnoid space, in the brain substance, or in the subdural or epidural space is readily recognized as an area of increased density. A typical deep intracerebral

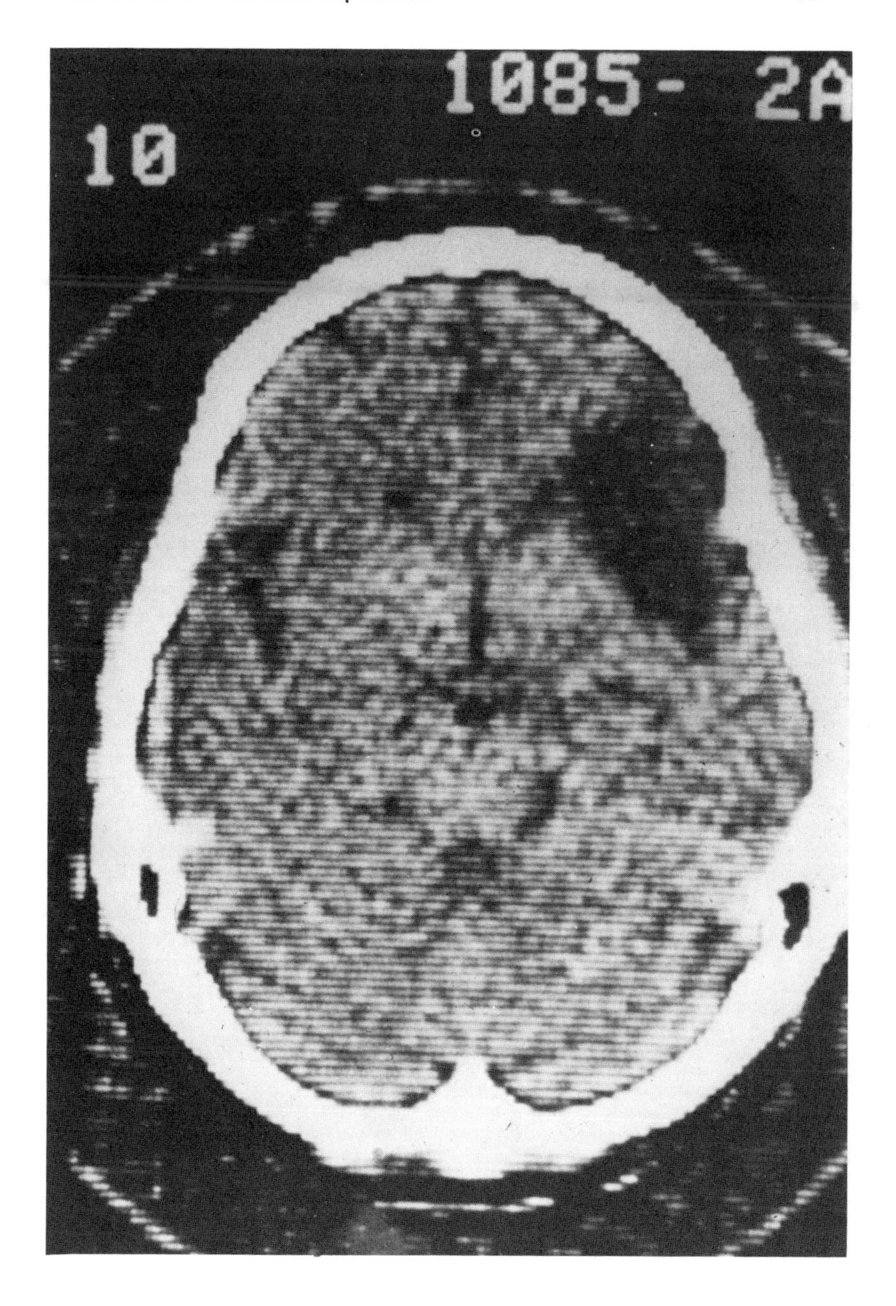

Figure 8-1. Middle cerebral infarction.

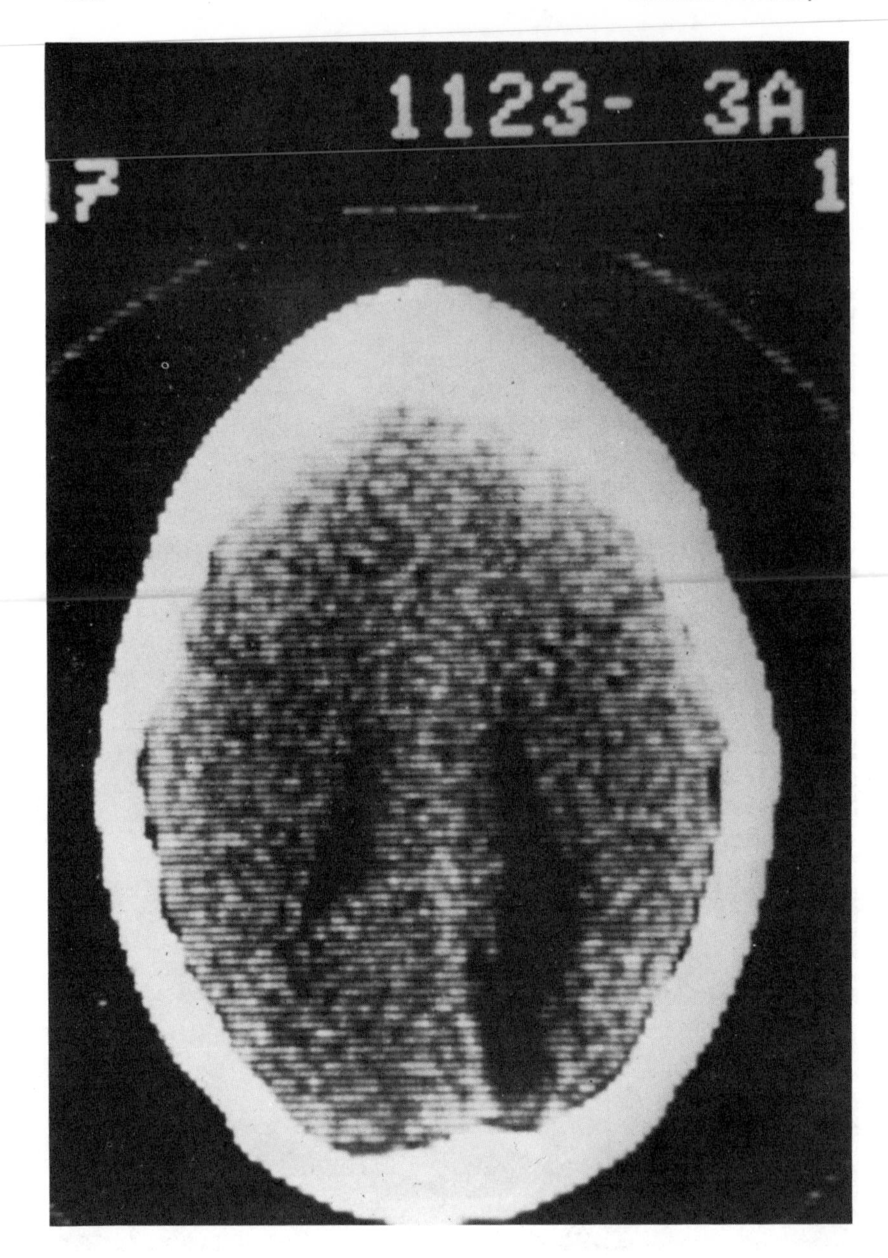

Figure 8-2. Posterior cerebral infarction.

hemorrhage is illustrated in figure 8-3. The size and position of such hemorrhages can be accurately determined by this noninvasive procedure. One of the

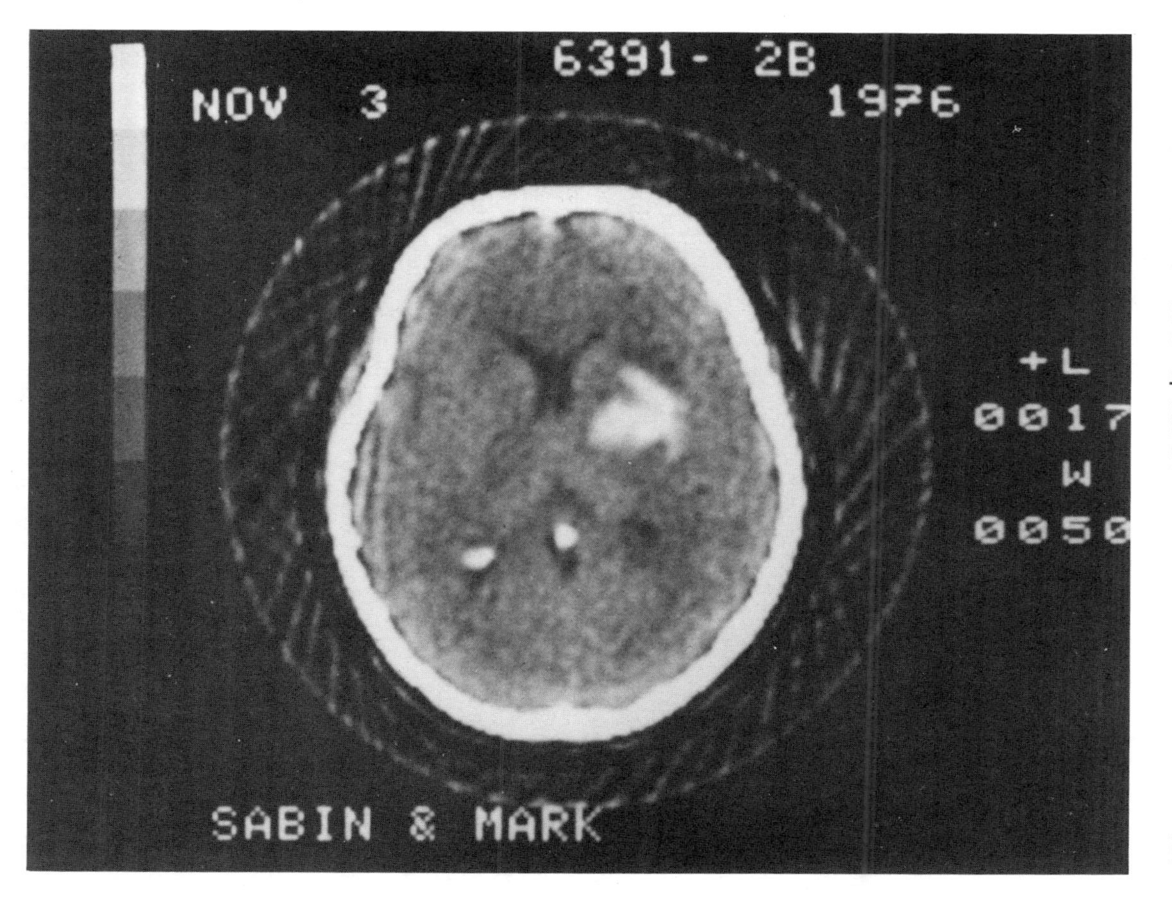

Figure 8-3. Deep intracerebral hemorrhage.

surprising findings to arise from widespread use of CT scanning is that a surprisingly large number of strokes that were clinically thought to be infarction have been demonstrated to be small hemorrhages on CT scans. This has important implications for physicians who use anticoagulant therapy in the acute stroke patient.

Figure 8-4 illustrates a vascular malformation. This lesion has not bled, but with the use of intravenous contrast material, the tangle of abnormal vessels has become opacified. While it is unusual to visualize a berry aneurysm, CT scanning often shows focal accumulation of blood near the site of aneurysmal bleeding, associated intracerebral hemorrhage, or the presence of blood within the ventricular system. When multiple aneurysms have been angiographically visualized, the CT scan is helpful in determining which one actually caused the episode of subarachnoid hemorrhage.

The usual radioisotope scan is also used to evaluate the stroke patient. When the blood-brain barrier has been disrupted, as in a cerebral infarct, the increased uptake of the isotope is often conveniently outlined by this technique. Electroencephalography is also helpful in evaluating the electrical activity in the region of injury. Lumbar puncture is necessary to examine cerebrospinal fluid pressure and constituents and is ordinarily part of the acute examination. Doppler studies of the blood flow in the carotid arteries and cerebral blood flow studies and thermography are newer developments in the evaluation of the individual with cerebrovascular disease. All three are designed to give an estimate of regional areas of decreased flow. Newer isotope flow studies sequentially map the appearance of isotope over the brain and provide an estimate of gross differences in regional blood flow (McHenry, 1977).

Treatment of the Stroke Victim

The treatment of stroke varies considerably depending on the cause and the overall status of the patient. The most effective measure is to prevent stroke altogether. The assiduous treatment of hypertension has proved to be the most effective preventive measure in reducing the incidence of both cerebral hemorrhage and cerebral infarction.

Aspirin, anticoagulants, and surgical correction of carotid artery disease can reduce TIAs in the carotid distribution, but the evidence that ultimate stroke is prevented by any one of these measures is less certain.

Once a stroke has occurred, a diagnostic and treatment program must be instituted immediately. The patient should monitor his or her cardiac status if the possibility of arrhythmia or myocardial infarction is likely. Proper fluid balance, particularly in obtundation, must be maintained. Brain edema may

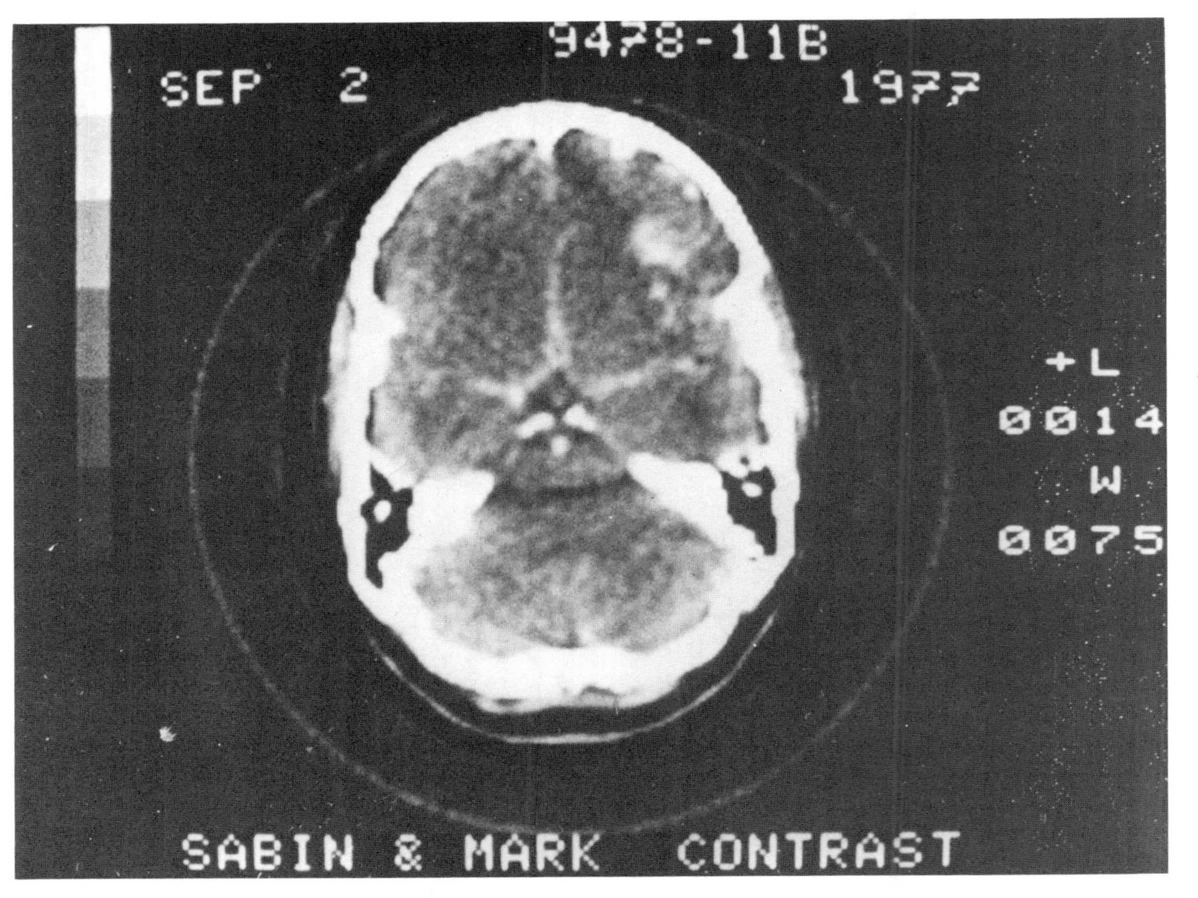

Figure 8-4. Vascular malformation with tangle of abnormal vessels.

require treatment with osmotic agents or steroids. Control of hypertension must be achieved. A rehabilitation program should be started early in the hospitalization to include physical therapy, fitting of braces, speech therapy, and vocational evaluation.

Early neurosurgical consultation is wise in cases of intracranial hemorrhage; in subarachnoid hemmorrhage the best form of treatment is to surgically isolate or obliterate the aneurysm. With the advent of microneurosurgical techniques and bipolar electrodes, some vascular malformations are now surgically resectable. Removal of cerebellar hemorrhage may prevent fatal compression of the brainstem. Controlled trials indicate that carotid surgery in acute cerebral infarction should not ordinarily be attempted.

There are several interesting cerebrovascular problems for the dentist. Head position during dental work can be of crucial importance. Vertebral arteriography, even on young people, demonstrates a decrease in vertebral artery flow with extension of the neck. The vertebral arteries course within the foramina of the cervical vertebrae up to Cl where they extend medially to reach the undersurface of the brainstem before fusing into the basilar artery at the level of the pons. Hypertrophic cervical degenerative bone disease, so common in the elderly, further contributes to mechanical deformation of the vertebral arteries with neck extension. A cervical collar that maintains a neutral neck position often proves to be a simple effective treatment for many elderly patients with TIAs in the vertebral-basilar distribution. The dentist should, therefore, be especially painstaking in assuring that an elderly patient's head be maintained in a neutral position for all dental work. Otherwise the patient may develop dimness of vision or blindness, sensations of flashing lights, defects in visual fields, double vision, vertigo, ringing in the ears, nausea, vomiting, slurred speech, or even loss of consciousness. Light general anesthetics that cause muscle relaxation can exacerbate this problem. The more upright the patient's posture, the more exaggerated the tendency toward decreased cerebral flow. If such symptoms develop, the patient should be immediately placed in the horizontal position with elevated legs.

Administration of local dental anesthesia can cause neurological disturbances (Blaxter and Britten, 1967). Since the injections are usually made near the inferior or superior alveolar branches of the internal maxillary artery, the anesthetic passes through deep orbital anastomoses between the external and internal carotid systems and then enters the ophthalmic artery. Elderly patients with artherosclerotic stenotic lesions in their carotid arteries are particularly likely to have also developed an extensive system of collateral circulation from the external to the internal carotid system. They are apt to experience neurological episodes accompanying local injections of anesthetics. Actual infarctions of the retina have been reported and have been attributed to the embolization from the oil base of some anesthetics (Walsh and Hoyt, 1969).

Giant cell arteritis or temporal arteritis is an idiopathic disease that causes inflammation of the arteries in the distribution of the external carotid artery or, less often, in the internal carotid artery (Wilkinson and Russell, 1972). It only occurs in elderly patients and most often begins with headaches in the distribution of the temporal artery, which are often swollen and tender. One devastating symptom of the disease is involvement of the ophthalmic artery and consequent blindness. Other arteries supplying the brain may be effected and cause stroke. The disease can be treated with steroids with good results. Although this disease is rare, the dentist should be aware of the occasional early involvement of the arteries supplying the tongue or the mastication muscles. Immediate signs of necrosis appear as a result of infarction of the tip of the tongue, resulting in extreme pain. When the mastication muscles are deprived of blood flow, the patient may complain of a peculiar intermittent claudication of these muscles. As the patient chews, the demands for increased blood supply to these muscles cannot be met by the diseased arteries and a painful ischemic state develops.

The pain subsides when the patient stops chewing. Either infarction of the tip of the tongue or intermittent claudication of the mastication muscles is diagnostic of giant cell arteritis. The patient needs emergency medical attention as soon as the diagnosis is considered. An immediate biopsy of the temporal artery and corticosteroid therapy are indicated to prevent blindness and stroke (Meadows, 1966).

Other mechanical problems associated with swallowing and chewing occur as a consequence of stroke. Patients with facial paralysis may have a tendency to accumulate food and debris on the side of the paralysis which causes a deterioration in oral hygiene. Patients with infarcts in the lateral part of the medulla have severe difficulty in swallowing, persistent hiccups, and sensory changes in the face or mouth, although no hemiplegia is present.

Patients with bilateral damage to the corticobulbar tracts may experience severe difficulty in swallowing and speaking, accompanied by relative immobility of the tongue and palate. The gag reflex may have a high threshold, but once triggered the response is exaggerated. Dental work may be difficult in such patients because of their poor handling of secretions and abnormal reflexes. The problem is compounded by a bizarre syndrome called emotional incontinence, which causes periods of automatic laughing or more often crying in response to minimal emotional stimuli. This abnormal reaction is not well correlated with the actual feeling state of the patient, but is a reflex release of the motor component of these emotional responses.

Other patients may have a small focal lesion that interrupts certain cerebellar pathways and causes palatal myoclonus. These patients exhibit constant beating movements at the rate of 100 to 160 per minute affecting the palate, tongue, lips, larynx, diaphragm, and sometimes the eyes. The dentist may witness a constant beating of the palate which may be associated with defective speech and swallowing.

Many patients show striking disorders of communication and responsiveness following a stroke which the dentist can readily recognize. Patients with right hemisphere lesions often become quite apathetic regarding their disabilities and may be totally unaware of their disability or at least quite unconcerned about it. This inappropriate lack of concern may extend to disabilities other than the neurologic disorder and interfere with cooperation in a therapeutic regimen outlined by the dentist.

Patients with communication disorders may also be extremely trying for the dentist. It is important to understand that in some forms of aphasia comprehension is perfectly intact even though the output of speech is grossly defective. Sometimes, when almost all language comprehension is abolished, the patient may show an unusual preservation of knowledge of commands having to do with total body and midline body movements (Geschwind, 1965). Such a patient may obey commands like "open your mouth," or "stick out your tongue," while being totally unable to obey any commands requiring individual limb or digit movements. These individuals may lack any concern or insight into the extent of their language predicament. Aphasic patients who have great trouble understanding spoken language may be responsive to communication through gestures. All aphasic patients, however, face problems in producing written language.

Infarction or ischemia is viewed as a result of an abnormality in the vessel walls, the constituents of the blood, or disorders of circulation. Spontaneous intracranial hemorrhage occurs from bleeding aneurysms, vascular malformations, or ruptured blood vessels in the hypertensive patient. The contributions of CT are especially informative for accurately diagnosing these diseases, which is essential for proper treatment.

Specific syndromes of relevance to the dentist have been discussed; namely, conditions interfering with the motor function of the muscles involved in speaking, chewing, and swallowing. Other syndromes that may warn of oncoming stroke such as those associated with temporal arteritis should and can be recognized by the practicing dentist. It is important to recognize behavioral changes caused by stroke that may severely affect the proper management of the patient.

References

Blaxter, P.L. and Britten, M.J.A. Transient Amaurosis After Mandibular Nerve Block. *Brit Med J* 1:681-691, 1967.

Fisher, C.M. Lacunes: Small, Deep Cerebral Infarcts. *Neurology* 15:774-784, 1965.

Geschwind, N. Disconnexion Syndromes in Animals and Man I and II. *Brain* 88:237-294; 585-644, 1965.

McHenry, L.C., Jr. Role of Special Testing in Cerebrovascular Disease. In

Thompson, R.A. and Green, J.R. (Eds.), *Advances in Neurology,* vol. 16 (New York: Raven, 1977), pp. 81-96.

Meadows, S.P. Temporal or Giant Cell Arteritis. *Proc Royal Soc Med* 59:329-333, 1966.

New, P.F.J. Computed Tomography: Experience at the MGH. In Whisnant, J.P. and Sandok, B.A. (Eds.), *Cerebral Vascular Diseases* (New York: Grune and Stratton, 1975), pp. 203-221.

Romanul, F.C.A. and Abramowicz, A. Changes in Brain and Pial Vessels in Arterial Border Zones; A Study of 13 Cases. *Arch Neurol* 11:40-65, 1964.

Walsh, F.B. and Hoyt, W.F. *Clinical Neuro-Opthalmology,* 3rd ed. (Baltimore: Williams and Wilkens, 1969), pp. 250-2502.

Wilkinson, I.M.S. and Russell, R.R. Arteries of the Head and Neck in Giant Cell Arteritis. *Arch Neurol* 27:378-391, 1972.

The Chemical Senses and Aging

Morley R. Kare and *Philip R. Zelson*

In the play "As You Like It" Shakespeare described the last stage of life as being "second childishness and near oblivion, sans teeth, sans eyes, sans taste, sans everything." Perhaps Shakespeare did not specifically include the sense of smell in his description of the final stage of man because most people use the word "taste" to encompass the sensations of olfaction and gustation. In fact, they are describing *flavor*, which is a combination of sensations from these two senses. Even though little is known about the effects of aging on olfaction, there is evidence that the most elderly individuals maintain an ability to perceive odors. Recent observations of a group of twelve people, reported to be between 96 and 117 years of age and evenly divided by sex, indicate that they were all able to perceive odor. Eleven of these twelve individuals correctly identified the test perfume as being floral.

It has been estimated from a number of studies, including an informal dental clinic survey, that at any time between 1 and 2 percent of the population suffers from a malfunctioning of one of the chemical senses. In the elderly, the incidence of malfunctioning, possibly related secondarily to the effects of medication or disease, has been estimated to be higher than 2 percent (Wank and Brightman, 1973).

Special problems complicate the understanding of the role of the chemical senses in body physiology. Many diseases and drugs have been reported to modify perception; for example, carcinoma (Carson and Gormican, 1976); diabetes (Schelling et al., 1965); malnutrition (Langan and Yearick, 1976); periodontal disease; artificial dentures (Manly et al., 1952); amphetamines; penicillamine (Henkin, 1969); and antithyroid agents. Since it is difficult to find many 80-year-old individuals in our society whose health is totally unimpaired and who are not taking medication, it becomes equally difficult to evaluate the true effect of aging on taste functions.

One of the most confusing aspects of evaluating the status of taste or smell is understanding the terminology used. When one reads of a taste deficit, it may represent a change in a detection, recognition, or preference threshold. Frequently investigators fail to delineate the nature of the deficit. The confusion is further complicated by testing techniques that vary with individual investigators (Pfaffman, Bartoshuk, and McBurney, 1971). It is then extremely difficult for the nonspecialist to evaluate an individual's taste or smell responses to food.

The problem of test methods and terminology is compounded by the large normal variation among individuals in perceiving taste or odor stimuli. When two people share an identical breakfast, they do not necessarily share an identical series of sensations. An individual who adds seven teaspoons of sugar to his or her coffee may experience the same sweetness sensation as the individual who adds only one teaspoon. Yet, both of these individuals may be within a normal range.

Differences between taste and odor perception among the species are even greater than between humans (Kare and Beauchamp, 1977). Therefore, interpretation of taste data obtained from animals must be evaluated with caution. Contrary to the advertised image, animals do not necessarily share sense impressions common to people. For example, many animals including lions, tigers, jaguars, leopards, chickens, armadillos, and hedgehogs do not perceive the common sugars as a pleasant sensation (Kare and Beauchamp, 1977). Therefore, interpretation of animal taste data has limited meaning to human taste perception.

Taste is commonly used to define a mixture of gustatory and nongustatory sensory inputs rather than the simple application of a taste stimulus to a receptor. For example, when one says a "soft drink" tastes good, one is referring to the complex effect produced by stimulating a variety of sensory modalities. The carbonation stimulates the pressure receptors in the oral cavity and the low pH probably provides pain and a mild acid stimulus. Additionally, most soft drinks are consumed cold, providing a thermal effect. The taste difference between cold as opposed to warm milk or beer is common knowledge. Finally, there is information from the 10 percent sucrose plus the added flavor. Collectively these multiple sensations produce the phenomenon we call taste.

Vision and audition can also modify taste. Imagine your reaction to a black-yoked egg or a glass of blue milk; the unnatural color of foods can influence one's reaction to a taste stimulus. Vickers and Bourne (1976) have reported sound as having an important role in food perception. They measured the acoustical patterns produced by crisp and wilted foods. Foods such as carrots, potato chips, celery, and lettuce each have a characteristic sinusoidal frequency. All crisp foods produce audible patterns with a large amplitude, whereas wilted foods are much less noisy (Kapur and Collister, 1970). Since visual and auditory deficits are common in the aged, it is conceivable that a good deal of described or imagined oral sensory diminution is related to a loss in audition or vision rather than to a decrease of stimulation transmitted via the taste receptors.

Precisely when taste begins to function in the development of an individual varies with the species. At birth the possum is without taste buds; they appear about sixteen days later. On the other hand, taste buds are discernible in the 7-week-old human fetus. Saccharin was introduced into the amniotic fluid of the 7-month-old fetus and was reported to stimulate the consumption of the fluid

(Snoo, 1937). In our laboratory, taste studies were carried out with infants 1 to 3 days old (Desor, Maller, and Turner, 1973). The newborn infants preferred sugars at concentrations similar to those of an adult. Furthermore, they discriminated between different simple sugars and concentrations of sugars. One can conclude that sweet perception is an innate or congenital sense in humans. The adolescent prefers a higher concentration of sucrose than does an adult (Desor, Greene, and Maller, 1975). This could be related to the caloric demands of a greater expenditure of energy. Unlike vision, taste is generally described as functioning at one level through middle age.

Arey, Tremaine, and Monzingo (1935) examined cadavers of subjects 74 to 85 years of age and reported a 60 percent loss in the number of taste cells. They suggested that, of those structures present, only about half appeared to be functional. Assuming this to be correct, a person who reaches 80 years of age can expect to have the use of only one of five taste receptors. These numbers were determined solely from the tongue, though we know taste receptors are distributed throughout the oropharyngeal area. A decline in several taste cells, however, does not in itself indicate declining taste sensitivity.

At the Monell Chemical Senses Center we conducted a study to measure the effect of age on the ability to distinguish among taste stimuli, and on taste preferences. There were three groups designated to participate: a group of individuals 40 to 45 years old, a second group 65 to 70 years, and a third group 80 to 85 years of age. Only noninstitutionalized individuals were selected as subjects. While it was desirable to select subjects in perfect health and receiving no medication, a reasonable compromise of this criterion in the aged group was necessary. Our taste testing procedure was based on the method of Harris and Kalmus as modified by Desor and Maller (1975). Reagent grade chemicals were used to establish sensitivity thresholds. In the same session V-8 juice with three levels of sodium chloride (sodium free, normal, and high salt), Hershey chocolate (made with low, normal, and high sucrose content), Tang with three levels of sourness, and a similar product with three levels of bitterness were used.

Taste ingredient differences in the food products were substantial (20 percent reduction or addition of sucrose). Though there was no restriction in the time allowed for a subject to make a response, older subjects progressed much more slowly through the testing regimen than did the control group. Under normal living conditions, time spent tasting can be adjusted by the subject, so it would probably be a mistake to include such criteria in measuring sensitivity. Furthermore, perception of taste in the elderly might be reduced if taste sensations compete for attention with other sensory stimuli (visual, auditory, tactile, and thermal).

Our results suggest that, under ideal testing conditions the aged maintain a high level of taste sensitivity and preference. There were no differences among the groups in their taste preferences behavior or in discriminations of concentration in the food products used. Only the detection threshold for salt was significantly decreased with age, particularly in the male. There were other small numerical declines in sensitivity with age, though none proved to be statistically significant.

Taste cells have a life expectancy of approximately ten days. Young cells, despite a reduction in numbers with age, appear to function adequately (Wolstemholme and Knight, 1970). The human sense of taste is so important that a sufficient number of functioning cells are present from birth through old age. The question then arises, "What are the functions of taste?"

The role of taste and smell in maintaining the body's nutrition is frequently overlooked. The digestive system normally accepts nutrients to regulate body homeostasis. The maintenance of nutritional balance is largely attributed to a postabsorptive phenomenon. The mouth serves in certain species as a specialized structure for prehension, where provision is made for mastication and salivation. Beyond this, the oral cavity is generally considered to be of little or no consequence to the digestive system.

The importance of the oral cavity should not be overlooked, however. It determines what nutrients will enter the digestive system, meters and monitors the quality and quantity of food consumed, and, consequently, is involved in many aspects of digestion. When food enters or even approaches the oral cavity, salivary secretion is stimulated. Saliva facilitates tasting by adding solvents, enzymes, and lubricants to the food bolus. Clinical problems arising from xerostomia (dry mouth) emphasize the importance of saliva in humans (Henkin et al., 1972).

Generally a consideration of the role of human taste focuses on hedonic functions. The taste of foods can influence the character and time of chewing as well as the pattern of swallowing. Strong taste stimuli slow gastric contractions as well as enhance intestinal motility (Kare, 1969).

Nicolaidis (1969) reported that at the first step of feeding, at the peripheral level taste initiates early and anticipatory metabolic modifications. The fasting respiratory quotient (RQ) is 0.7 and approaches 1.0 after feeding. This is attributed to metabolic needs after absorption of nutrients. The precise time of the change in the fasting RQ coincides with oral stimulation. Apparently the preparation of the digestive tract for the reception of food may be initiated in part by taste.

Fischer et al. (1972) have reported that immediately after oral administration of glucose to a dog, there is a rise in the circulating immunoreactive insulin (IRI). A second rise occurs moments later and in about twenty minutes the circulating IRI rise parallels the hyperglycemia induced. Yet if the glucose is administered intravenously, the first two releases of IRI are omitted. Furthermore, if the sugar is given orally and escapes through an esophogeal fistula, only the initial two releases of IRI occur. These results support the hypothesis that oral stimulation, possibly taste, is involved in the early release of metabolic hormones.

Testing dogs with gastric and intestinal fistulas, Kare (1969) reported that the nature of a taste stimulus can substantially influence both the volume and protein content of exocrine pancreatic secretion. Application of an appealing sucrose solution appreciably increased volume and protein content of pancreatic secretion when compared to an offensive quinine mixture.

Recently, Naim, Kare and Merritt (1978) administered taste stimulus cellulose mixtures to dogs both orally and intragastrically through a fistula. These experiments were designed to separate the effects of pregastric factors on exocrine pancreatic secretion from the effects of gastric stimulation. An appealing oral stimulus was effective in increasing pancreatic secretion, but an offensive stimulus was not. Neither stimuli created any difference in pancreatic flow when gastrically administered.

The significance of these various effects of taste on the digestive processes in the elderly warrants serious consideration. Winick (1976) observed that certain diseases associated with the gastrointestinal tract are more common in the elderly. A reduction in the over-optimum supply of digestive enzymes, sluggish tract activity, and the prevalence of diabetes are commonly associated with the elderly. Consequently, taste stimuli and their effects on the digestive system assume an especially important role in the health of the elderly in more efficient food utilization (Naim, Kare, and Ingle, 1978).

Certain drives are substantially reduced in the aged population. Dehydration is frequent because the impetus to consume fluids is modest or absent. Taste stimuli could motivate the elderly to consume fluids. Since most of us need little encouragement to eat or drink, the concept of a metabolic need for sensory stimulation to initiate consumption is foreign.

In reviewing the various reports on special lunch programs for the aged, the only problems mentioned were the delivery of the food and social aspects concerning table arrangements. Yet the taste of the food was totally overlooked, even though there is considerable evidence that the sensory qualities of the food may be of critical importance in encouraging the elderly to consume nutritious foods.

It is true that problems of hypertension and diabetes are preeminent in the aged population. The use of appealing foods that provide strong taste stimulants such as salt are then contraindicated. There is also concern about catering to the sweet tooth of the elderly. Research at the Veterans Administration, however, has described an intensely sweet protein, monellin, that may substitute as a viable alternative to carbohydrate sweeteners (Morris and Cagan, 1972). Monellin consists of ninety-one amino acids and no carbohydrates. Perhaps this sweet protein substitute will also play an important role in the prevention of dental caries and research in diabetes.

Similarly, there is no reason why we must assume that a salty taste can only be produced by salts. Up to now, most salt substitutes have been largely taste failures. Until monellin was characterized, proteins were described as tasteless. A concerted research effort on taste should be able to identify compounds such as monellin, that will produce needed gustatory stimulation without the associated deleterious physiological side effects.

We have difficulty providing adequate nutrition and changing diets for the young because nutritional quality is seldom a criterion for selecting novel foods. In the elderly the problem changes to one of inflexible food habits. With an understanding of the sensory qualities of food, however, these problems can be surmounted.

The oral cavity is the responsibility and the unique concern of dental medicine. No physiological system is more integral to this area than taste. We have reviewed some of the functions of taste in digestion and suggest that the function of taste is probably of increased importance in the elderly. The chemical senses in the aged should be a special challenge to the science and practice of dental medicine.

References

Arey, L.B., Tremaine, M.J., and Monzingo, F.L. The Numerical and Topographical Relations of Taste Buds to Human Circumvallate Papillae Throughout the Life Span. *Anat Rec* 64:9-25, 1935.

Carson, J.S. and Gormican, A. Taste Acuity and Food Attitudes of Selected Patients with Cancer. *J Am Diet Assn* 70:361-365, 1976.

Desor, J.A., Greene, L.S., and Maller, O. Preferences for Sweet and Salty in Adolescent and Adult Humans. *Science* 190:686-687, 1975.

Desor, J.A. and Maller, O.sTaste Correlates of Disease–Cystic Fibrosis. *J Pediatr* 87:93-97, 1975.

Desor, J.A., Maller, O., and Turner, R.E. Taste in Acceptance of Sugars by Human Infants. *J Comp Physiol Psychol* 84:496-501, 1973.

Fischer, U., Hommel, H., Ziegler, M., and Lutzi, E. The Mechanism of Insulin Secretion After Oral Glucose Administration. *Diabetologia* 8:385-390, 1972.

Henkin, R.I. The Metabolic Regulation of Taste Acuity. In Pfaffman, C. (Ed.), *Olfaction and Taste* II. (New York: Rockefeller University Press, 1969), pp. 574-585.

Henkin, R.I., Talal, N., Larson, A.L., and Mattern, C.F.T. Abnormalities of Taste and Smell in Sjorgren's Syndrome. *Ann Intern Med* 76:375-383, 1972.

Kapur, K.K. and Collister, T. A Study of Food Textural Discrimination in Persons with Natural and Artificial Dentitions. In J. Bosma (Ed.), *2nd Symposium on Oral Sensation and Perception* (Springfield: Charles C. Thomas, 1970), pp. 332-339.

Kare, M.R. Digestive Functions of Taste Stimuli. In Pfaffman, C. (Ed.), *Olfaction and Taste* (New York: Rockefeller University Press, 1969), pp. 586-592.

Kare, M.R. and Beauchamp, G.K. Taste, Smell and Hearing. In Swenson, M.J. (Ed.), *Dukes' Physiology of Domestic Animals* (Ithaca: Cornell University Press, 1977).

Langan, M.J. and Yearick, E.S. The Effects of Improved Oral Hygiene on Taste Perception and Nutrition of the Elderly. *J Gerontol* 31:413-418, 1976.

Manly, R.S., Pfaffman, C., Lathrope, D., and Kaiser, J. Oral Sensory Thresholds of Persons with Natural and Artificial Dentitions. *J Dent Res* 31:305-312, 1952.

Morris, J.A. and Cagan, R.H. Purification of Monellin, the Sweet Principle of *Dioscoreophyllum Cumminsii. Biochim Biophys Acta* 261:114-122, 1972.

Naim, M., Kare, M.R., and Ingle, D.E. Diet Palatability and Growth Efficiency: Evidence for a Physiological Interrelationship in Rats. *Life Sci* 23:2127-2136, 978.

Naim, M., Kare, M.R., and Merritt, A.M. Effects of Oral Stimulation on the Cephalic Phase of Pancreatic Exocrine Secretion in Dogs. *Physiol Behav* 20:563-570, 1978.

Nicolaidis, S. Early Systemic Responses to Orogastric Stimulation in the Regulation of Food and Water Balance: Functional and Electrophysiological Data. *Ann NY Acad Sci* 157:1176-1203, 1969.

Pfaffman, C., Bartoshuk, L.M., and McBurney, H. Taste Psychophysics. In Biedler, L.M. (Ed.), *Handbook of Sensory Physiology,* vol. 4, pt. 2 (New York: Springer-Verlag, 1971).

Schelling, J.L., Tetrault, L., Lasagna, L., and Davis, M. Abnormal Taste Threshold in Diabetes. *Lancet* 1:508-512, 1965.

Snoo, K. de Das trinkende Kind im Uterus. *Geburtshilfe Gynaekologie Monatsschrift* 195:88-97, 1937.

Vickers, Z. and Bourne, M.C. A Psychoacoustical Theory of Crispness. *J Food Sci* 41:1158-1164, 1976.

Wank, H. and Brightman, V. The Prevalence of Atypical Facial Position and Other Disorders of Oral Sensation. IADR 51st annual meeting, Washington, DC, Abstract 701:234, 1973.

Winick, M. *Nutrition and Aging. Current Concepts in Nutrition.* vol. 4 (New York: John Wiley and Sons, 1976).

Wolstemholme, G.E.W. and Knight, J. (Eds.), *C.B.A. Symposium on Taste and Smell in Vertebrates.* (London: J.A. Churchill, 1970).

Part II
Oral Problems

10 Oral Pathology in the Aging Individual

Gerald Shklar

There is a gradual alteration in the morphology and physiology of many oral tissues with aging. These changes may predispose the involved tissues to a variety of pathologic conditions. Although very few oral diseases are characteristic of the elderly, many pathologic states are seen with greater frequency than in younger individuals.

Two fundamental questions concerning the aging process cannot be easily answered at this time. The most interesting is whether aging itself is a pathologic or a physiologic process. If aging, in its multifaceted manifestations, is a disease process, it might be prevented or at least treated and cured once we have an appropriate understanding of the basic pathogenesis and etiology. It is basic to our current scientific approach that all diseases will be controlled; the problems to be solved involve an understanding of the nature of the disease and its cause or causes. On the other hand, if aging is understood as a physiologic state, then we would be forced to accept it as part of human existence and be powerless to prevent or reverse the process. This concept implies that human beings might be genetically programmed for a certain life span, during which certain cells and organ systems begin to degenerate as the end of programmed existence approaches.

The second question concerns different rates of aging. The aging process is accelerated or retarded by various factors. If we can understand these modifying influences, we could conceivably delay the aging process, even if the basic mechanisms are genetically predetermined. Many individuals are vigorous, both physically and intellectually, well into their seventies, while others begin to deteriorate in their fifties. Many people 70 years old have excellent oral health; their teeth and periodontal tissues are in good condition, and the oral mucosa is clinically normal.

General Oral Features in Aging

The aging process affects most oral tissues and results in the gradual appearance of alterations visible at the clinical level.

Alveolar Bone

Alveolar bone reflects changes seen in other parts of the skeletal system and gradually undergoes osteoporotic changes in the aging process (figure 10-1). The

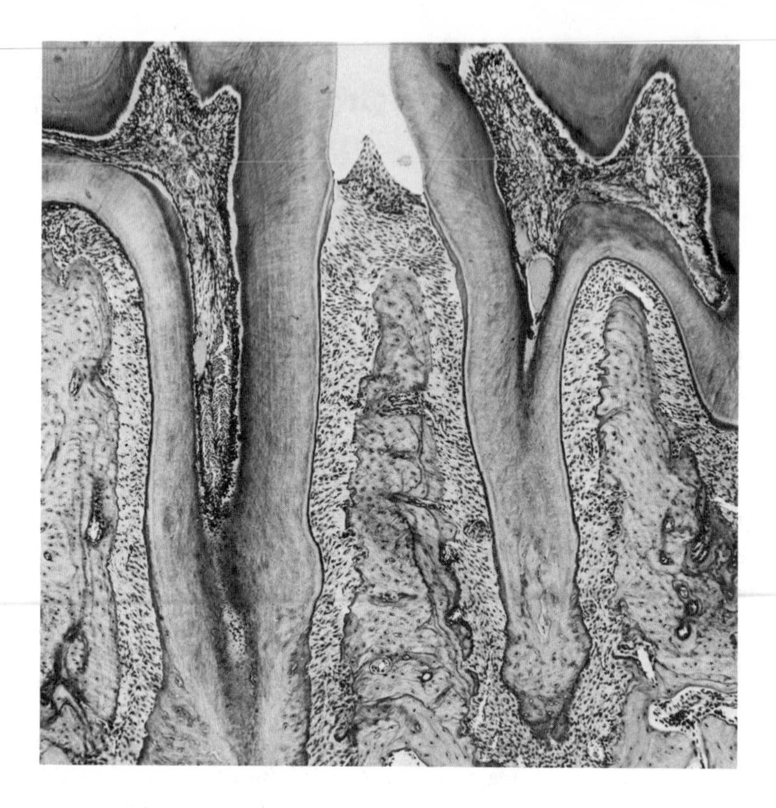

Figure 10-1. First and second molars of normal young rodent with interdental septum of bone and periodontal tissues. (Hematoxylin-eosin, x 80.)

effect is antianabolic rather than catabolic. There is a negative effect on osteoblastic or bone formation activity rather than an increase in osteoclastic activity or resorption (figures 10-1 through 10-3). The causative factor(s) for this alteration in bone metabolism is not known, but is probably comparable to the general effect of aging noted on cells and tissues throughout the body. It is similar to the results seen with antianabolic activity, such as the administration of corticosteroid hormones, estrogen deprivation in women, and radiation. Normally, there is a dynamic equilibrium between bone formative and resorptive activity; or the anabolic and catabolic activity in metabolic terms; and osteoblastic and osteoclastic activity, in histologic terms. In aging, the equilibrium shifts towards resorptive activity because the activity of the osteoblastic cells is depressed. Thus, the antianabolic activity produces bone resorption. The endosteal surfaces of bone are more sensitive to metabolic influences than the periosteal surfaces,

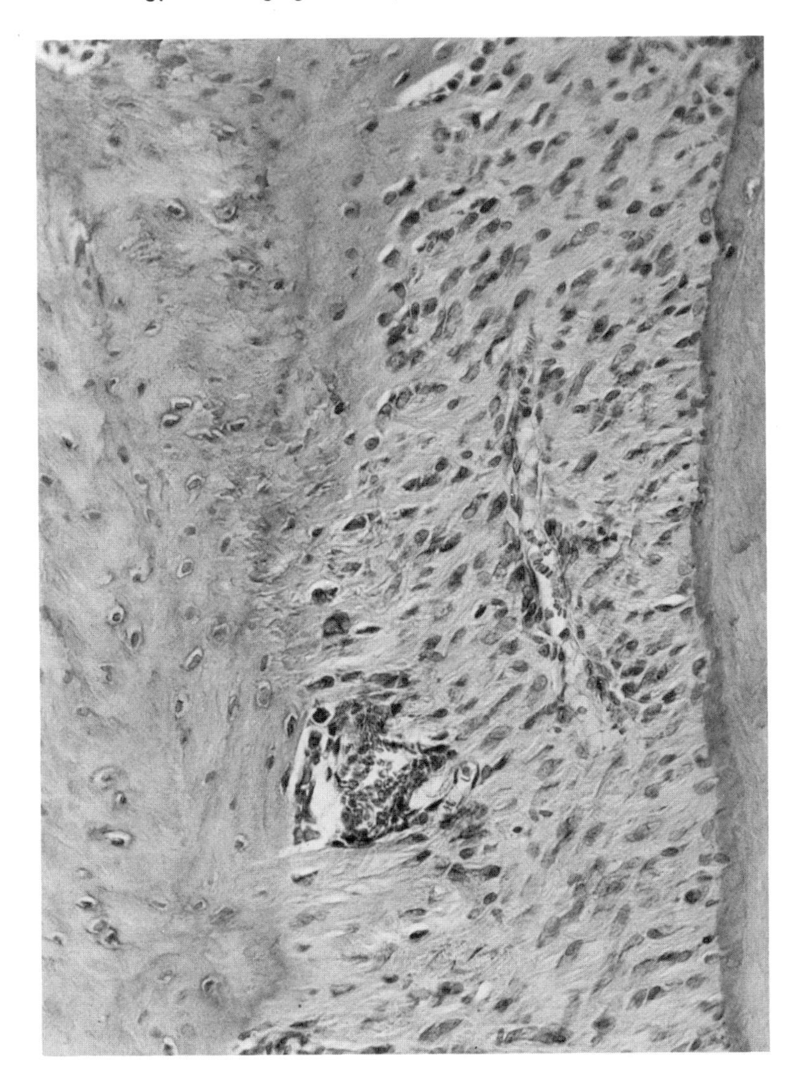

Figure 10-2. Mesial surface of alveolar bone, periodontal membrane, and cementum of second molar tooth in young rodent. The periodontal membrane is highly cellular and osteoblasts are seen along the surface of the newly formed bone. (Hematoxylin-eosin, x 200.)

and extensive bone loss occurs primarily within the tissue rather than at the surface. The bone therefore becomes porous (figure 10-4). This process is called

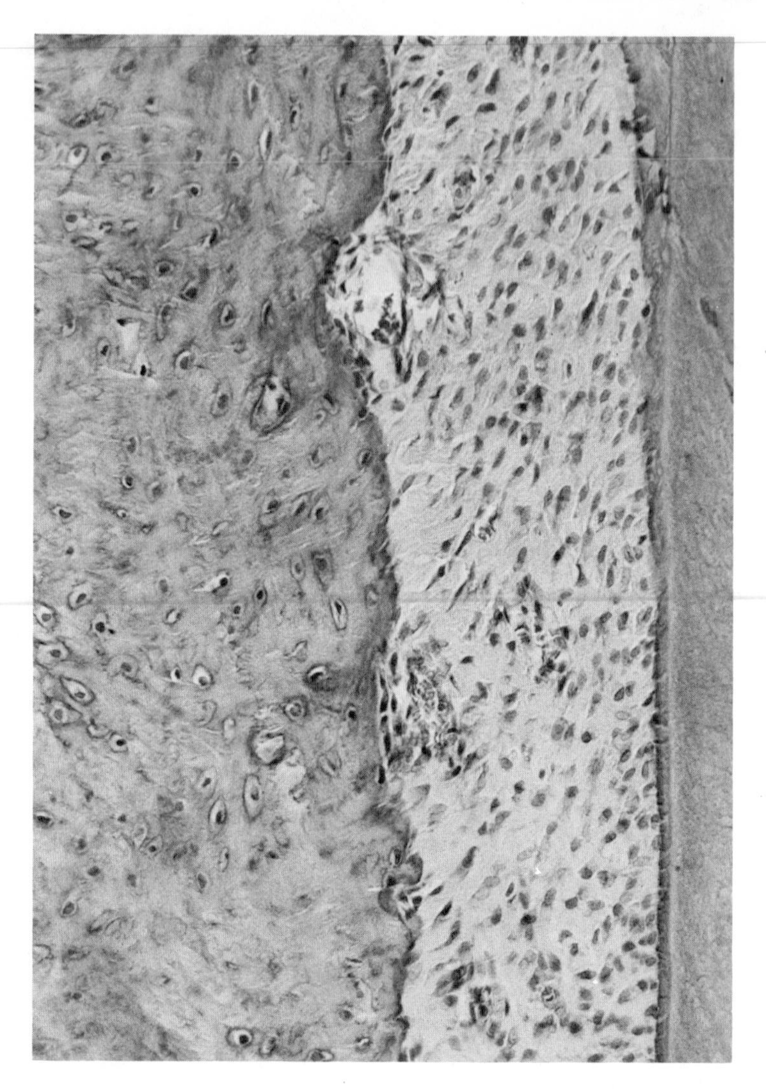

Figure 10-3. Mesial surface of alveolar bone in aged rodent. The bone surfact is inactively and sharply outlined. Few osteoblasts are seen and the periodontal membrane is less cellular. (Hematoxylin-eosin, x 200.)

osteoporosis and is one of the common conditions noted in older persons. In persons with osteoporosis, the periosteal or periodontal surfaces of alveolar bone are less resistant to harmful local oral factors such as trauma, inflammation, or disease. These favor local bone resorption by stimulating osteoclastic activity,

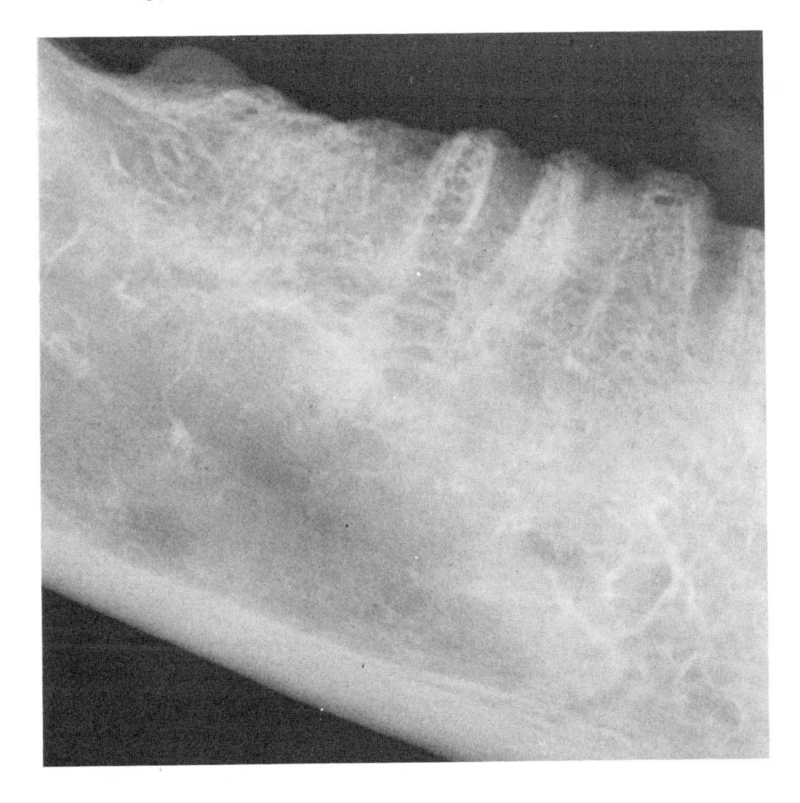

Figure 10-4. Radiograph of edentulous mandible in 80-year-old male showing large trabecular spaces consistent with diagnosis of osteoporosis. Skeletal survery showed similar findings in other bones.

and the osteoporotic process becomes exaggerated if the bone is already affected. Thus osteoporosis favors the development of periodontitis, or chronic periodontal disease, and in certain situations alveolar ridge resorption. In recent years, it has been shown with experimental animals that anabolic steroids can alter the antianabolic changes associated with aging (Shklar, 1974). There are encouraging reports regarding the use of anabolic steroids in humans. These exciting findings may alter many of our present concepts toward the inevitability of osteoporosis occurring in older persons.

Oral Mucosa

In the aging process the stratified squamous epithelium of the oral mucosa becomes relatively thin and atrophic. In tissues that normally exhibit keratinization, such as the palatal mucosa, there is a flattening of the rete pegs and a greater frequency of edema plus a tendency towards increased keratinization. Specialized epithelial structures, such as the filiform and fungiform papillae on the dorsum of the tongue often undergo atrophy. The tongue then has a smooth appearance. Taste perception decreases as a result of the lingual papillary atrophy (Fikentscher et al., 1977). The oral epithelium also exhibits increasing amounts of glycogen, and the connective tissue beneath the epithelium presents degenerative alterations in collagen. The collagen bundles appear hyperchromatic, separated, and, occasionally, irregular or fragmented (figures 10-5 and 10-6).

Salivary Glands

Salivary gland tissue also becomes atrophic with aging. The acinar cells of the glands frequently appear hyperchromatic and the acini are often replaced by connective or adipose tissue with a concommitant decrease in glandular tissue. Less saliva is produced, creating varying degrees of xerostomia. This xerostomia cannot be treated adequately, since the tissue function has been lost and cannot be restored.

Tissue Healing

Tissue healing is often depressed in old age, particularly in the restoration of alveolar bone following injury or surgical intervention (Darvish, Shklar, and Shiere, 1972). Experimental extraction wounds have been shown to heal more rapidly following the use of an anabolic steroid (Tennenbaum and Shklar, 1970). These agents may eventually play an important role in stimulating the healing response of bone.

Oral Diseases in Aging Subjects

Oral diseases and disorders that one associates with old age are attrition of teeth, chronic periodontal disease, xerostomia, mucositis and mucosal atrophy, leukoplakia and malignant neoplasia.

Attrition

Attrition or the gradual wearing down of teeth occurs throughout life and is manifested in old age. The problem is compounded by tooth loss and the

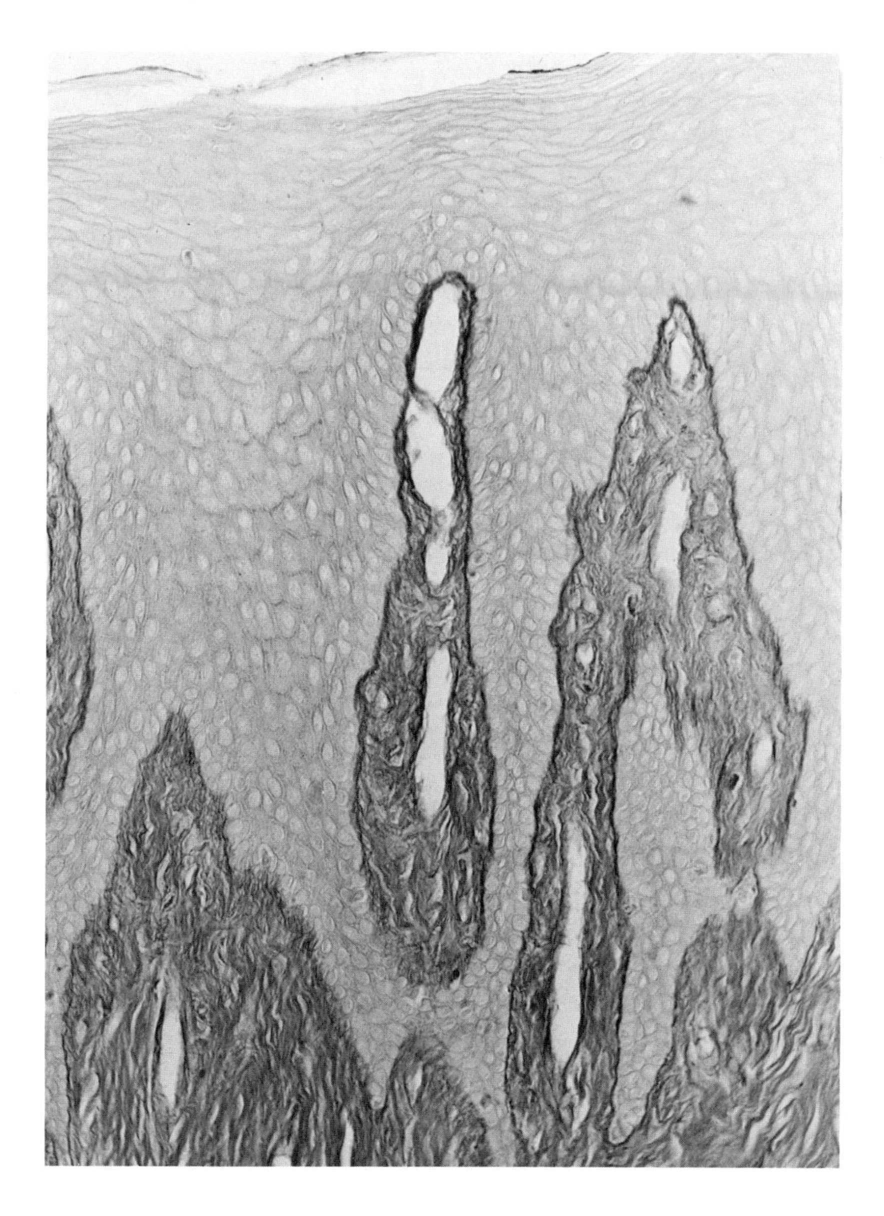

Figure 10-5. Oral mucosal epithelium and underlying connective tissue in a child. Epithelium is free of glycogen and shows deep rete pegs. The connective tissue is densely fibrillar. (Periodic acid-Schiff, × 200.)

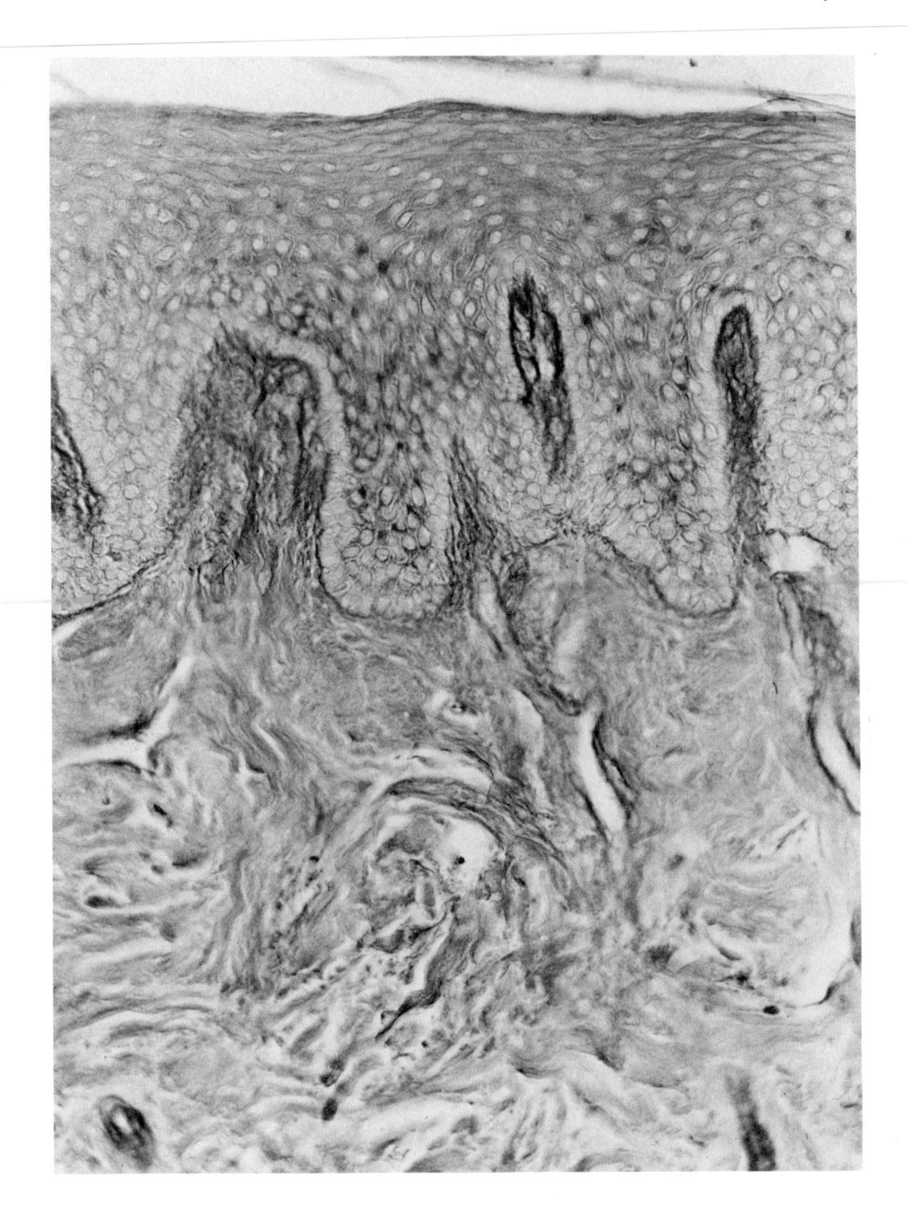

Figure 10-6. Oral mucosal epithelium and underlying connective tissue in a 70-year-old adult. The epithelium is thin with flattened rete pegs. Glycogen is present. The connective tissue is disoriented and demonstrates collagen degeneration. (Periodic acid-Schiff, × 200.)

resultant decrease in masticatory function, so that increased occlusal stress is placed on the remaining teeth.

Attrition results in a loss of vertical dimension, a problem compounded by tooth loss and the nonreplacement of missing teeth by prosthetic appliances. Loss of vertical dimension results in overclosure of the mandible, giving the characteristic facial picture of senescence—protruding raised chin and wrinkled perioral skin. The deep fissures at the commissures of the lips become irritated and inflammed, particularly in those who drool because of some loss of labial control. This cheilitis or cheilosis is difficult to treat and usually is not the result of a vitamin B deficiency in the older patient, although the cheilitis (cheilosis) of vitamin B deficiency must always be considered. Loss of vertical dimension may also result in "so called" temporomandibular joint disorders, although this possible cause has been overemphasized. This pain syndrome is usually due to muscle spasm and is more correctly referred to as the myofascial pain dysfunction syndrome (Laskin and Greene, 1972). Osteoarthritis involving the temporomandibular joint may be a cause of temporomandibular joint dysfunction and pain, but this is relatively uncommon.

Chronic Periodontal Disease

Znamensky (1902) pointed out almost a century ago that periodontal disease was caused by a variety of local irritative factors acting on periodontal tissues that in some way had a lowered resistance. An "osteoporousical atrophy" acted as a "favorable soil" for the development of periodontal disease, with a gingivitis extending into underlying tissue to produce apical migration of epithelial attachment, periodontal pockets, periodontal membrane destruction, and resorption of alveolar bone. The probability of some underlying systemic predisposing cause or causes of periodontal disease has been understood by most of the major periodontal investigators, such as Gottlieb (1927), Glickman (1972), and Goldman (1953). Experimental pathology has demonstrated that classic periodontal disease with gingival inflammation, periodontal pocket formation, and alveolar bone loss could be induced in experimental animals with diabetes (Cohen, Shklar, and Yerganian, 1961) or animals debilitated by cold stress (Shklar, 1970). A combination of local irritants and systemic debilitation was demonstrated by several investigators to result in periodontitis (Stahl, Sandler, and Cahn, 1955). Periodontal disease is not only more common in aging human subjects, but is commonly found in aging experimental animals such as mice, rats, dogs, monkeys, and baboons.

Xerostomia

Xerostomia, or dry mouth, may be due to a large variety of etiologic factors (Bertram, 1967), but severe xerostomia is occasionally seen in elderly patients as the result of atrophy of salivary gland tissue—an aging change. The oral cavity is extremely dry, the mucosa appears red, dry, fissured, and often is coated with food and desquamating cells. The lips are crusted and the tongue demonstrates papillary atrophy (figure 10-7). There may also be dry throat and dysphagia. The only available therapy is the continuous use of artificial saliva, since the glandular tissue itself is atrophic. This type of xerostomia is similar to that caused by extensive radiation to the head and neck, with subsequent atrophy of salivary gland tissue. In the absence of saliva there is a tendency to develop extensive caries, particularly on the root surfaces of the anterior mandibular teeth (figure 10-8). Xerostomia is commonly seen in elderly patients receiving tranquilizing drugs. These pharmacologic agents may act to inhibit parasympathetic stimulation of the salivary glands. This xerostomia can often be resolved by the use of a different drug. Xerostomia can also occur in the depressed patient. Many elderly persons suffer from periodic depression.

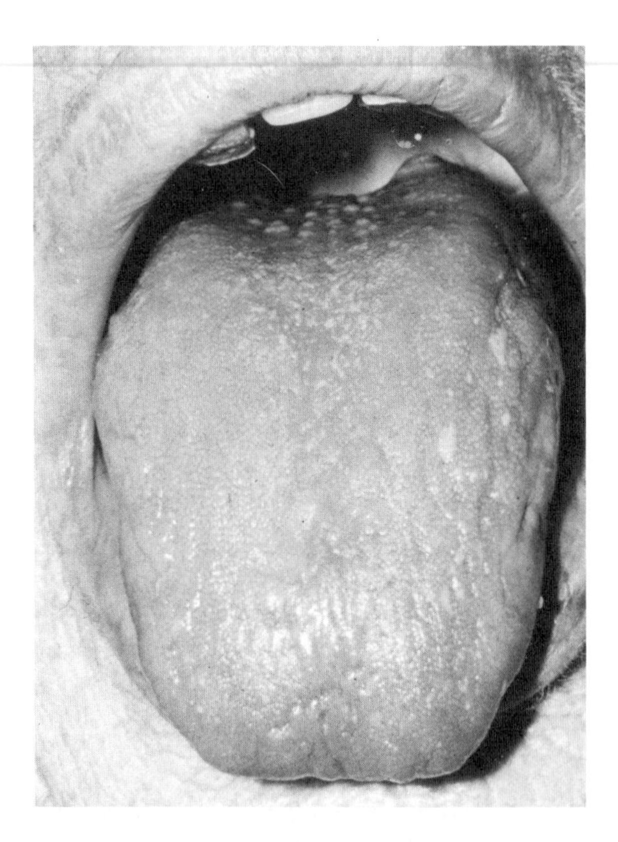

Figure 10-7 The tongue in xerostomia of aging. There is atrophy of lingual papilla, dryness, and accumulation of debris.

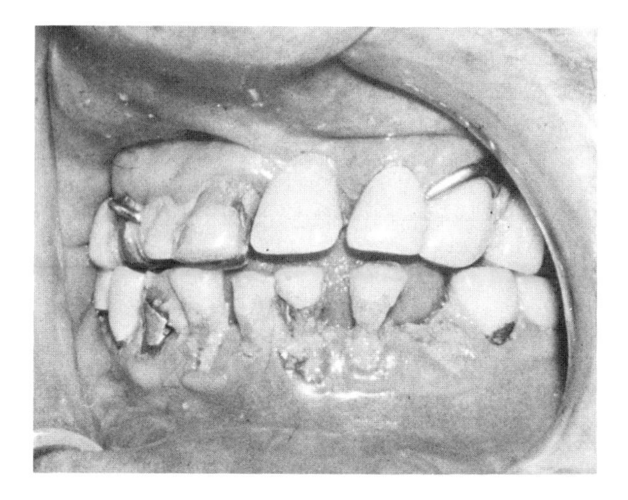

Figure 10-8. Severe root caries in xerostomia of aging.

Mucositis, Mucosal Atrophy

The thin, atrophic oral mucosa often seen in elderly subjects is less resistant to the irritation of oral noxious stimuli such as mechanical trauma, hot foods, and strong mouthwashes. A dry mouth may also favor the surface growth of bacteria. Atrophy of lingual papillae results in a smooth tongue that is highly susceptible to irritation, and the resultant glossitis produces burning and discomfort. These problems are not hysterical in origin, but result from the atrophic alterations in the tissue.

Mucositis is particularly severe in older patients receiving chemotherapy or radiation therapy for malignant neoplasia. The therapy itself can produce a mucositis as a toxic side effect, and the oral mucosa, with lowered resistance to irritation, responds with severe inflammation and ulceration. Chemotherapeutic drugs essentially are antimetabolites and have been shown experimentally to cause atrophy of the oral epithelium and connective tissue. Together with the atrophy of oral mucosa caused by aging, the combined effect can be extremely destructive, and healing notably delayed.

Psychosomatic Disease

Emotional stress plays a role in the cause or pathogenesis of many oral diseases and is probably the major etiologic factor in lichen planus. However. the elderly patient is more affected by neurotic oral symptomatology than by psychosomatic disease. Common oral symptomatology in depressed patients includes burning tongue (glossodynia, glossopyrosis), burning mucosa, and altered taste perception. (There are often complaints about a bad taste that cannot be described.) Many elderly people have a difficult role in our society and are unhappy and depressed. The oral cavity is a common target site for the resolution of emotional stress. Severe burning tongue in the absence of visible disease usually represents hysterical or neurotic symptomatology. Neurotic habits such as cheek biting may also occur in the elderly and result in more tissue damage than in young patients because of tissue atrophy and delayed healing.

Leukoplakia

Oral leukoplakia is a keratotic protective reaction of the mucosa to local irritation, usually smoking (figure 10-9). It is rarely seen in young subjects and apparently develops more readily in aging oral mucosa. Approximately 10 percent of leukoplakias present significant histologic evidence of dysplasia and are essentially preinvasive carcinomas, although the term precancerous leukoplakia is still used. Waldron and Shafer (1975), in a study of 3,256 cases of oral leukoplakia, found histologic evidence of carcinoma or severe dysplasia in 7.6 percent of cases and mild to moderate dysplasia in 12.2 percent of the cases. The most frequent occurrence of dysplasia was found in the age groups of 50 years

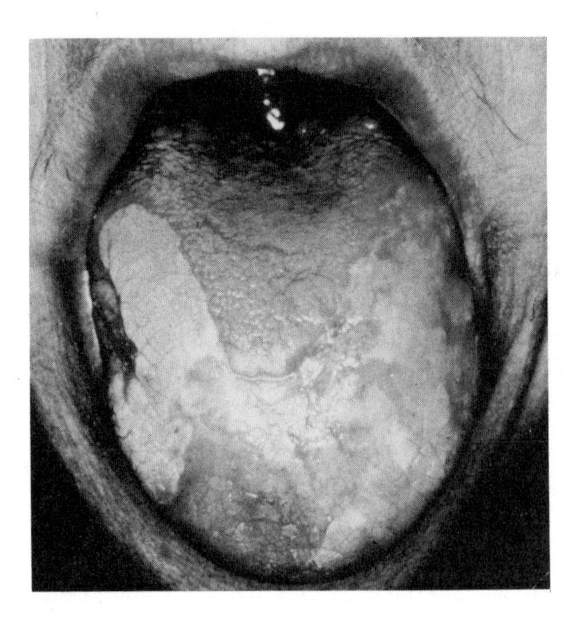

Figure 10-9. Leukoplakia of tongue.

and above. Leukoplakia with dysplasia is essentially carcinoma in situ and must be treated as such.

Oral Carcinoma

Oral cancer is usually the epidermoid or squamous cell variety (figures 10-10 and 10-11). It is rarely seen in young patients, but occurs in elderly men and less commonly in elderly women (Krolls and Hoffman, 1976), comprising 5 percent of all cancer of men and 2 percent of all cancer of women. Early diagnosis is the key to successful therapy; careful oral screening for lesions should be carried out in elderly patients with reasonable frequency, perhaps every six months. Any questionable lesion should be investigated by biopsy. Seventy percent of oral cancers can be cured by current techniques if the lesions are small and localized, while only 24 percent can be cured if the disease has spread. Routine oral screening and cytology examination may also be of value, since oral cytology discloses oral malignancy with 85 percent reliability (Shklar, 1974). The reliability of biopsy is virtually 100 percent and should be used when possible (Giunta, Meyer, and Shklar, 1969). The elderly man is a particularly high-risk subject if he smokes and drinks, since these two environmental hazards increase the risk of oral cancer substantially (Schottenfeld, Gantt, and Wyner, 1974).

Oral Response to Cancer Therapy

Elderly patients have an increased incidence of many forms of malignancy, and the radiation or chemotherapy used as therapy may result in oral disease, either as a primary mucositis due to radiation damage or drug toxicity, or as a secondary response to the effect of the radiation or antimetabolic drug on bone marrow, producing a leukopenia or thrombocytopenia. The oral lesions may include mucositis, extensive ulceration, hemorrhage due to the thrombocytopenia, and suppurative infection due to the leukopenia and immunosuppression. Candidiasis of the oral mucosa is a rare infection from a common oral inhabitant and nonpathogen. However, in patients treated with radiation or antimetabolites, the incidence of oral candidiasis is significantly increased. The fungus invades and destroys the oral mucosal epithelium and proliferates.

Oral Manifestations of Systemic Disease

Nutritional deficiencies (usually vitamin B) may appear in the elderly patient who lives alone and whose diet is poor. Iron deficiency anemia may be seen in post menopausal women as a unique deficiency or combined with dysphagia in

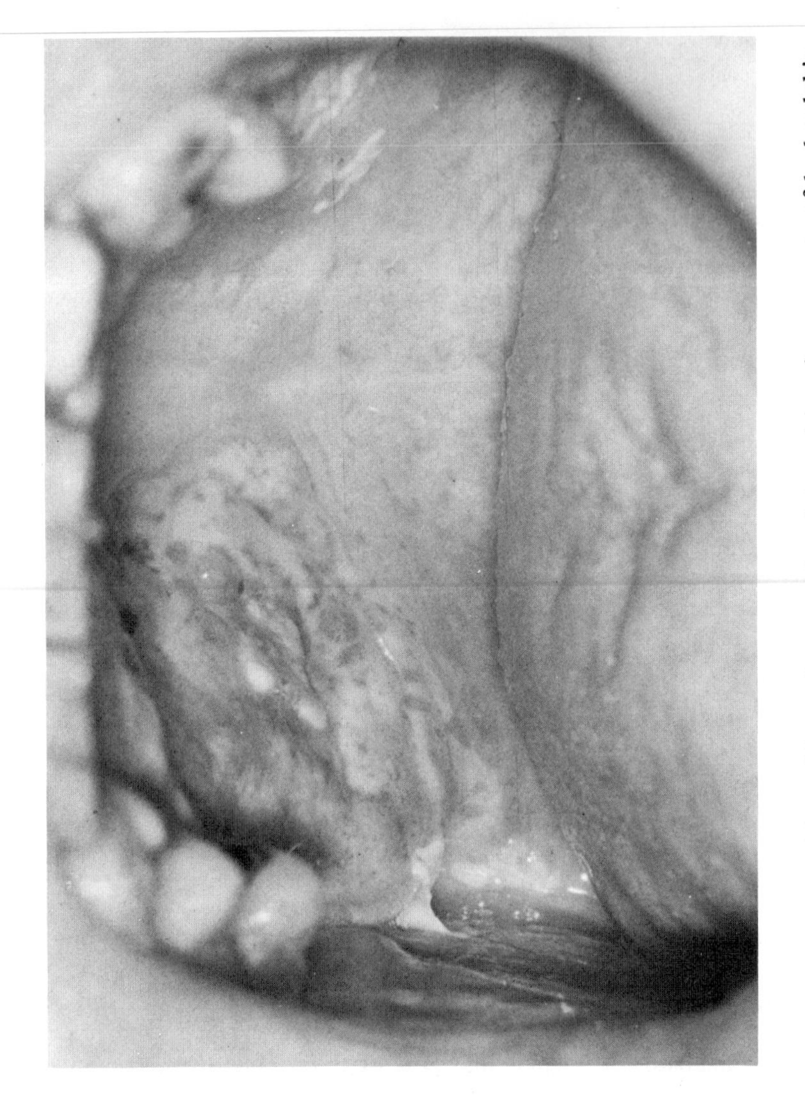

Figure 10-10. Epidermoid carcinoma of palate arising in an area of leukoplakia.

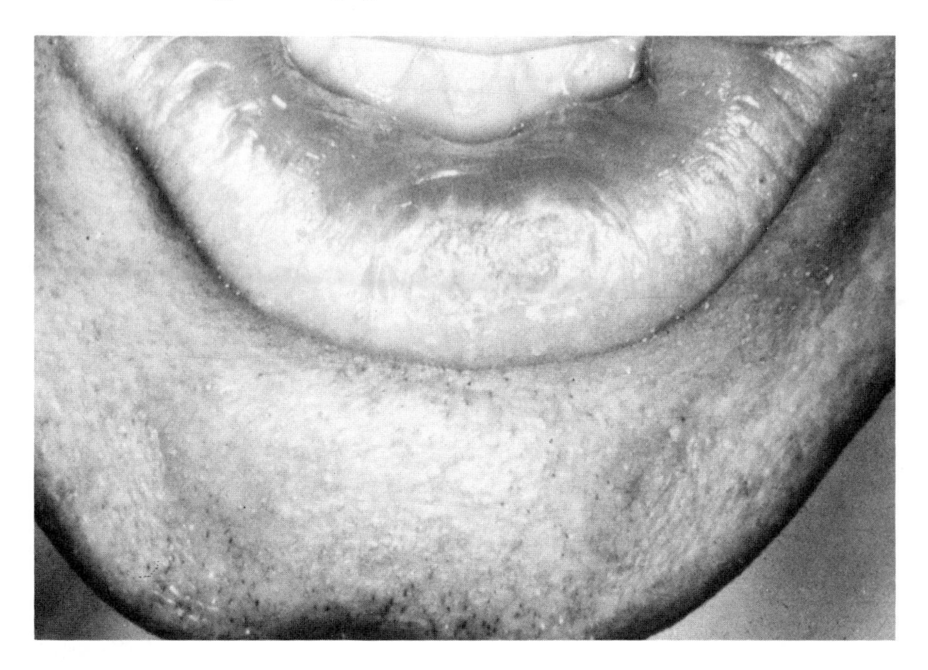

Figure 10-11. Epidermoid carcinoma of lip arising in an area of actinic cheilitis.

the Plummer-Vinson syndrome. A menopausal stomatitis or gingivitis is a rare feature of estrogen depletion in the elderly woman.

Vitamin B deficiency appears as a combination of a red, atrophic glossitis and an angular cheilitis (figure 10-12). These changes result primarily from niacin deficiency, but acute pellagra is rare today, and if a deficiency exists because of a generally poor diet, it will usually involve the entire B group, including niacin (Shklar, 1974). Diagnosis is usually confirmed by placing the elderly patient on therapeutic doses of multivitamins and observing the resolution of the oral changes. Vitamin C deficiency results in scurvy in severe form. The oral manifestations consists of gingival inflammation with hyperplasia and multiple hemorrhagic lesions. Scurvy is extremely rare today, but occasional cases are seen in elderly patients living by themselves and who forget to eat foods containing vitamin C.

Iron deficiency anemia is seen in young or middle-aged women, but may be more severe in elderly women. The oral changes may be notable, including atrophic glossitis. In the Plummer-Vinson syndrome there is a mucositis of the oropharynx and dysphagia in addition to the oral manifestations and anemia.

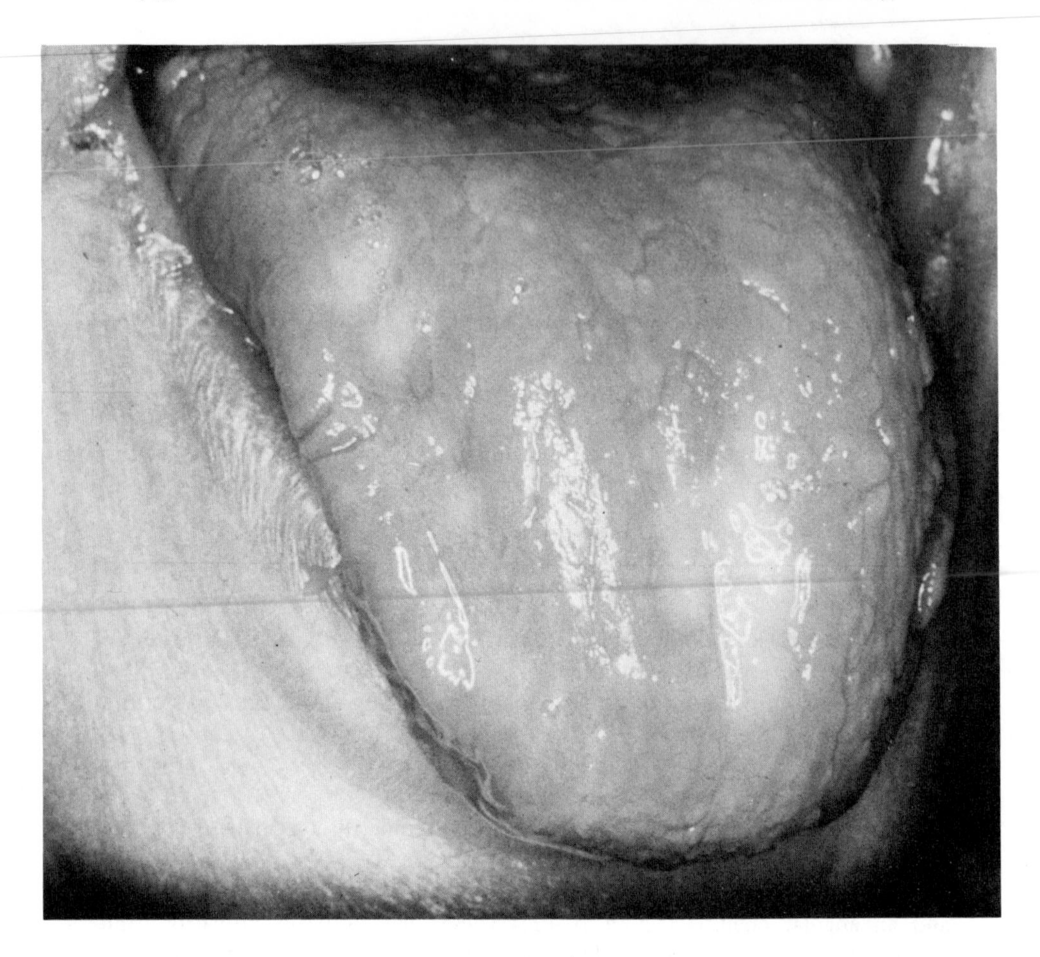

Figure 10.12. Atrophic glossitis and angular chelitis seen in vitamin B deficiency.

Oral manifestations may occur in postmenopausal women in the form of an erosive or desquamative gingivitis. However, this form of desquamative gingivitis is rare. So-called desquamative gingivitis may be found in a variety of systemic diseases and is most commonly seen in lichen planus and mucous membrane pemphigoid.

Paget's disease, although a relatively rare bone disease of unknown origin is seen with increasing frequency in the aging patient (figure 10-13). In addition to widespread skeletal involvement, there may be involvement of the jaws, with enlargement, spacing of teeth, and dense radiopacity on intraoral radiographs.

In summary, these atrophic changes may affect the oral tissue of elderly patients and lead to disease or predispose the patient to certain types of disease. However, there are few oral diseases found only in the elderly. Many aging

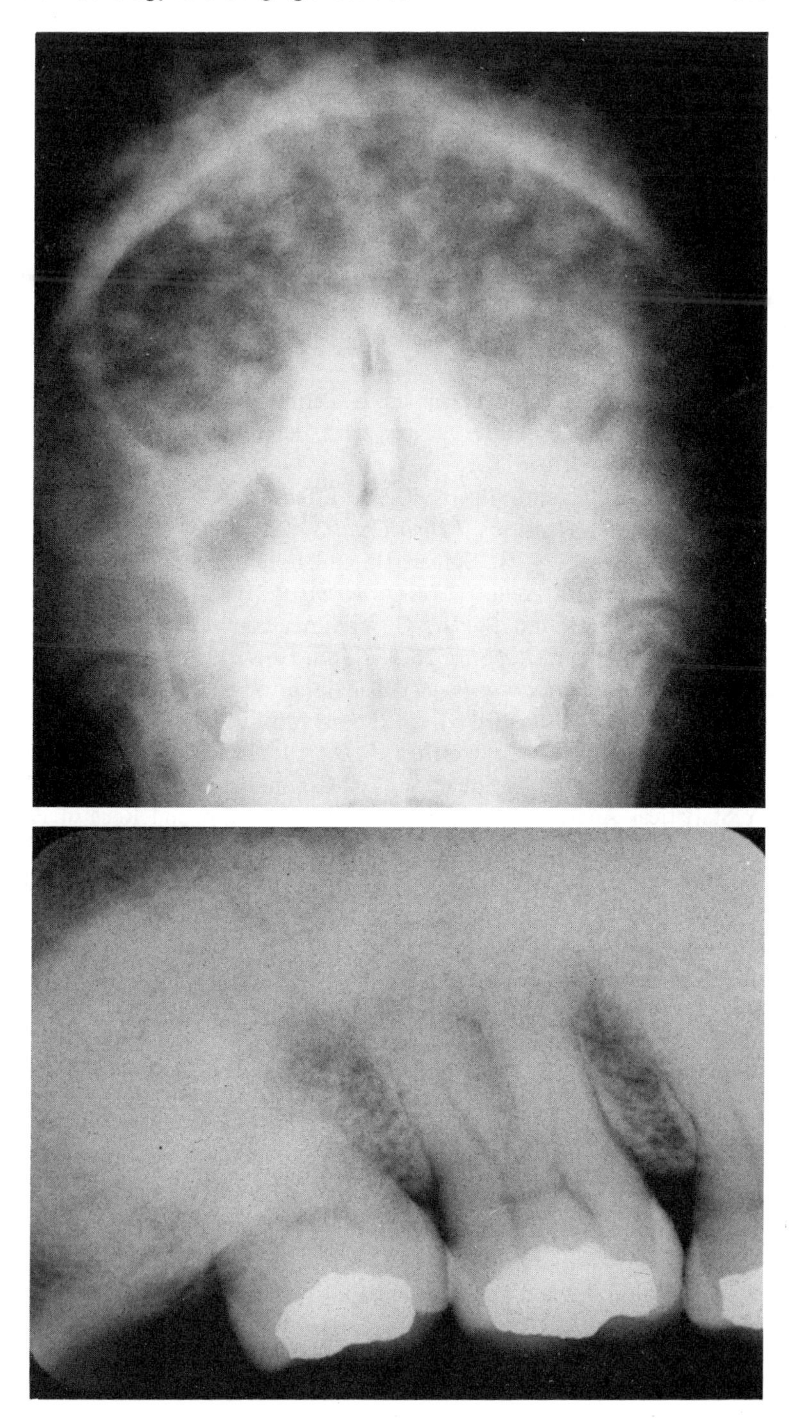

Figure 10-13. Radiographs of skull and maxilla in an elderly patient with Paget's disease of bone.

individuals are relatively free of oral disease, and their healing response to trauma is no worse than that seen in young patients. Of the conditions found more frequently in the elderly, oral cancer and the precancerous leukoplakia are the most serious and require appropriate preventive programs if the current mortality and morbidity is to be significantly reduced.

References

Betram, U. Xerostomia: Clinical Aspects, Pathology, and Pathogenesis. *Acta Odont Scand* 25:1-126, 1967.

Cohen, M.M., Shklar, G., and Yerganian, G. Periodontal Pathology in a Strain of Chinese Hamster. *Cricetulus griseus,* with Hereditary Diabetes Mellitus. *Am J Med* 31:864-867, 1961.

Darvish, M., Shklar, G., and Shiere, F. The Effect of Age on Extraction Wound Healing in Syrian Hamsters. *J Dent Child* 39:384-389, 1972.

Fikentscher, R., Roseburg, B., Spinar, H., and Bruchmuller, W. Loss of Taste in the Elderly: Sex Differences. *Clin Otolaryngol* 2:183-189, 1977.

Giunta, J., Meyer, I., and Shklar, G. The Accuracy of Oral Biopsy in the Diagnosis of Cancer. *Oral Surg* 28:552-566, 1969.

Glickman, I. *Clinical Periodontology* (Philadelphia: W.B. Saunders Co., 1972).

Goldman, H.M. *Periodontia,* 3rd ed. (St. Louis: Mosby, 1953).

Gottlieb, B. Tissue Changes in Pyorrhea. *JADA* 14:2178-2207, 1927.

Krolls, S.O. and Hoffman, S. Squamous Cell Carcinoma of the Oral Soft Tissues: A Statistical Analysis of 14,253 Cases by Age, Sex and Race of Patients. *JADA* 92:571-574, 1976.

Laskin, D.M. and Greene, C.S. Influence of the Doctor-Patient Relationship on Placebo Therapy for Patients with Myofascial Pain Dysfunction (MPD) Syndrome. *JADA* 85:892-894, 1972.

Mosadomi, H.A., Shklar, G., Loftus, E., and Chauncey, H.H. Effects of Smoking and Age on the Keratinization of Palata Mucosa—A Cytologic Study. *J Oral Surg* 46:413-417, 1978.

Schottenfeld, D., Gantt, R.C., and Wyner, E.L. The Role of Alcohol and Tobacco in Multiple Primary Cancers of the Upper Digestive System, Larynx and Lung: A Prospective Study. *Prev Med* 3:277-293, 1974.

Shklar, G. The Effects of Aging Upon Oral Mucosa. *J Invest Dermatol* 47:115-120, 1966.

Shklar, G. Systemic Influences in the Etiology of Periodontal Disease in Animal Models. *J Periodont* 45:567-573, 1974.

Shklar, G., Cataldo, E., and Meyer, I. Reliability of Cytologic Smear in Diagnosis of Oral Cancer: A Controlled Study. *Arch Otolaryngol* 91:158-160, 1970.

Shklar, G. and McCarthy, P.L. *The Oral Manifestations of Systemic Disease.* (Boston: Butterworth, 1976).

Stahl, S.S., Sandler, H.C., and Cahn, L. Effects of Protein Deprivation Upon Oral Tissues of Rat and Particularly Upon Periodontal Structures Under Irritation. *Oral Surg* 8:760-768, 1955.

Tennenbaum, R. and Shklar, G. The Effect of an Anabolic Steroid on the Healing of Experimental Extraction Wounds. *Oral Surg* 30:824-834, 1970.

Waldron, C.A. and Shafer, W.G. Leukoplakia Revisited: A Clinicopathologic Study of 3,256 Oral Leukoplakias. *Cancer* 36:1386-1392, 1975.

Znamensky, N.N. Alveolar Pyorrhea–Its Pathological Anatomy and Its Radical Treatment. *J Brit Dent Assoc* 23:585-604, 1902.

11 Functional Taste and Food Intake Changes with Aging

Krishan K. Kapur, Sharon Wallace, Carol Conway, and *Howard H. Chauncey*

In the recently published *Dietary Goals for the United States,* limitation of salt and sugar use was mandated (U.S. Senate Select Committee on Nutrition and Human Needs, 1977). Limiting salt intake was recommended because high salt diets are linked to exacerbation of, if not directly to the development of, hypertension (Dahl, 1972; Kannel and Dawber, 1971). While no role has been defined for sugar in the development of metabolic diseases (Danowski, 1979), the recommendation for limiting its use was based on the belief that, in certain circumstances, it can supplant more nutritious dietary constituents and induce caries formation (Finn and Glass, 1975). Resistance to salt and sugar restriction can be anticipated, since these are the two most popular flavorings added to foods after preparation.

Perhaps the most dramatic change in American diets since the early 1900s has been the increase in the amount of refined sugar used. This is primarily a result of the greater use of processed foods which contain sugar (Friend and Page, 1974). The issue of sugar and salt intake and sweet and salt-seeking behavior is clouded due to the use of many processed foods that contain sugar and/or salt but do not have a primarily salty or sweet flavor (Cantor and Cantor, 1977; Cullen, Paulbitski, and Oace, 1978).

Salt and sugar are basic tastes. They excite specific receptors on the tongue and are appreciated without aid from other sensory systems (Pfaffman, Bartoshuk, and McBurney, 1971). There is debate as to how specific taste responses to salt and sugar are related to human physiologic needs. In certain diseases, salt craving occurs due to a physiological need; humans can tolerate otherwise noxious quantities (Lepkovsky, 1977). Similarly, glucose deficit is associated with a preference for sweet-tasting solutions and foods, but the mechanisms underlying these phenomena are not well understood (LeMagnen, 1977). Investigation of specific hunger in humans is complicated because the use of salt and sugar may be conditioned by early sensory, social, or cognitive experiences (Beauchamp and Maller, 1977). Dietary data is generally difficult to assess (Marr, 1971), and a variety of techniques are used for measuring taste preferences and thresholds (Mieselman, 1972).

Because measurement techniques are unwieldy, few investigators have attempted to relate intake and threshold. Awareness of a decreased number of taste buds in the elderly (Arey, Tremaine, and Monzingo, 1935), and a greater frequency of oral complaints reported by older persons (Cohen and Gitman, 1959) have fostered the belief that diminished taste perception may be one cause of flagging appetites and poor nutrient intake observed among these individuals (Soremark and Nilsson, 1972). It has thus been assumed that the ability of older people to regulate their nutrient intake is diminished. However, certain recent studies have shown that there may be a minimal or no decline in sucrose detection threshold with age, but that a decline in salt detection does appear in elderly individuals (Kare and Wallace, 1976).

The study described in this chapter was undertaken to determine whether an association of age with taste thresholds for salt and sugar could be demonstrated in a population of healthy men, and whether the use of salt and sugar could be related either to taste thresholds or to salivary composition. The study is unique in the taste literature in that comprehensive data regarding the oral health and physical health of these subjects was also available.

Methods

Subjects

One hundred fifty-three participants from the Veterans Administration Longitudinal and Cross-Sectional Study of Oral Health in Healthy Veterans volunteered to participate in this study. This "Longitudinal Dental Study" (LDS) was initiated in 1969 as an adjunct to the Veterans Administration Normative Aging Study (NAS) (Bell, Rose, and Damon, 1966, 1972) and utilizes twelve hundred of the two thousand NAS subjects (Kapur et al., 1972).

The LDS includes salivary analysis, preference for taste, texture, ease of chewing, and ingestion frequency for thirteen foods as well as masticatory performance tests. The age distribution of the participants ranged from 25 to 75 years. Selection of the NAS subjects was based on health criteria. They represented a broad range of socioeconomic strata.

Saliva Collection and Analysis

Stimulated parotid and whole saliva collections were made at random in the morning or afternoon, at least 1½ hours postprandial. Ten milliliters of rubber-band stimulated whole saliva was collected. Subsequently, a vacuum-maintained metal collection device was positioned over the orifice of Stensen's duct. The gustatory stimulus was a sour lemon flavored lozenge. [Regal Crown Imported Lemon Sours, Murray Allen Imports, New York City, NY] Each subject was given a one minute acquaintance interval of stimulation to clear the collection apparatus and allow the gland to accommodate to stimulation. After the acquaintance interval, the plastic collection tubule was transferred to a graduated tube and 10.0 ml of parotid fluid was collected. The lozenge was changed every five minutes to maintain a constant level of stimulation. Flow rate (ml/min/gland) was calculated by recording the time necessary to collect the standard 10.0 ml volume.

Immediately after collection the saliva pH value and bicarbonate level were measured. Bicarbonate was determined by the automated method for the estimation of carbon dioxide detailed by Skeggs (1960), while the pH was measured using a Corning Model 12 Research pH meter. The saliva sample was then stored at 4°C until the remaining variables could be measured, usually twenty-four hours. Sodium and potassium were measured by flame photometry (I.L. Digital Flame Photometer). Calcium and inorganic phosphorus were determined by the automated method of Kessler and Wolfman (1964); the latter procedure involved a modification of the method described by Fiske and Subbarow (1925). Chloride analysis was conducted by the procedure described by Cotlove, Trantham, and Bowman (1958).

Ponderal Index

The ponderal index is a ratio of height, in inches, to the cube root of the weight in pounds. It is used to characterize relative leanness (U.S. Public Health Service, 1970), and is frequently used as an important anthropometric measure in biomedical studies (Damon and Seltzer, 1972). This measure was available for all study participants.

Salt and Sugar Intake Scoring

The one hundred fifty-three participants from the LDS completed a comprehensive food intake questionnaire designed to elicit use frequency of high salt and sugar food items, perceived desire for sweets and perceived table salt use. Intake scores for salt and sugar were developed for each participant from their response to the questionnaire.

Threshold Determination

The total number of subjects tested for taste thresholds was 65. Each subject was presented with twenty paper cups. Ten contained 10 ml of distilled deionized water, while ten contained 10 ml of tastant solution at room temperature. Each subject was asked to swish the liquid in his mouth and report whether the solution was "plain" or "salt," or "plain" or "sugar." Samples of

Table 11-1
Sugar Threshold Determination

Concentrations of Sucrose Solutions Used to Determine Threshold	*Assigned Threshold Value*
.001 M	
	.003 M
.005 M	
	.0075 M
.010 M	
	.0125 M
.015 M (starting concentration)	
	.0175 M
.020 M	
	.025 M
.030 M	
	.035 M
.040 M	

water and the test solution were presented prior to the first test cup to task orient the subjects. During the testing, subjects were advised whether they were correct or incorrect after each cup trial. Presentation order for water and tastant trials in each concentration series was random. The base or starting tastant solution was the .015 M concentration. The concentration series are presented in tables 11-1 and 11-2. When the subject responded correctly on sixteen or more of the twenty trials at one concentration, a lower concentration was used for the next twenty-cup trial; if less than sixteen correct responses were obtained, the next higher concentration was used. Testing continued until a break—sixteen or

Table 11-2
Salt Threshold Determination

Concentrations of NaC1 Solutions Used to Determine Threshold	*Assigned Threshold Value*
.0001 M	
	.0005 M
.001 M	
	.003 M
.005 M	
	.0075 M
.010 M	
	.0125 M
.015 M (starting concentration)	
	.0175 M
.020 M	
	.030 M
.040 M	
	.060 M
.080 M	

Table 11-3
Determinants of Salt Intake Score (A)

Score Contribution	*Question*
	How often do you add salt to your food at the table?
1	Never
2	Occasionally
3	Most of the time
4	Always
	Do you usually salt your food before you taste it?
0	No
4	Yes
	How would you describe your use of salt?
1	Do not use
2	Light
3	Moderate
4	Heavy

more correct responses in an ascending series, or fifteen or fewer correct responses in a descending series—was obtained. Threshold was defined as the concentration midway between the two test concentrations where the break occurred (Desor and Maller, 1975).

Findings

The first contributions to the salt intake score were the coded equivalents of the answers to the three questions shown in table 11-3. Table 11-4 shows the first contributions to the sugar intake score: a "sweet tooth" rating, the number of teaspoons of sugar used per day in coffee or tea, and the number of desserts consumed per week.

Table 11-4
Determinants of Sugar Intake Score (A)

1. On a scale where 1 = I dislike sweets and 5 = I have a real sweet-tooth, where do you fit?

1	I dislike sweets
2	
3	Neutral
4	
5	I have a real sweet-tooth

2. How many cups of coffee, tea do you drink per day?
   How many spoons of sweetening do you use? in coffee in tea
3. How many times per week do you eat desserts?

Table 11-5
Food Intake Pattern Questionnaire

Use the codes below to report your meal pattern for working days. Write the times you usually eat. Write the number code for the kind of meal you typically eat at that time. . . . PLEASE READ ALL THE CHOICES BEFORE YOU BEGIN.

Codes for Kind of Meal:

1 = Light breakfast (three items or less—example: coffee, juice, toast)
2 = Full breakfast (four items or more—example: coffee, juice, cereal, milk)
3 = Fruit or vegetable snack (examples: apple, carrot sticks)
4 = Sweet snack (examples: donut, brownie, cookies, cake, ice cream, candy)
5 = Salty snacks (examples: saltines, chips, pretzels, popcorn)
6 = Light lunch or supper meal
7 = Heavy luncheon or dinner meal
8 = Mini meal (examples: bowl of soup, cheese and fruit, half sandwich)
9 = Beverage alone

For Working Days:		**Code Number:**
Time I arise on working days:	am/pm	
Time I first eat or drink something:	am/pm	What I usually have at that time:
Time I next eat or drink:	am/pm	What I usually have at that time:

Table 11-5 shows the format used to elicit a food intake pattern for both working and leisure days. The number of times that codes 4 and 5, sweet and salty snacks, were reported on the form contributed to the sugar and salt intake scores. Reported intake frequency of salty snacks ranged from 0 to 4 times per day, while sweet snacks ranged from 0 to 3 times per day.

Table 11-6
Determinants of Salt Intake Score (B)

Write the one LETTER CODE that best describes how often you use each item, in the box provided.

Items Used, Daily	*Used Less than Daily, but Used,* Every Week	*Used* Less Often
A = 4 or more times/day	E = 6 times/week	K = 2-3 times/month
B = 3 times/day	F = 5 times/week	L = rarely or never
C = 2 times/day	G = 4 times/week	
D = 1 time/day	H = 3 times/week	
	I = 2 times/week	
	J = 1 time/week	

☐ Salted snacks (chips, nuts, crackers)
☐ Cheese (not cottage)
☐ Canned soup
☐ Pickles, olives, relish
☐ Catsup, mustard
☐ Lunchmeat or franks (salami, bologna, liverwurst, etc.)
☐ Ham, bacon, sausage

Table 11-7
Subject's Food Intake Diary

Food Diary for:
Name ______________________ **Date** ____________

Time I got up: ____________

Time I Ate and/or Drank	*Items I Ate and/or Drank*	*How Prepared*	*Approximate Amount*

Table 11-6 shows the source of another major contribution to the salt intake score. Coded equivalents for the answers to the questions shown were added into the salt score. A similar series was used for sugar. Letter codes A through C were given a value of 3; D through G were assigned a value of 2; H through J were given a value of 1; and K and L were considered to be 0. Subjects were also asked how often they would like to use these items. Responses to this question also contributed to the total respective scores using the same coding structure.

Table 11-7 shows the format used to record a twenty-four hour intake diary. The number of high sugar and salt items entered on this diary were added to the intake scores. Score contributions from this source ranged from 0 to 8 times per day for salt and 0 to 6 for sugar. A high salt item was defined as a food or beverage that would be excluded from a sodium restricted diet, while a high sugar item was defined as a serving of a food or beverage that would be excluded from a diabetic diet.

Table 11-8
Age versus Threshold Levels

	Sucrose Threshold		
Age	*.0125 or Less*	*.0175 or Greater*	*Number of Subjects*
<50	15	16	31
50-59	9	15	24
60+	4	6	10
	28	37	65

$\chi^2 = .70$ NS

	NaCl Threshold		
Age	*.0125 or Less*	*.0175 or Greater*	*Number of Subjects*
<50	21	10	31
50-59	17	7	24
60+	2	8	10
	40	25	65

$\chi^2 = 8.67$ $p < .05$

The range of total salt scores for the test population was 2 to 33 with a mean of 17.06, while the range of total sugar scores was 2 to 64, with a mean of 24.83. These scores were divided into triads and representatives from each triad were tested for taste threshold. The total number of subjects tested for taste thresholds was sixty-five. More subjects from the top and bottom score triads were recruited to improve the opportunity for observing differences.

For purposes of analysis, the salt and sugar intake score parts were weighted and summed to form a standardized composite score. This was done to compensate for variation in the scaling of the various score parts. Cross-tabulations were generated between age, threshold values, standardized intake scores, and salivary composition variables. Table 11-8 shows that no association is observed between age and sucrose threshold. By contrast, among the oldest subjects tested a tendency toward elevated salt thresholds is observed. Table 11-9 shows that age is not related to sugar intake, but that a trend toward lower intakes of salt in men over 60 occurs. Table 11-10 shows that individuals with high sucrose thresholds tend to use less sugar, while no apparent relationship exists between salt threshold and intake.

To help elucidate the relationship between sucrose threshold and sugar use, the subjects were divided on the basis of their ponderal index, which is a measure of height relative to weight. Table 11-11 shows that subjects with a ponderal index below the median (12.39) for the one hundred fifty-three questionnaire respondents show no relationship between sucrose preference and sugar intake, while the leanest subjects appear to account for the counter-intuitive effect of sucrose threshold on sugar intake.

Table 11-9
Age versus Intake

	Standardized Sugar Intake Score			
Age	*−1.98 to −.58*	*−57 to .47*	*.48 to 3.31*	*Number of Subjects*
<50	20	16	21	57
50-59	20	17	17	54
60+	11	19	12	42
	51	52	50	153

$x^2 = 3.71$ NS

	Standardized Salt Intake Score			
Age	*−2.11 to −.49*	*−.48 to .34*	*.35 to 3.30*	*Number of Subjects*
<50	14	25	18	57
50-59	16	18	20	54
60+	21	9	12	42
	51	52	50	153

$x^2 = 9.18$ $p<.05$

Table 11-10
Threshold versus Intake

	Sucrose Threshold		
Standard Sugar Intake Score	*.0125 or Less*	*.0175 or Greater*	*Number of Subjects*
−1.98 to −.58	7	22	29
−.57 to .47	9	6	15
.48 to 3.31	12	9	21
	28	37	65

$\chi^2 = 7.69$ $p < .05$

	NaCl Threshold		
Standard Salt Intake Score	*.0125 or Less*	*.0175 or Greater*	*Number of Subjects*
−.211 to −.49	14	9	23
−.48 to .34	13	7	20
.35 to 3.30	13	9	22
	40	25	65

$\chi^2 = .16$ NS

Table 11-11
Ponderal Index as a Function of Intake and Threshold

Ponderal Index < 12.39

	Sucrose Threshold		
Standard Sugar Intake Score	*.0125 or Less*	*.0175 or Greater*	*Number of Subjects*
−1.98 to −.04	10	10	20
−.03 to 3.31	7	7	14
	17	17	34

$\chi^2 = 0$ NS

Ponderal Index > 12.39

	Sucrose Threshold		
Standard Sugar Intake Score	*.0125 or Less*	*.0175 or Greater*	*Number of Subjects*
−1.98 to −.04	3	15	18
−.03 to 3.31	8	5	13
	11	20	31

$\chi^2 = 4.82$ $p < .05$

Table 11-12
Salt Saliva Content Versus NaC1 Taste Threshold

	Whole Saliva Chloride		
NaC1 Threshold	*7.5 to 19.6*	*19.7 to 48.6*	
<.0126	22	14	36
>.0174	6	16	22
	28	30	58

$\chi^2 = 4.98$ $p < .05$

Although no significant relationship between sucrose threshold and salivary composition was found, table 11-12 shows that the salivary schloride level related to the NaC1 taste threshold.

Discussion

The information obtained in this study did not indicate an age-related change in either sucrose threshold or sugar intake. On the other hand, the sodium chloride threshold appeared to increase with age, and a tendency for older men to consume less salt was observed. The latter may be related to voluntary salt restriction undertaken as a preventive health care practice. In young subjects, salt intake may be guided, in part, by the chloride environment of the oral cavity. Whole saliva chloride levels were significantly lower for persons with a low sodium chloride taste threshold. Schecter, Horwitz, and Henkin (1974) found an increased preference for salt in persons with hypertension. The interaction between diet, NaCl taste threshold, salivary composition, age, and disease warrants further study.

An observation of extreme interest was that persons with high sucrose thresholds reported less sugar use. Since a previous report indicated that heavy individuals tend to seek less sweets (Mieselman, 1977), the current test group was subdivided according to its median ponderal index. No relationship between threshold and intake was noted among the participants below the median ponderal index, however persons above the median ponderal index showed a statistically significant relation betweeen sucrose threshold and sugar intake. Among the individuals, persons with the higher sucrose thresholds tended to have lower intake scores. While the possibility of reporting bias among heavy individuals must be considered (Rodin, 1977), Gawecki et al. (1976) found that sucrose taste thresholds correlate positively with sugar use. Consistent with the finding here, Grinker (1977) found an aversion to high concentrations of sugar in overweight adults.

These preliminary findings do not provide substantive support for any theories regarding the interplay of the multiple biomedical, physical, sociologic, and psychologic factors responsible for variations in food selection. They do, however, suggest potentially productive areas for future focus.

References

Arey, L.B., Tremaine, M.J., and Monzingo, F.L. The Numerical and Topographical Relations of Taste Buds to Human Circumvallate Papillae Throughout the Life Span. *Anat Rec* 64:9-25, 1935.

Beauchamp, G.K. and Maller, O. The Development of Flavor Preferences in Humans. In Kare, M.R. and Maller, O. (Eds.), *The Chemical Senses and Nutrition* (New York: Academic, 1977), pp. 291-310.

Bell, B., Rose, C.L., and Damon, A. The Veterans Administration Longitudinal Study of Healthy Aging. *Gerontologist* 6: 179-184, 1966.

Bell, B., Rose, C.L., and Damon, A. The Normative Aging Study: An Interdisciplinary and Longitudinal Study of Health and Aging. *Aging Human Dev* 3:5-17, 1972.

Cantor, S.M., and Cantor, M.B. Socioeconomic Factors in Fat and Sugar Consumption. In Kare, M.R. and Maller, O. (Eds.), *The Chemical Senses and Nutrition,* (New York: Academic, 1977), pp. 429-444.

Cohen, T., and Gitman, L. Oral Complaints and Taste Perception in the Aged. *J Gerontol* 14:294-298, 1959.

Cotlove, E., Trantham, H.V., and Bowman, R.C. An Instrument For and Method For Automatic Rapid, Accurate, and Sensitive Trituration of Chloride in Biologic Samples. *J Lab and Clin Med* 51:461-468, 1958.

Cullen, R.W., Paulbitski, A., and Oace, S.M. Sodium Hypertension and the U.S. Dietary Goals. *J Nutr Ed* 10:59-60, 1978.

Dahl, L.K. Salt and Hypertension. *Am J Clin Nutr* 25:231-244, 1972.

Damon, A. and Seltzer, C.C. Anthropometry in the Normative Aging Study of Healthy Veterans. *Aging Human Dev* 3:7-76, 1972.

Danowski, T.S. Sugar and Disease. *J Kans Med Soc* 80:36-38, 1979.

Desor, J.A. and Maller, O. Taste Correlates of Disease: Cystic Fibrosis. *J Peds* 87:93-97, 1975.

Finn, S.B. and Glass, R.B. Sugar and Dental Decay. *World Rev Nutr Diet* 22:304-326, 1975

Fiske, C.H. and Subbarow, Y. The Colorimetric Determination of Phosphorous, *J Biol Chem* 66:375-400, 1925.

Friend, B. and Page, L. Levels of Use of Sugars in the United States. In Sipple, H.L. and McNutt, K.W. (Eds.), *Sugars in Nutrition*, The Nutrition Foundation Monograph Series. (New York: Academic, 1974), pp. 93-107.

Gawecki, J., Urbanowicz, M., Jaszka, J., and Mazur, B. Feeding Habits and Their Physiological Determinants. *Acta Physiol Pol* 27:455-460, 1976.

Grinker, J.A. Effects of Metabolic States on Taste Parameters and Intake. In Wieffenbach, J.M. (Ed.), *Taste and Development: The Genesis of Sweet Preference* (Bethesda, MD: DHEW (NIH) Publication No. 77-1068, 1977), pp. 295-308.

Kannel, W.B. and Dawber, T.R. Hypertension and Cardiovascular Disease: The Framingham Study. In Onesti, G., Kim, K.E., and Mayer, J.H. (Eds.), *Hypertension Mechanisms and Management,* The 26th Hahnemann Symposium. (New York: Grune and Stratton, 1971), pp. 93-117.

Kapur, K.K., Glass, R.L., Loftus, E.R., Alman, J.E., and Feller, R.P. The Veterans Administration Longitudinal Study of Oral Health and Disease. *Aging Human Dev* 3:125-137, 1972.

Kare, M. and Wallace, S. Taste Thresholds in Aging. Personal communication, 1976.

Kessler, G. and Wolfman, M. An Automated Procedure for the Simultaneous Determination of Calcium and Phosphorous. *Clin Chem* 11:624-627, 1964.

LeMagnen, J. Sweet Preference and the Sensory Control of Caloric Intake. In Wieffenbach, J.M. (Ed.), *Taste and Development: The Genesis of Sweet Preference,* (Bethesda, MD.: DHEW (NIH) Publication No. 77-1068, 1977), pp. 355-366.

Lepkovsky, S. The Role of the Chemical Senses in Nutrition. In Kare, M.R. and Maller, O. (Eds.), *The Chemical Senses and Nutrition* (New York: Academic, 1977), pp. 422.

Marr, J.W. Individual Dietary Surveys. *World Rev Nutr Diet* 13:105-164, 1971.

Mieselman, H.L. Human Taste Perception. *CRC Critical Reviews in Food Technology* 89:119, 1972.

Mieselman, H.L. The Role of Sweetness in the Food Preference of Young Adults. In Wieffenbach, J.M. (Ed.), *Taste and Development: The Genesis of Sweet Preference* (Bethesda, MD.: DHEW (NIH) Publication No. 77-1068, 1977), pp. 269-279.

Pfaffman, C., Bartoshuk, L.M., and McBurney, D.H. Taste Psycho-Physics. In Biedler, L. (Ed.), *Handbook of Sensory Physiology,* vol. 10, pt. 2. (New York: Springer-Verlag, 1971), pp. 75-101.

Rodin, J. Implications of Responsiveness to Sweet Taste for Obesity. In Wieffenbach, J.M. (Ed.), *Taste and Development: The Genesis of Sweet Preference* (Bethesda, MD.: DHEW (NIH) Publication No. 77-1068, 1977), pp. 295-308.

Schechter, P.J., Horwitz, D., and Henkin, R.I. Salt Preference in Patients with Untreated and Treated Essential Hypertension. *Am J Clin Med* 267:320-326, 1974.

Schiffman, S. Food Recognition by the Elderly. *J Gerontol* 32:586-592, 1977.

Skeggs, L.T., Jr. The Determination of Carbon Dioxide in Blood Serum. *Ann NY Acad Sci* 87:650-657, 1960.

Soremark, R. and Nilsson, B. Dental Status and Nutrition in Old Age. In Carlson, L.A. (Ed.), *Nutrition in Old Age* (Uppsala: Almquist and Wiksell, 1972), pp. 147-164.

U.S. Public Health Service. DHEW (PHS) Publication No. 1000, Series 11, No. 35. *Vital and Health Statistics: Skinfolds, Body Girths, Biacromial Diameter and Selected Anthropometric Indices of Adults: U.S. 1960-1962.* Washington, D.C., 1970.

U.S. Senate Select Committee on Nutrition and Human Needs. *Dietary Goals for the United States,* 2nd ed. Washington, D.C.: U.S. Government Printing Office, 1977.

12 A Saliva Substitute for Dry Mouth Relief

Ira L. Shannon

Xerostomia and its sequelae are significant problems in the aging patient. While the dry mouth syndrome may result from many different causes or, for that matter, be completely unexplainable in an individual instance, the classic xerostomic patient is the individual who has received radiotherapy for a malignancy in the head or neck area. Oral health maintenance in such patients is very demanding and requires the full cooperation and effort of the patient, plus a time and effort commitment on the part of the clinician that far exceeds routine oral health supervision.

Most of the intraoral problems in the irradiated patient are directly related to the degree of salivary flow rate depression experienced. It is therefore appropriate to briefly consider the quantitative effect of irradiation on saliva production. Figure 12-1 presents the unstimulated whole saliva flow rate for ten irradiated patients (white males; 47 to 67 year age range). These patients received a mean dose of 4432 rads (SD = 900) over a six-week period (Shannon, Starcke, and Wescott, 1977a). Prior to irradiation, thirty-seven control saliva samples were collected from these ten subjects, and one hundred fifty-nine collections were made during the six-week period of active radiotherapy. The pretreatment mean flow rate was 0.722 ml per minute. Six weeks later this mean had fallen to 0.036 ml per minute. The usual radiotherapy protocol at our hospital calls for doses of 225 rads given on four successive days (Monday through Thursday), followed by a rest period of three days (Friday through Sunday), with repetition of that schedule until the total dose planned has been given.

After the first week of treatment there was an average decrease of 60 percent in the unstimulated whole saliva flow rate in these ten patients. During treatment weeks two through six, the flow rate decrease averaged 71 percent, 76 percent, 81 percent, 9 percent, and 95 percent, respectively, from the control mean. Thus, after six weeks of radiotherapy the saliva flow rate was only 5 percent of its normal value. The course of radiotherapy is customarily not complete within a six-week period and the flow rate usually continues to decrease to the point that, where in many of our patients, it is virtually impossible to collect a measurable amount of unstimulated whole saliva.

It has been suggested that the parotid gland, whose secretion is almost totally serous, is more sensitive to radiation than the other glands (Rubin and Doku, 1976; Silverman and Chierici, 1965; Eneroth, Henrikson, and Jakobsson,

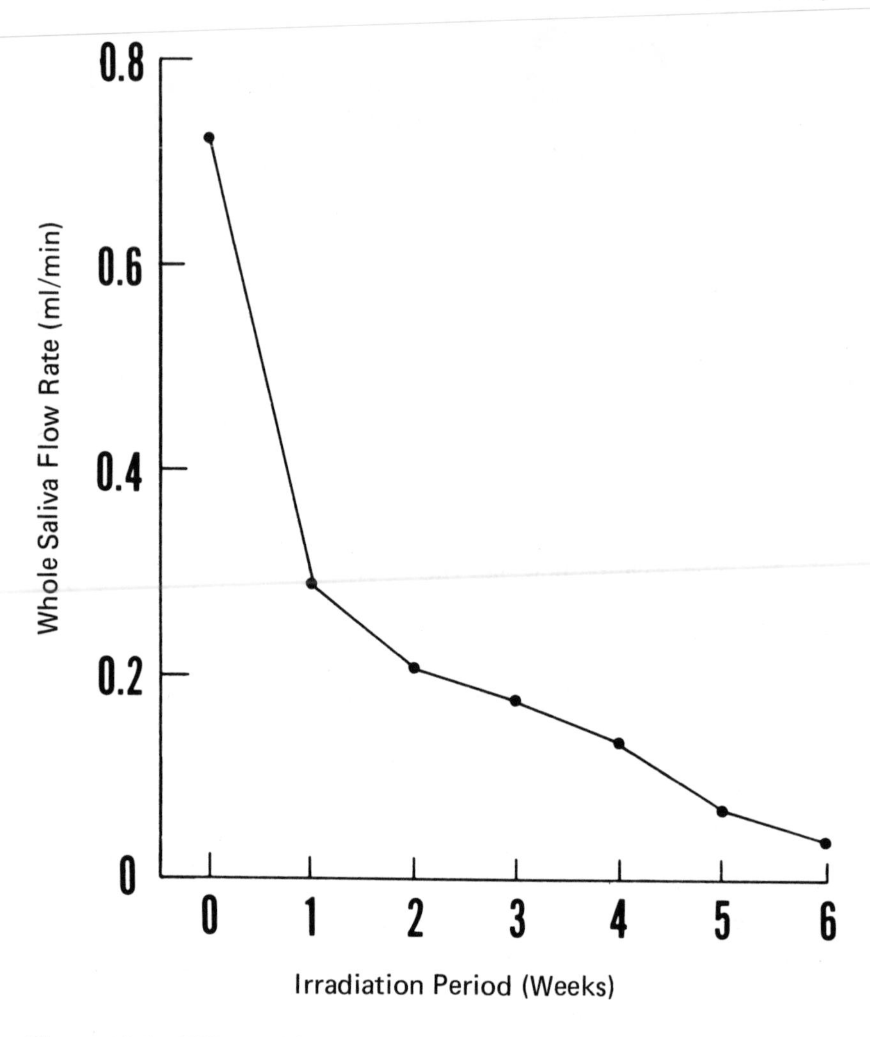

Figure 12-1. Effect of irradiation therapy on unstimulated whole saliva flow rate.

1972a, 1972b). Since it has also been reported that caries development in experimental animals is in direct proportion to the amount of serous glandular tissue extirpated (Cheyne, 1939), we conducted studies involving the resting human parotid secretion during radiotherapy (Shannon, Trodahl, and Starcke, 1978a). For seven patients the pretherapy flow for the unstimulated parotid gland ranged from 0.012 to 0.073 ml per minute with a mean of 0.045 ml per minute (SD = 0.023). This is an acceptable baseline figure since in previous work (Shannon, 1967) with over four thousand healthy young adult men we found a comparable mean value of 0.040 ml per minute (SD = 0.031). Approximately twenty-four hours after the first radiotherapy treatment (225 rads) the mean had decreased to 0.023 ml per minute (SD = 0.022), and after the second treatment, of the same magnitude, the mean was only 0.001 ml per minute (SD = 0.002). After 450 rads there was no resting parotid flow in six of the seven patients, and in the seventh the rate of flow was only 0.005 ml per minute (table 12-1). Thus, the human parotid gland is exquisitely sensitive to irradiation; the response is rapid and virtually complete. These changes are not rapidly reversible, since the collections were made twenty-four hours after radiation. This deprivation of fluid from the serous glandular elements explains the ropy, sticky, viscous nature of the residual oral fluid generally seen in these patients.

A devastatingly destructive form of dental caries is characteristically observed in head and neck irradiation patients who do not participate in a vigorous program of oral hygiene maintenance and chemical preventive dentistry. The development of this caries process can be prevented by having the patient apply a stabilized 0.4 percent stannous fluoride gel on a daily basis (Wescott, Starcke, and Shannon, 1975). Early investigators felt that there might well be a direct effect of irradiation on enamel, but research in this laboratory (Shannon, in press) and others' strongly indicates that the severely depressed salivary gland function is the fundamental cause underlying intraoral changes.

Another significant and unfortunately neglected factor in the irradiated patient is the development of painful mucositis that can severely restrict oral hygiene procedures and progress to the point that it interferes with nutritional adequacy. In some patients the mucosa may become cracked, hemorrhagic, and so painful that swallowing becomes difficult. Changes are commonly less severe, they are extremely distressful. Characteristically these patients shift to a soft

Table 12-1
Resting Parotid Flow Rate Responses to Radiotherapy

		Resting Parotid Flow Rate (Ml/Min)			
	Pretreatment			*Number of Treatments (225 rads)*	
Patient Number	*Number of Samples*	*Mean*	*SD*	*1*	*2*
1	3	.057	.006	.030	0
2	3	.073	.028	.040	0
3	3	.040	.013	.010	.005
4	2	.030	.000	.001	0
5	2	.070	.014	.060	0
6	3	.012	.004	.005	0
7	3	.032	.003	.012	0

SD = Standard deviation.

diet, usually with a high carbohydrate content, in an effort to meet nutritional requirements. Thus the oral health problem is compounded.

While there is general agreement that irradiated patients must receive vigorous topical fluoride therapy to combat caries, little progress has been made toward the development of a therapeutic answer to soft tissue problems. It is with this phase of the care of the irradiated patient that we were greatly concerned. Table 12-2 presents directions for compounding VA-OraLube, a saliva substitute solution developed in the VA Oral Disease Research Laboratory, specifically in response to the treatment requirements of veteran patients. Table 12-3 gives similar information for the preparation of a dry concentrate that can be used to prepare the saliva substitute. Logistically this is the preferred approach, since the concentrate can be shipped to clinicians dry, in plastic bags. The clinician can then add ½ gallon of water, shake vigorously and, after the mixture is allowed to stand for several hours, the OraLube preparation is ready to use.

While the primary purpose of the saliva substitute was to provide relief for the troublesome soft tissue symptoms, it was realized that it might be possible to add a remineralizing potential to the solution. Since patients would be using this material several times a day, the potential for rehardening damaged tooth surfaces is obvious. Several laboratory studies of rehardening potential were conducted and the results are recounted.

Figure 12-2 presents the results of a control experiment. The bar on the left indicates Knoop Hardness Number (KHN) mean of 291 for twenty intact enamel surfaces. After the surfaces had been exposed to 0.01 M acetic acid–potassium hydroxide solution (pH 5.0) at 37°C for four hours, the surfaces were softened

Table 12-2
VA OraLube Saliva Substitute
(2.0 PPM F)

Ingredient	*Quantity*
KCl	2.498 gm
$NaCl$	3.462 gm
$MgCl_2$	0.235 gm
$CaCl_2$	0.665 gm
K_2HPO_4	3.213 gm
KH_2PO_4	1.304 gm
Methyl p-hydroxybenzoate	8.0 gm
Flavoring	16.0 gm
70% Sorbitol (Sorbo)	171.0 gm
Na carboxmethylcellulose	40.0 gm
NaF	17.68 mgm
FD&C Red 40 Dye (2%)	1.0 ml
Water, qs ad	4000.0 ml

PPM = parts per million.

to a mean level of 227 KHN. When the softened surfaces were treated for sixty minutes with the saliva substitute that did not contain Ca, P, or F, the resulting hardness mean was 226 KHN. This indicated a lack of effect on the microhardness by the incomplete solution.

Figure 12-3 presents similar results when the "complete" OraLube solution was tested and the fluoride concentration was adjusted to 5.0 parts per million (ppm). The acid-potassium hydroxide exposure softened the enamel surfaces by 25.9 percent in these twenty teeth, and treatment with the complete saliva substitute brought about a significant ($P < .01$) increase in hardness of 5.3 percent. This was the first indication of a rehardening potential for the saliva substitute and was a heartening development.

The next experiment employed groups of twelve teeth, each, which were treated with the complete OraLube ($F = 5.0$ ppm) for fifteen, thirty, or sixty minutes. The initial mean hardness for all thirty-six teeth was 287.9 KHN. Acid-potassium hydroxide exposure brought about a 24.3 percent softening, with a mean of 218.0 KHN. Subsequent treatment of the softened enamel for fifteen, thirty, or sixty minutes rehardened the surfaces by 3.1 percent, 4.0 percent, and 5.5 percent, respectively. These increases were statistically significant (figure 12-4).

Figure 12-5 presents additional data illustrating the effect of each specific component in the saliva substitute formula. Exposure of twenty-four enamel surfaces to acid-potassium hydroxide softened the intact enamel by 20.4 percent, to a mean value of 227.2 KHN. Treatment with complete OraLube for one hour induced a 5.2 percent ($P < .01$) rehardening of the enamel. When combinations of Ca, P, or F were omitted, however, there was interference with

Table 12-3
VA OraLube Dry Concentrate

Ingredient	*Quantity (Grams)*
Carbowax	2000
KC1	125
NaC1	173
$MgCl_2 \cdot 6H_2O$	12
KH_2PO_4	65
FD&C Red #40	1.45
$CaCl_2 \cdot 2H_2O$	39
K_2HPO_4	161
Methyl p-hydroxybenzoate	200
Powdered cheri-beri	700
NaF	.884

This concentrate is sufficient to prepare one-half gallon of saliva substitute containing 2.0 ppm F.

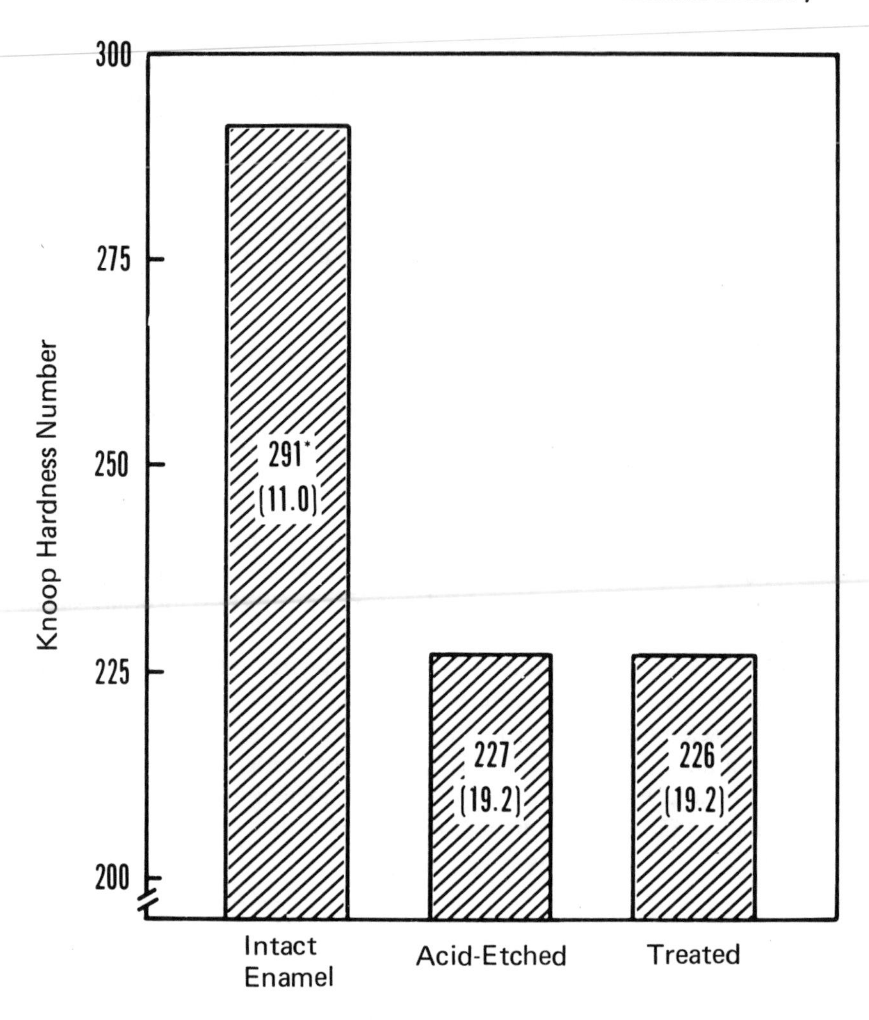

Figure 12-2. No hardness change in softened enamel treated with VA-OraLube without Ca, P, or F.

the rehardening process. It was clear that for the desired effect to occur it was necessary to include all three components.

Since the viscosity of topical fluoride solutions has a significant effect on performance, it was pertinent to evaluate the role of viscosity in the rehardening process. With the information that the complete OraLube formula would reharden softened enamel at about 5 percent, we omitted the viscosity-imparting binder (sodium carboxymethylcellulose) and found that under the same experimental conditions softened enamel was rehardened by 4.6 percent. When the dry

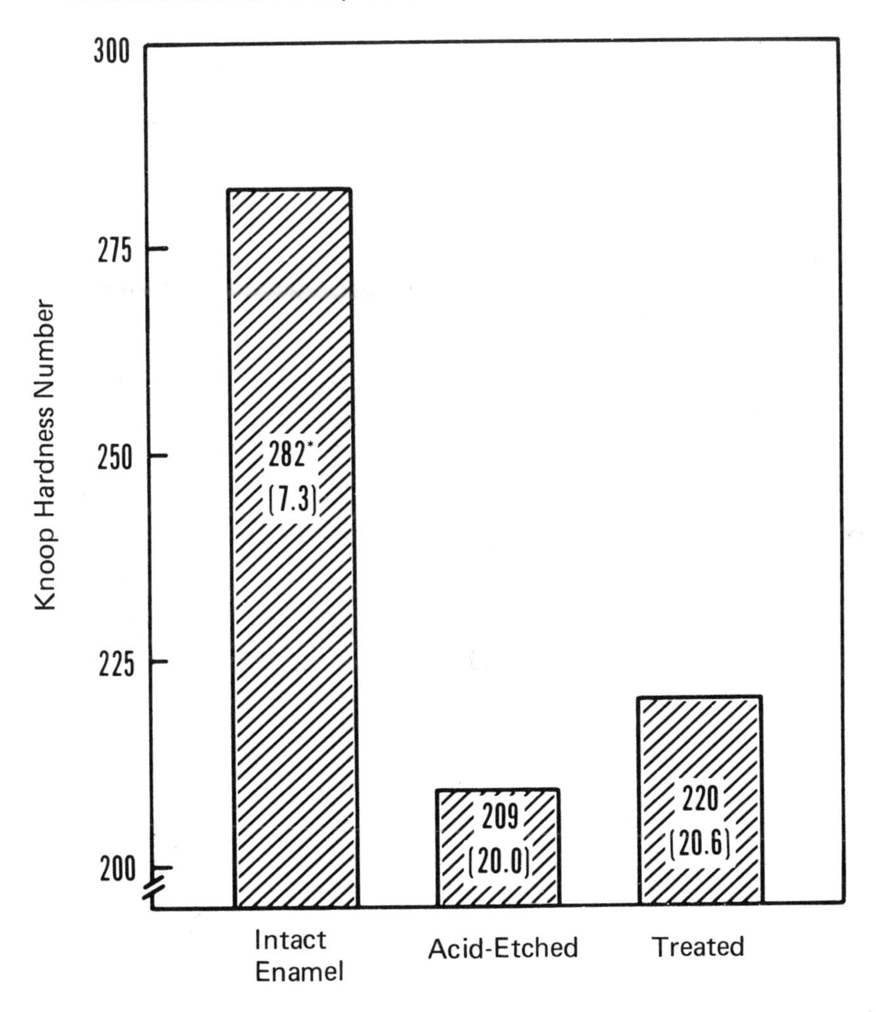

Figure 12-3. Rehardening of softened enamel by 1-hour treatment with VA-OraLube saliva substitute.

concentrate (with carbowax as binder) was employed to prepare OraLube enamel rehardened at a rate of 5.6 percent. Thus viscosity, a factor essential to soft tissue symptom relief, did not interfere with enamel rehardening potential. Also distributing OraLube in dry concentrate form would not detract from its performance in rehardening.

An experiment was undertaken to compare rehardening with OraLube I (the original formula), OraLube II (prepared from dry concentrate), and freshly collected human whole saliva. The results are presented in table 12-4. The two

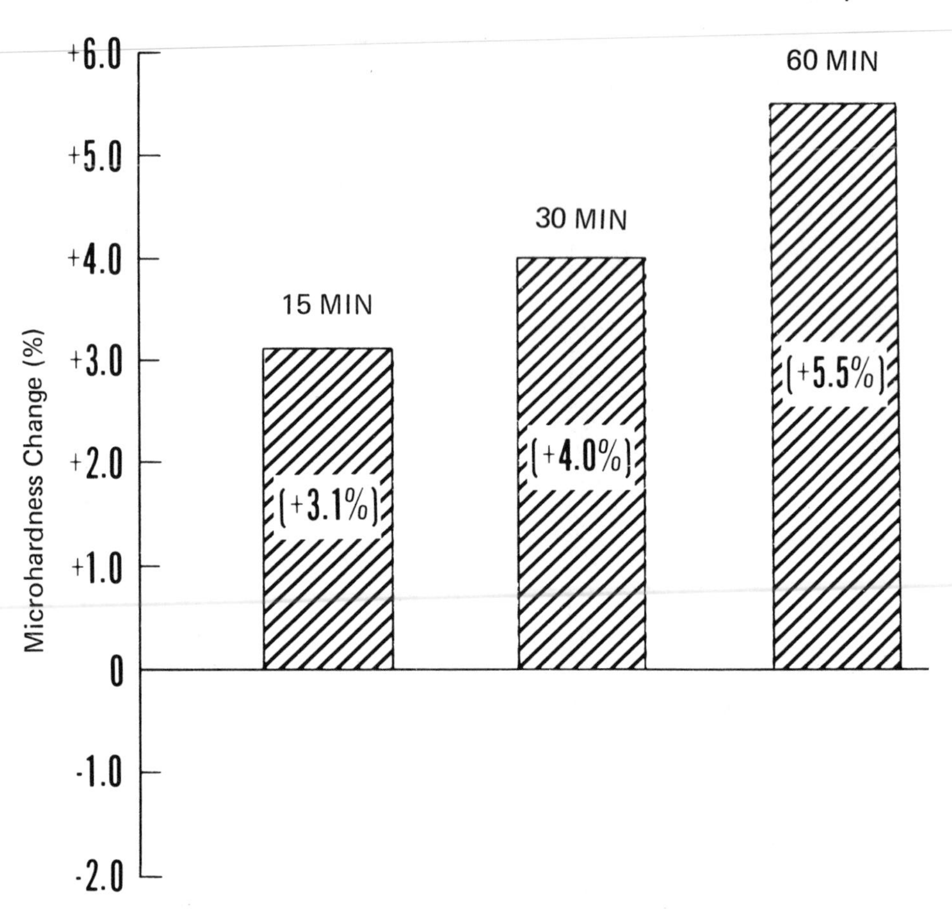

Figure 12-4. Effect of duration of treatment on enamel microhardness.

OraLube preparations rehardened at rates slightly above 5 percent, and whole saliva rehardened at a rate of about 7 percent. The rehardening potential of saliva is authenticated in the research literature. This study indicated that biological rehardening was being approached by the synthetic preparations. When it is considered that patients apply OraLube several times daily, the potential for a significant reparative effect is clear.

Another experiment involved selection of a fluoride concentration to provide maximal rehardening effect. Groups of six enamel surfaces were treated with OraLube containing either zero, 1, 2, 3, 4, or 5 ppm F. There were no other changes in the constituents. Treatment with OraLube containing no F softened the enamel surface insignificantly, by 1.2 percent (figure 12-6). The solution containing 1.0 ppm F induced 5.1 percent rehardening; this figure was increased

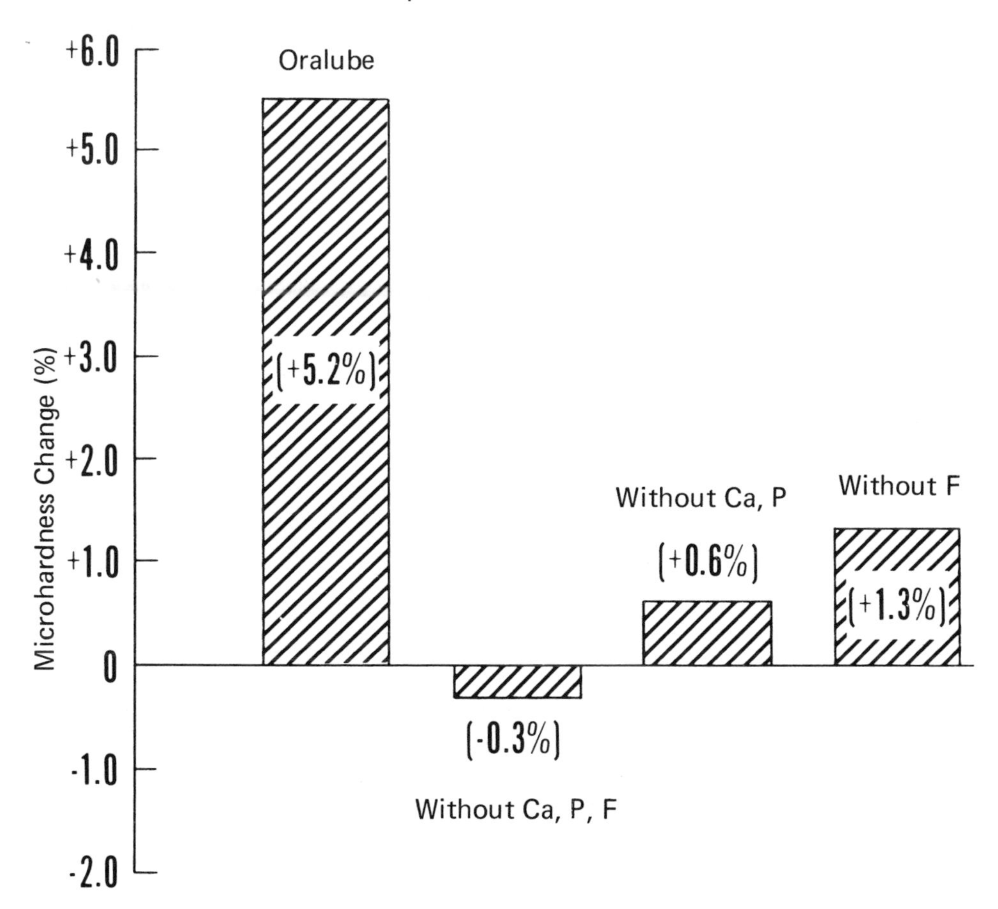

Figure 12-5. Effect of complete and deficient OraLube on enamel microhardness.

to 12.5 percent when the concentration was elevated to 2.0 ppm. Further increases in the F level did not significantly increase the rehardening capacity of the OraLube solution. As a result of this and several similar experiments, OraLube now is formulated to contain 2.0 ppm F.

Of prime importance in the performance characteristics of OraLube is whether or not it relieves soft tissue problems in irradiated xerostomic patients. We reported a study of twenty-two patients who had been using OraLube for periods ranging from four weeks to three months (Shannon, McCrary, and Starcke, 1977b). These patients were followed closely and their comments carefully considered. A principal consideration was the adjustment of viscosity to the point that symptom relief would be provided. Viscosity characteristics were held to a level that plaque-like accumulation of material on the soft tissues

Table 12-4
Comparison of OraLube and Whole Saliva as Rehardening Solutions

	Enamel Microhardness (KHN)				
	Softened Enamel		*After Treatment*		
Test Solution	*Mean*	*SD*	*Mean*	*SD*	*Change of Treatment*
OraLube (I)	211	25.0	222	25.3	+5.2%
OraLube (II)	209	20.0	220	20.6	+5.5%
Whole Saliva	236	6.8	253	9.0	+7.3%

would not be a problem. Taste response was monitored, but this aspect was found to be a relatively minor consideration. The overwhelming concern of the patients receiving radiotherapy was relief from the lack of lubrication formerly provided by saliva. Since it was impossible to dictate an application program that would be appropriate for all patients, we stipulated unrestricted use but encouraged application only when a true intraoral requirement was felt. A gratifying response came from all twenty-two patients. When given the choice of continuing on the medication or resuming their previous program of treatment, all twenty-two chose to remain on OraLube.

A second clinical study (Shannon, Trodahl, and Starcke, 1978b) involved one hundred twenty-five xerostomic patients who used OraLube over a four-month period. Subjective relief of intraoral soft tissue problems was virtually universal and no complaints or problems of consequence were reported. Patients consistently noted that their mouths were much more comfortable and that they did not have to repeatedly sip water to obtain relief. Those who had complained of dry, sore throat also reported consistent relief. The duration of beneficial effect varies from one to three or more hours.

The product has now been evaluated in all types of xerostomic patients in thirty VA facilities and by several nonaffiliated radiotherapists. It can be stated with confidence that OraLube has proven to be a valuable adjunct in maintaining oral health in xerostomic patients. Not one single report to the contrary has been received. Based on these clinical and laboratory results, the product is now being made available for patient care at VA medical centers throughout the country.

There are equally important applications to other types of patients. A manuscript (Fann and Shannon, 1978) has been published recommending the use of OraLube in patients on psychiatric medications that characteristically bring about a severe salivary flow rate depression (for example, the tricyclic depressives). OreLube can also be used by general surgery patients in preventing the dry, sore throat that is often seen when antisialagogues are administered as a

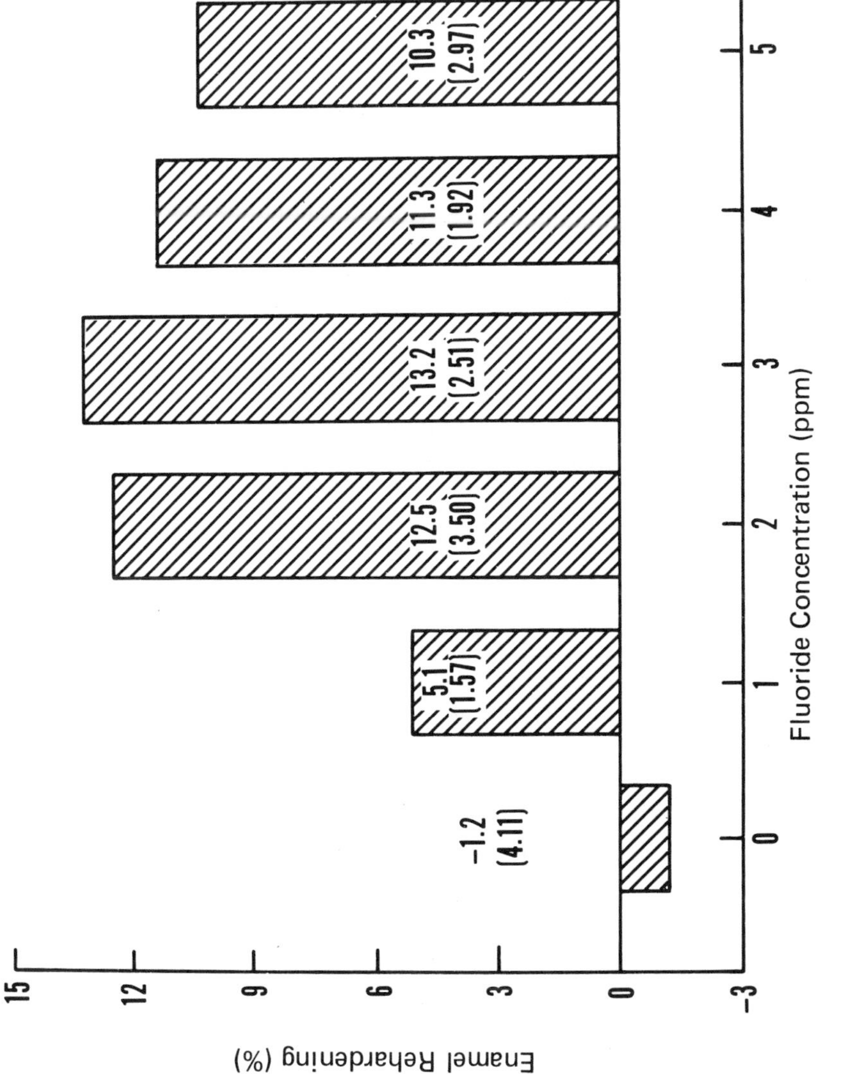

Figure 12-6. Effect of fluoride concentration on rehardening of enamel.

preoperative medication. The patient can be treated with OraLube at the time of premedication and in the recovery room as soon as treatment can be safely administered. Xerostomia associated with a number of systemic diseases (such as Sjogren's syndrome) will respond to similar care.

A saliva substitute with electrolyte levels and physical characteristics based on normal values for human mixed saliva has been developed, primarily for relief of soft tissue complications in patients receiving radiotherapy for malignancy of the head and neck.

Substantial relief of soft tissue problems has been reported by virtually all patients in two clinical studies. Patients given the choice of remaining on this medication or shifting back to their former regimen all elected to continue the use of the saliva substitute.

In addition to the ability to deal with soft tissue problems successfully, the saliva substitute also induces a significant rehardening of softened enamel surfaces. Since patients apply the solution several times daily, this rehardening capacity presents a significant added protective potential.

References

Cheyne, V.A. a Description of the Salivary Glands of the Rat and a Procedure for Their Extirpation. *J Dent Res* 18:457-468, 1939.

Eneroth, C., Henrikson, C.O., and Jakobsson, P.A. Effect of Fractionated Radiotherapy on Salivary Gland Function. *Cancer* 30:1147-1153, 1972a.

Eneroth, C., Henrikson, C.O., and Jakobsson, P.A. Preirradiation Qualities of a Parotid Gland Predicting the Grade of Functional Disturbance by Radiotherapy. *Acta Otolaryngol* 74:436-444, 1972b.

Fann, W.E., and Shannon, I.L. Treatment of Dry Mouth in Psychiatric Patients. *Am J Psychiatry* 135:251-252, 1978.

Rubin, R.L., and Doku, H.C. Therapeutic Radiology—the Modalities and Their Effects on Oral Tissues. *JADA* 92:731-739, 1976.

Shannon, I.L. A Formula for Human Parotid Fluid Collected Without Exogenous Stimulation. *J Dent Res* 46:309, 1967.

Shannon, I.L., Starcke, E.N., and Wescott, W.B. Effect of Radiotherapy on Whole Saliva Flow. *J Dent Res* 56:693, 1977a.

Shannon, I.L., McCrary, B.R., and Starcke, E.N. A Saliva Substitute For Use by Xerostomic Patients Undergoing Radiotherapy to the Head and Neck. *Oral Surg* 44:656-661, 1977b.

Shannon, I.L., Trodahl, J.N., and Starcke, E.N. Radiosensitivity of the Human Parotid Gland. *Proc Soc Exp Biol Med* 157:50-53, 1978a.

Shannon, I.L., Trodahl, J.N., and Starcke, E.N. Remineralization of Enamel by a Saliva Substitute Designed For Use by Irradiated Patients. *Cancer* 41:1746-1750, 1978b.

Shannon, I.L., Wescott, W.B., Starcke, E.N., and Mira, J.G. Laboratory Study of Cobalt-60 Irradiated Human Dental Enamel. *J Oral Med* 33:23-27, 1978.

Silverman, S. and Chierici, G. Radiation Therapy of Oral Carcinoma. I. Effects on Oral Tissues and Management of the Periodontium. *J Periodont* 36:478-484, 1965.

Wescott, W.B., Starcke, E.N., and Shannon, I.L. Chemical Protection Against Postirradiation Dental Caries. *Oral Surg* 40:709-719, 1975.

13 The Acid Etch Technique in Geriatric Dentistry

I. Leon Dogon

Restorative dentistry has two major goals: to place restorations in teeth to produce an effective seal between the enamel and the restorative material, and to eliminate the possibility of bacterial penetration around the restoration with subsequent secondary decay. No adhesive material alone can clinically provide effective sealing to dental tissues for a prolonged period of time. By conditioning the tooth surface with acid, however, the bond between the restorative material and enamel can be significantly increased. Buonocore, in 1955, was the first person to demonstrate markedly improved retention of methyl methacrylate resin to enamel after a thirty-second application of 85 percent orthophosphoric acid. Currently this bond is restricted to the tooth's enamel surface. This method of adhesion is known as the acid etch technique and is now widely used in restorative and preventive dentistry as well as orthodontics.

The acid etch technique is relatively simple; however, its effectiveness is dependent on many parameters including the material used to clean the surface of the tooth prior to etching, the efficacy of the etchant, the chemical and physical nature of the tooth enamel, the area and surface of the enamel that is etched, and the properties of the resin materials used to provide the sealing and tooth restoration. The most frequent reason for failure of this technique is contamination of the etched enamel surface with water, saliva, blood, or any other agent prior to placement of the resin coating. Various uses of this method for geriatric patients are discussed.

The Etched Tooth Surface

A variety of acids have been used to produce a well-conditioned tooth surface. These include lactic, citric, pyruvic, and orthophosphoric acids. The most suitable surface for sealing is obtained with orthophosphoric acid (Silverstone, 1974; Silverstone et al., 1975), and the range of concentration that provides the most homogeneous etch without removing excessive enamel surface is between 30 and 40 percent, for sixty seconds (Silverstone and Dogon, 1976). This etching treatment of the enamel increases the enamel porosity to enable suitable resins to penetrate the pores and mechanically attach to the enamel. To enhance the etchant's effectiveness, the tooth should be cleaned prior to etching. Cleaning agents containing oils, glycerine, or fluoride tend to leave a film on the tooth surface that diminishes the effectiveness of the etchant. It is preferable to apply pumice powder and water with either a prophylaxis brush or rubber cup. Teeth in fluoridated communities or in older patients tend to be more resistant to acid etching, and, consequently, the etching time should be increased to one hundred twenty seconds. This is also true of deciduous teeth where the enamel prisms are oriented slightly differently from permanent teeth, requiring more time for an effective etch. In addition, deciduous teeth contain a considerably higher organic content than permanent teeth, making them more difficult to acid etch.

It is important to understand the microstructure of enamel to provide an effective seal when using the acid etch technique. The enamel prisms in all permanent teeth are oriented at right angles to the surface; therefore, the surface of the tooth is the most suitable place to etch, providing greater surface area and deeper pore penetration into the prisms. For example, if a Class III restoration is to be placed in an incisor the etching should not be restricted to the cut surfaces of the enamel. The etching should extend over the labial and lingual surface of the enamel. The restoration should extend into the enamel surface that surrounds the margins of the restoration. A feather-edge rather than a butt joint should be used. Jorgensen and his associates (1975) and Mitchem and Granum (1976) demonstrated that enamel prisms fractured in restorations when only the cut margins of the cavity preparations were etched. This enamel damage can be prevented by acid etching the surface of the enamel surrounding the restoration and finishing with a feather-edge to cover the etched enamel.

Resin Requirements for the Acid Etch Technique

Once an adequately etched enamel surface is obtained, it is of prime importance to have a material that will penetrate into the enamel pores, created by the etch, to effectively seal the enamel. Studies with resins of varying viscosities from 180 to over 10,000 centipoise have demonstrated that the viscosity of the resins is of major importance to the penetrability of the material into the etched enamel (Dogon, 1975, 1976, 1978). Teeth specimens sealed with the resins of varying viscosities have been viewed by both light (figure 13-1 A and B) and electron microscopy (figure 13-2, 13-3). They indicate that the most effective range of viscosity is from 150 to 450 centipoise which provides the deepest penetration (figure 13-4). In addition, a higher frequency of penetration and tag formation is obtained with the resins within this range of viscosity (figure 13-5). It is of considerable importance to place an intermediary resin of relatively low viscosity

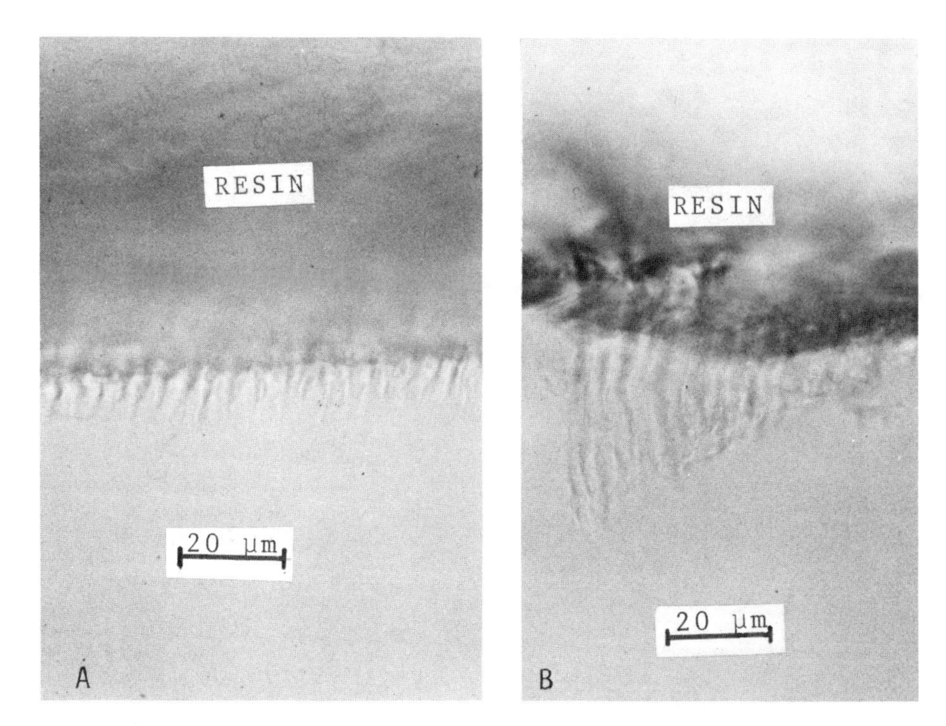

Figure 13-1. Demineralized resin coatings of teeth of 500 (A) and 430 (B) centipoise. The surface shows a relatively evenly distributed row of tags having an average length of 8 mu in (A) and 35 mu in (B).

(below 450 centipoise) over the etched enamel prior to the placement of restorative resins.

Effectiveness of the Seal

To demonstrate the efficacy of the seal obtained with the use of intermediary resins of low viscosity, Class I cavities were cut in extracted premolar teeth and different resin restorative materials were placed with and without etching. The teeth were stressed by thermal cycling in a calcium isotope, sectioned and radiographed. The results clearly demonstrated that it was possible to seal the restoration and eliminate penetration of the isotope (table 13-1, figure 13-6) only by using resins of relatively low viscosity prior to restoring with a composite resin.

This superior seal has been demonstrated by many other authors when using intermediary resins (Eriksen and Buonocore, 1976; Speiser and Kahn, 1979).

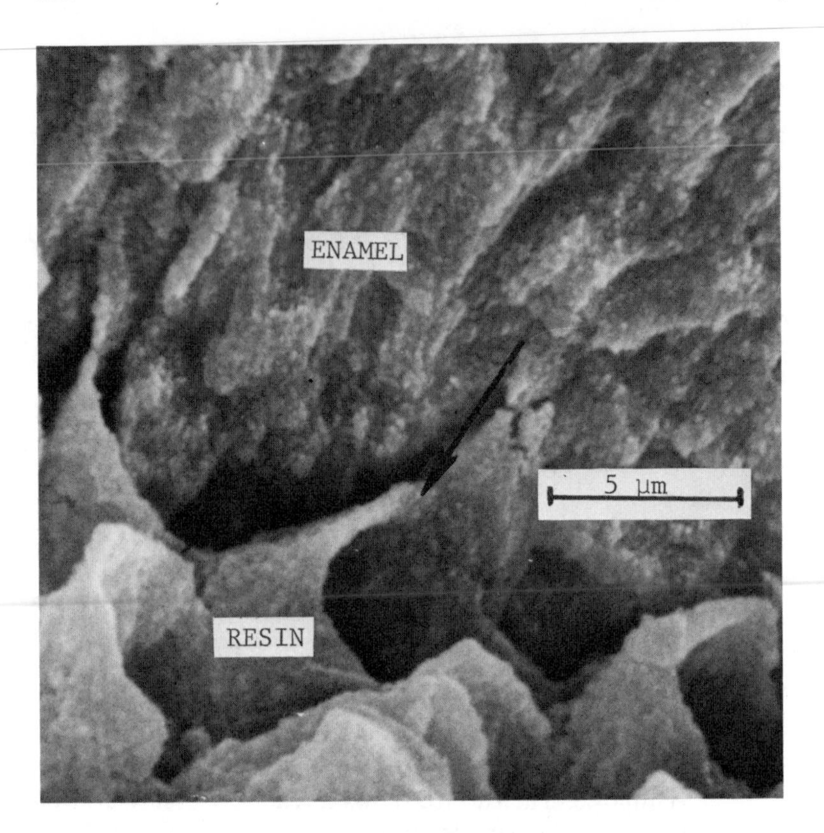

Figure 13-2. Scanning electron micrograph of the enamel resin interface of a specimen coated with a resin of 3,840 centipoise (cps) viscosity. Note the lack of penetration of the resin into the etched enamel and the attachment to only one side of the etched prism (*arrow*).

From a clinical standpoint, this seal is essential to eliminate secondary caries around anterior restorative materials as well as preventing caries occurrence in occlusal pits and fissures. When viewing these specimens in the scanning electron microscope, no fracture of enamel surrounding the preparations was observed, in comparison to that seen by Jorgensen, Asmussen, and Shimokobe (1975) and Mitchem and Granum (1976) when they etched the cut enamel surface only.

Restorative, Preventive, and Orthodontic Uses of the Acid Etch Technique

The acid etch technique is currently being used extensively for a variety of restorative and preventive measures. The sealing of pits and fissures has proven

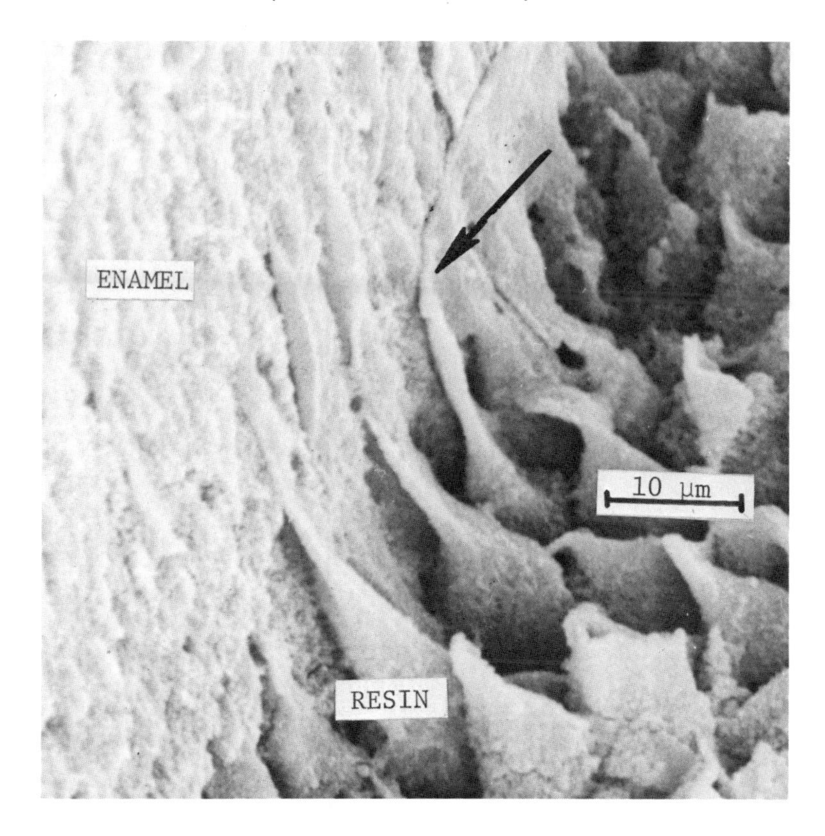

Figure 13-3. Scanning electron micrograph of the enamel resin interface in a specimen coated with a resin of 240 cps viscosity (Enamel Bond 3M Co.). The resin extends deeply into the etched enamel and fills the space provided by the etching. The resin tags are over 45 mu in length (*arrow*).

to be an efficient preventive procedure, substantiated by many clinical trials (Rock, 1975; Horowitz, Heifetz, and Poulsen, 1977; *Sealants,* 1973). Fractured anterior teeth and anterior esthetic restorations have been improved markedly by using this technique in combination with composite restorative materials (Dogon, Nathanson, and Henry, 1976). In a comparison study of Class III and Class IV restorations involving one hundred thirty-six nonetched restorations and five hundred twenty-three etched restorations with an intermediary low viscosity resin, the most striking observation was the difference in secondary caries incidence and marginal discoloration over the three-year period of the study (Nathanson and Dogon, 1977). There were secondary caries in 15 percent of the nonetched restorations and 0.8 percent of the etched ones. Forty-five percent of the nonetched restorations showed varying degrees of marginal discoloration compared with only 15 percent of the etched group (table 13-2).

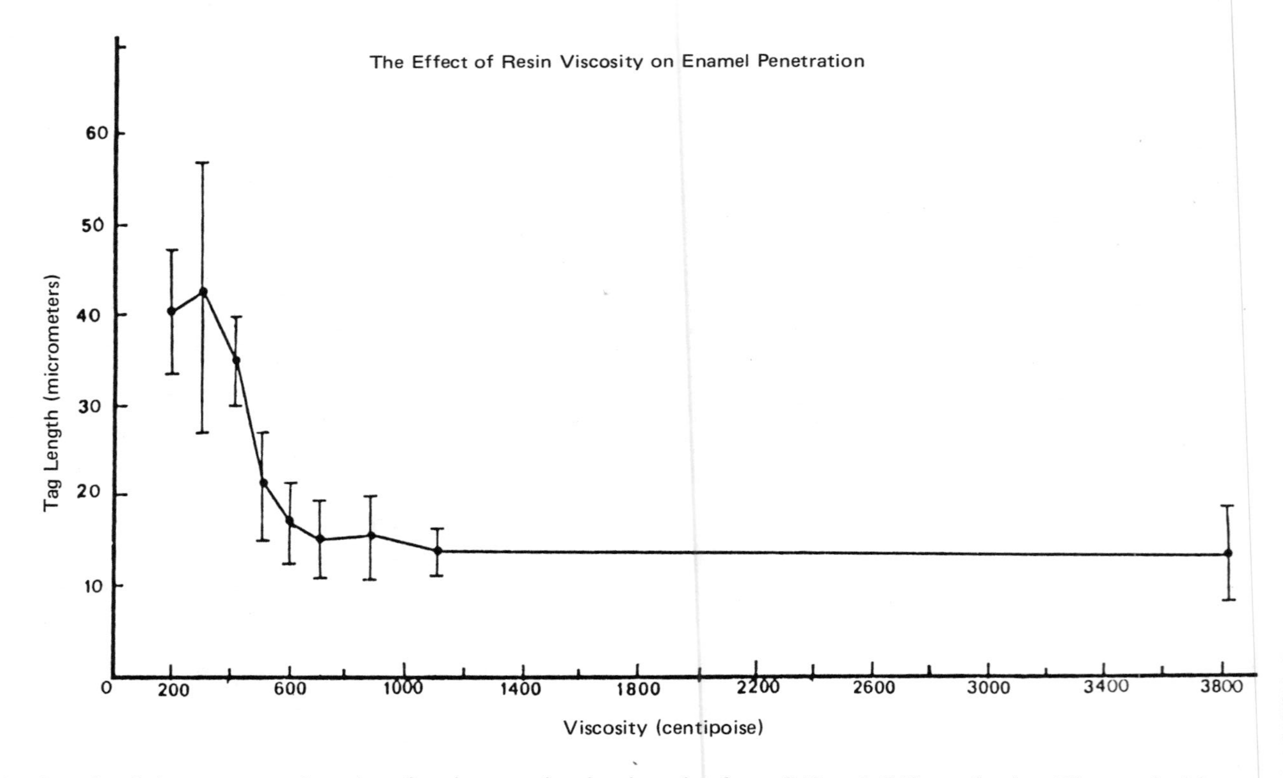

Figure 13-4. Graph of the mean tag lengths of resins ranging in viscosity from 240 to 3,840 centipoise. The vertical bars are the standard deviations of the tag lengths of the different resin viscosities. No significant difference in tag lengths are noted in resins about 500 cps.

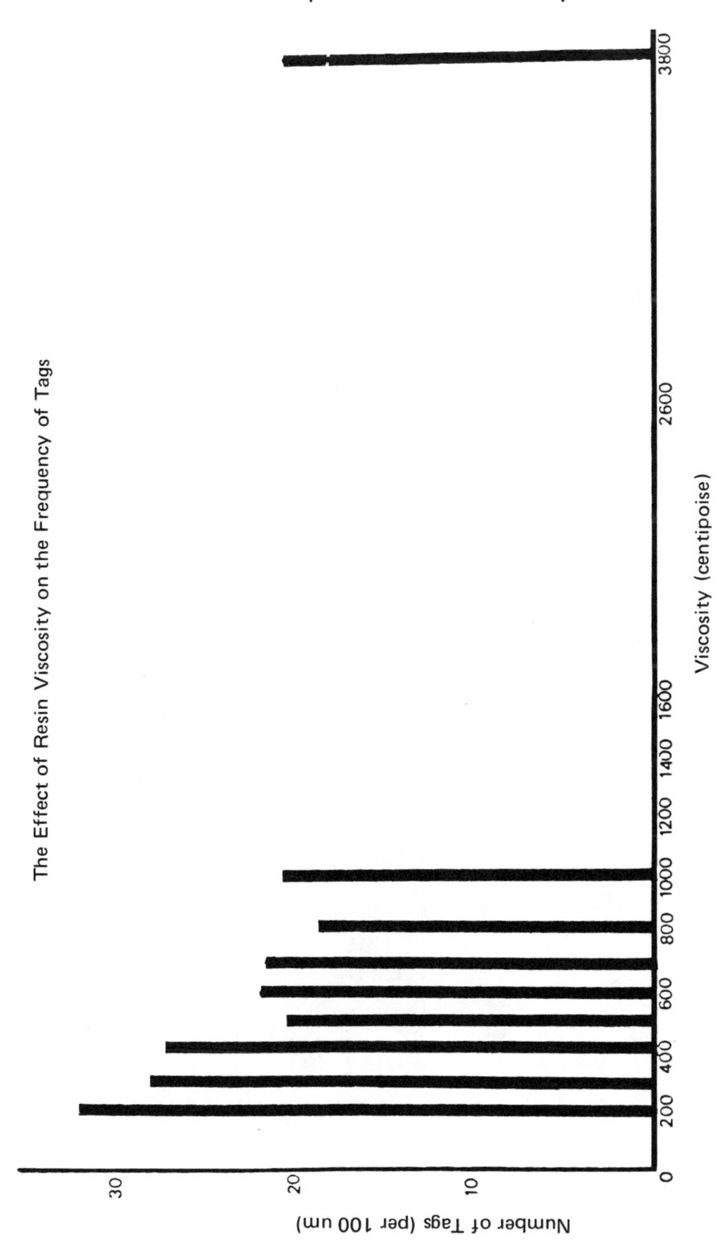

Figure 13-5. Bar graph showing the frequency of tags formed with resins of viscosities ranging from 240 to 3,840 cps. Note the resins below 500 cps form more numerous tags per 100 mu of enamel surface than resins of viscosity over 500 cps.

Table 13-1
Seal Effectiveness in Eliminating Isotope Penetration

Enamel Surface Treatment	*Restoration*	*Isotope (^{45}Ca) Penetration*			
		Severe	*Moderate*	*Slight*	*None*
None	Composite	15	–	–	–
37% H_3PO_4 (60 secs)	Composite	3	12	–	–
37% H_3PO_4 (60 secs)	Dilute Composite	–	–	13	2
37% H_3PO_4 (60 secs)	E.B. and Composite	–	–	–	15
37% H_3PO_4 (60 secs)	Nuva Seal and Composite	–	–	–	15

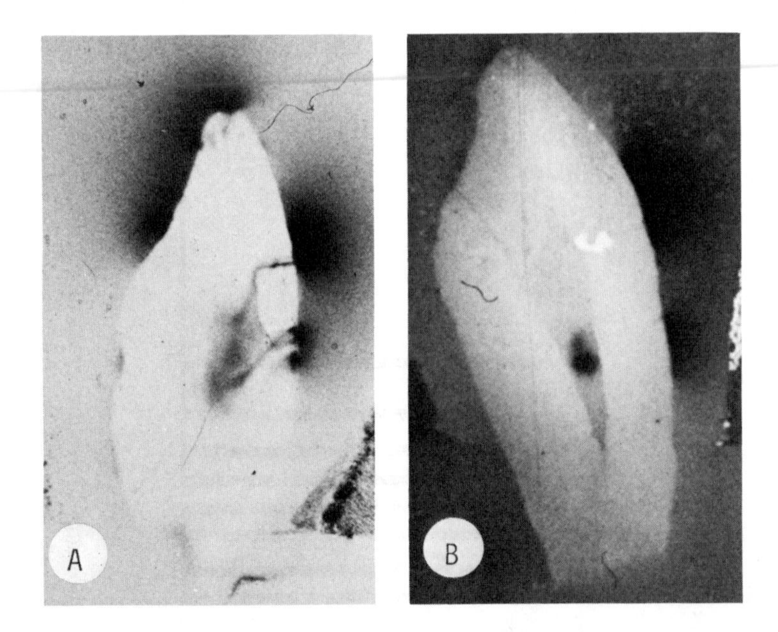

Figure 13-6. Contact autoradiograph of teeth after thermal cycling (6°C-60°C) in which a composite resin restoration was placed without etching (A) and a composite resin placed after the enamel surrounding the preparation was etched with 37% H_3PO_4 for 60 seconds and coated with Enamel Bond (3M Co.)(B). Note the severe penetration into the dentin at the base of the restoration in (A) and the isotope concentrated on the tooth surface without any evidence of penetration in (B).

Table 13-2
Comparison of Acid-Etched and Non-Acid-Etched Class III and Class V Restorations

Method	*Total Number of Restorations*	*Recurrent Decay Restorations*	*%*	*Marginal Discoloration Restorations*	*%*
Nonetched (No intermediary resin)	136	20	15	61	45
Etched (intermediary resin)	523	4	0.8	78	15

This finding is important when providing both an effective and esthetic anterior restoration. The acid etch technique is recommended when using resin restorative materials. The bonding of attachments directly to teeth is widely used in orthodontics. Though the methods for this use of the acid etch technique have been well documented (Brandt, Servoss, and Wolfson, 1975; Moin and Dogon, 1977), problems still remain in the removal of the adhesive from the tooth after bonding.

Uses in Older Patients

The acid etch technique as previously described is a rapid and simple procedure enabling extensive restorations of single teeth in one visit. The enamel of teeth in older patients tends to be considerably more resistant to decalcification because of the incorporation of increased levels of trace elements into the surface. The etching period, therefore, should be prolonged to two minutes with a 30 to 40 percent solution of orthophosphoric acid. It is equally important to maintain an uncontaminated etched surface prior to placement of the low viscosity resin when treating older patients.

There are four basic uses of the acid etch technique in older patients.

1. Restoration of severely broken-down teeth. Both vital and nonvital root-treated teeth can be adequately restored, provided some enamel remains to bond the restorative material to the tooth. The acid etch technique can be used in combination with composite restorative materials. Teeth can be restored to a functional state for relatively long periods and be readily repaired by reetching and the addition of more composite restorative material.

2. Cervical erosion. By acid etching the enamel for three to four minutes incisally to the area of erosion and coating with a low viscosity resin, restorations can adequately be placed and retained in these areas. It should be

noted that the dentin or cementum of vital teeth should never be treated with acid.

3. Periodontal splinting. Periodontally involved mobile teeth can be adequately splinted by means of the acid etch technique. These splints are able to immobilize the loose teeth and are considerably more esthetic and comfortable than other modes of temporary splinting.

4. Single tooth replacement. Missing single anterior tooth replacements can be accomplished for reasonable periods (three or more years) by means of acid etching either acrylic denture teeth or teeth fabricated from composite resin restorative materials to the adjacent abutment teeth. This provides a quick, esthetic replacement for single missing teeth without the need for extended chair-side time and at low cost to the patient.

The introduction of the acid etch technique into the restorative, preventive, and orthodontic fields has resulted in very safe, effective, and simple methods of treatment. This technique enables rapid, effective treatment with a minimum of armamentarium and materials. Frequently, this technique enables groups such as the aged and handicapped to be treated more effectively. Strict adherence to the basic principles described is important for the ultimate success in using this technique to its maximum potential.

References

Brandt, S., Servoss, J.M., and Wolfson, J. Practical Methods of Bonding, Direct and Indirect. *J Clin Orthod* 9:610-635, 1975.

Buonocore, M.G. A Simple Method of Increasing the Adhesion of Acrylic Filling Materials to Enamel Surfaces. *J Dent Res* 34:849-853, 1955.

Dogon, I.L. Studies Demonstrating the Need For an Intermediary Resin of Low Viscosity For the Acid Etch Technique. In Silverstone, L.M. and Dogon, I.L. (Eds.), *Proveedings of the Viscosity For the Acid Etch Technique.* Proceedings of the International Symposium on the Acid Etch Technique (St. Paul: North Central, 1975), pp. 100-118.

Dogon, I.L. The Influence of Viscosity on the Penetration of Resin into Acid Etched Enamel. *J Dent Res* 55:B138, 1976.

Dogon, I.L., Nathanson, D., and Henry, P. A Long Term Clinical Evaluation of Class IV Acid Etched Composite Resin Restorations. *54th General Meeting IADR Abstracts* 708:B238, 1976.

Dogon, I.L. Resin Systems in the Acid Etch Technique. In *Scanning Electron Microscopy,* vol. II, 1978, Sem Inc., AFM O'Hare, IL.

Erikson, H.M. and Buonocore, M.G. Marginal Leakage with Different Composite Restorative Materials in vitro: Effect of Cavity Design. *J Oral Rehabil* 3:315-322, 1976.

Horowitz, H.S., Heifetz, S.B., and Poulsen, S. Retention and Effectiveness of an Adhesive Sealant After Five Years. *J Dent Res* 56:B69, 1977.

Jorgensen, K.D., Asmussen, E., and Shimokobe, H. Enamel Damage Caused by Contracting Restorative Resins. *Scand J Dent Res* 83:120-122, 1975.

Mitchem, J.C. and Granum, E.D. Fracture of Enamel Walls by Composite Resin Restorations Following Acid Etching. *Oper Dent* 1:130-136, 1976.

Moin, K. and Dogon, I.L. Indirect Bonding of Orthodontic Attachments. *Am J Orthod* 72:261-275, 1977.

Nathanson, D. and Dogon, I.L. A Long Term Clinical Study of Non-Acid Etched Vs. Acid Etched Composite Resin Restorations. *55th General Session, Special Issue B, IADR Abstracts,* 340:B137, 1977.

Rock, W.P. Sealant Trials in the United Kingdom. In Silverstone, L.M. and Dogon, I.L. (Eds.), *Proceedings of the International Symposium on the Acid Etch Technique.* (St. Paul: North Central, 1975), pp. 176-180.

Sealants–Special Issue. *Journal of the American Society for Preventive Dentistry* 3:19, 1973.

Silverstone, L.M. Fissure Sealants. Laboratory Studies. *Caries Res* 8:2-26, 1974.

Silverstone, L.M., Saxton, C.A., Dogon, I.L. and Ferjerskov, O. Variation in the Pattern of Acid Etching of Human Dental Enamel Examined by Scanning Electron Microscopy. *Caries Res* 9:373-387, 1975.

Silverstone, L.M. and Dogon, I.L. The Effect of Phosphoric Acid on Human Deciduous Enamel Surface in vitro. *J Int Assoc Dent Child* 7:11-15, 1976.

Speiser, A.M. and Kahn, M. The Etched Butt-Joint Margin. *J Dent Child* 44:42-45, 1977.

14 Oral Surgery and the Geriatric Patient

Walter C. Guralnick

The impact of geriatric dentistry on oral surgical practice is already apparent. It is estimated that by the year 2000, 15 percent of the U.S. population will be over 65 years of age. At present, the 11 percent of the population in the state of Massachusetts over the age of 65 uses 30 percent of hospital beds, 25 percent of the medications prescribed, and 30 percent of all health care dollars.

Geriatric dentistry has several distinctive characteristics. It deals with a particular age group rather than with a specific disease and, therefore, demands an understanding of normal biological and psychological aging. Furthermore, it requires a multidisciplinary approach, because the health and illness of elderly people is greatly influenced not only by biological and psychological factors, but also by social forces. Analyzing the problems of the geriatric patient demands a keen awareness of these forces. This is illustrated by the number of elderly patients requiring multiple extractions. Decisions must be made about their physical condition and ability to tolerate surgery and the psychological impact of edentulism. Additionally, there are considerations concerning the fabrication of dentures.

Many oral surgery procedures are particularly pertinent to the older patient: extractions, odontogenic infection, preprosthetic surgery, salivary gland disease, oral carcinoma, temporomandibular joint pathology, facial pain, and facial trauma. For example, an uncomplicated extraction (or multiple extractions) is a benign procedure in the healthy young adult. In the older, medically compromised patient, the site of operation (hospital or office), the anesthetic agent administered (local or general), and the tolerance limit of the patient combine to change a simple surgical procedure into a complex event (Goodman and Gilman, 1975). Therefore, it is essential to know a patient's medical problems by obtaining a complete medical history.

The history should be concise yet all-inclusive, identifying all medical problems and current medications. Several questions, clearly stated, will elicit this information.

1. Are you under a physician's care now or have you been during the last few years? If so, who is your doctor?
2. Are you now taking any medicines? What are they? (Knowing what drugs are being taken or were recently stopped provides a key to the patient's pathology and a guidepost to surgery.)

3. Are you allergic to anything, including drugs?
4. Have you ever had a serious bleeding episode?
5. Have you had any breathing problems such as asthma, emphysema, or tuberculosis? Do you sleep with more than one pillow?

Finally, to reinforce the previous questions, the patient should be asked about specific diseases by posing the following question.

6. Have you ever had any of the following illnesses?
   Heart problems, including cardiac surgery?
   Stroke?
   Rheumatic fever?
   Liver disease or jaundice?
   Kidney disease?
   High blood pressure?
   Diabetes?
   Anemia?

If there is still doubt about current medications or the patient's physical status, direct contact should be made with the patient's physician.

When treated calmly, considerately, and promptly in an office setting, most older, medically compromised patients can safely undergo minor oral surgery under local anesthesia. Excitement and increased blood pressure and pulse rate are alleviated better through good office ambience than by preoperative tranquilizers. The hypertensive patient who is well controlled by propranolol can be treated as a "normal" person if he is not unduly stressed. One should remember, however, that older people have less tolerance, even without disease, than younger people. Efficiency, consideration, and exercise of good judgment about the extent of surgery are important determinants of how well patients progress.

Multiple extractions may be performed safely over several office visits. With some patients, particularly those on anticoagulants, a single operation will avoid prolonged alteration of prothrombin time. Surgery for such patients is best performed in a hospital where the total procedure can be completed in one carefully monitored operation.

As a general rule, geriatric patients with more than six or seven teeth to be extracted should be considered for hospital admission. Psychosocial as well as physiological forces must be considered, for the older person may not have the social support necessary for even limited help at home. In addition, a general anesthetic is less stressful than the multiple injections required for local anesthesia, especially with multiple extractions in several quadrants of the mouth. Short, uncomplicated procedures are appropriate for the office, yet concomitant medical problems must be considered every time.

Anticoagulated patients are frequently treated for oral health problems. If the prothrombin time is at the therapeutic level of one and a half times normal, one or two simple extractions can be performed without alteration of the drug dosage. All that is required is careful handling of tissue, avoidance of undue trauma, and suturing of sockets. More extensive work will require interruption of anticoagulant therapy which must be supervised by the patient's physician.

There are a number of patients with angina who are taking either nitroglycerin or propranolol. If the patient has frequent angina attacks, nitroglycerin may be given prophylactically just prior to administration of the local anesthetic. Alternatively, intravenous sedation with a small dose of diazepam may also be used during the procedure. Finally, reassurance and psychological support are extremely important in reducing apprehension and stress.

Propranolol is a beta blocker whose action is quite different from that of nitroglycerin. Its use does not contraindicate local anesthesia (American Pharmaceutical Association, 1976). Hypotension and bradycardia may be encountered in patients taking more than 80 to 160 mg of propranolol per day, however. In a hospital setting this is not a major problem; however, in an office setting it could be. Two drugs useful in combating severe hypotension in a patient with beta blockade are dopamine and ephedrine. If hypotension and concomitant bradycardia persist, the office patient should be taken immediately to a hospital where intravenous therapy and support can be given.

The medical condition most frequently seen by the oral surgeon in geriatric practice is hypertension. Propranolol is a frequently prescribed antihypertensive drug for the *mildly* hypertensive patient. For more severe hypertension, methyldopa is another, perhaps more common, drug. Diuretics such as chlorothiazide and hydrochlorothiazide are frequently prescribed for mild hypertension, while the antiadrenergic drugs, reserpine and guanethidine, are prescribed less often than the others. It is important to note that it is wise *not* to use epinephrine for patients taking reserpine and guanethidine because the small amount present in the dental anesthetic could precipitate a hypertensive crisis. If handled properly, patients taking the other drugs discussed can safely undergo appropriate office surgery without anticipated complications.

Another group of medically compromised geriatric patients consists of those who have suffered a myocardial infarction (MI) or have had cardiac surgery. Unless it cannot be deferred, the post MI patient should not have oral surgery within six months of an infarct. During the first six months after a coronary, the myocardium is extremely sensitive to stress. Surgery performed during this period carries an inordinately high mortality rate. After one year, the patient is considered to be a relatively normal risk.

Cardiac surgery has several implications for oral surgery. Stringent chemoprophylaxis prior to any surgery is as important for patients who have had valves replaced as it is for those with valvular damage from rheumatic fever. On the other hand, patients who have had a coronary artery bypass to relieve unstable angina do not require preoperative antibiotics.

All patients with compromised hearts must be treated carefully and with precise knowledge of their current medication and cardiac status. Many individuals will be taking anticoagulants, including patients who have had cerebral vascular accidents. Judgments concerning safe procedures and medication alternatives should be based on history and laboratory data.

The patient with congestive heart failure (CHF) will be identifiable by either direct questioning or from clues supplied from his medication. In all probability, he or she will be taking one of the digitalis glycosides such as digitalis or digoxin. Patients with CHF are a definite surgical risk. There is potential for arrhythmias, tachycardia, and failure. Careful preoperative evaluation is essential and tender care is required.

Elderly patients are also treated for depression with drugs that can seriously interact with other medications. The most commonly used antidepressant drugs are the tricyclics: amitriptyline hydrochloride, imipramine hydrochloride, and doxepin hydrochloride. Since one of the side effects of tricyclics is orthostatic hypotension, caution should be exercised when a patient arises from the dental chair. Support should always be given and sudden movement avoided. In addition, since these drugs produce tachycardia, it is wise to avoid large amounts of local anesthetic with epinephrine.

Another group of antidepressant drugs is the monoamine oxidase (MAO) inhibitors; phenelzine dihydrogen sulfate and isocarboxazid. These can produce severe and serious side effects and drug interactions. Opiates, particularly meperidine hydrochloride, may cause hypertension, convulsions, and coma. Fortunately, few patients take MAO inhibitors, but those who do must be treated with extreme caution and in consultation with the patient's physician.

Phenothiazines, which include chlorpromazine and prochlorperazine, are antipsychotic drugs used in schizophrenia. The most frightening complication sometimes exhibited in an office setting is the dramatic though not dangerous acute dystonic reaction which can occur in the first weeks of treatment. It consists of rhythmic, intermittent muscle twitchings, and spasms of the facial muscles, the tongue, and the neck. A complication of the syndrome which is seen occasionally in hospital emergency wards is jaw dislocation. The treatment is intravenous or intramuscular administration of an antihistamine such as diphenhydramine hydrochloride. Patients taking phenothiazines, however, can be safely treated in an office.

Another category of patients frequently encountered in geriatric oral surgery have endocrine disorders, such as diabetes. The well-controlled diabetic can be treated as a normal patient; only minimal precautions are necessary. Appointments should be scheduled so that food intake is altered as little as possible, and antibiotics should be prescribed liberally when infection, or the potential for it, exists.

Patients with thyroid disease may present more serious problems in the ambulatory oral surgical situation. They are particularly sensitive to epinephrine and may have serious hypertensive reactions to even small amounts. It is recommended that local anesthetics without epinephrine be used.

Finally, the oral surgeon will see many geriatric patients taking steroids. For such patients, oral surgical procedures under local anesthesia are not contraindicated. If general anesthesia is required, however, additional steroids will be necessary and may be given by a readily determined regimen. For patients who have been on long-term steroids, within six months of surgery supplementary steroids must be administered to offset adrenalin depletion.

In addition to specific medical problems that influence the treatment of geriatric patients, there are many surgical procedures that directly concern the elderly. Resorbed ridges and difficulty in wearing dentures are common problems among older people (Davis, Delo, and Ward, 1975). When conventional dentures cannot be worn, several surgical procedures can be used to correct the situation. Vestibuloplasty with skin grafting (MacIntosh and Obsgeser, 1967) is helpful if there is sufficient basal bone to retain a denture after a labial sulcus is created and the floor of the mouth is lowered. Two other possibilities, perhaps even more valuable, are mechanical appliances—the subperiosteal implant and the staple denture.

The subperiosteal implant, developed and perfected by Goldberg and Gershhkoff (1952), is an excellent aid to denture retention. Its limitation is that it requires two operations, one to obtain a direct impression of the bony ridge and the other to insert the framework. Although this does not lessen its usefulness, it may prove overly stressful for people who are medically compromised. The staple denture, introduced by Small (1975), may offer a better solution for denture instability, since it can be inserted in a single, relatively simple operation. Both the subperiosteal implant and the staple denture have good long-term utility. The major obstacle to their use is their high cost. If this were reduced, their effectiveness would be even greater.

Temporomandibular joint (TMJ) problems are common in the geriatric population and range from myofascial pain dysfunction (MPD) syndrome to arthritic joints and chronic dislocation. The edentulous patient often has TMJ symptoms. It is imperative, therefore, that he or she have the occlusion restored, either by conventional dentures or by a combined surgical-prosthetic effort which will allow the use of dentures. Additionally, older patients often suffer the devastation of long-standing rheumatoid arthritis, which may affect the TMJ as well as other joints. Limitation of jaw motion and even ankylosis must be corrected surgically.

Osteoarthritis, or degenerative joint disease (DJD), is more common than rheumatoid arthritis. Its presence, even when demonstrated by x-ray, does not necessarily require surgical intervention. Periodic low-grade discomfort accompanying DJD is responsive to salicylates, heat, and rest. Occasionally, more protracted discomfort can be alleviated by the installation of steroids into the joint space. Though this can be useful, it should not be repeated more than once or twice. Finally, for the few patients in whom pain is intractable, a high condylectomy should be considered.

Salivary gland problems are seen regularly in the geriatric population. The elderly debilitated person with a long-standing illness and dehydration is a prime candidate for parotitis from or because of retrograde infection. This very painful condition, which has the potential for serious sequelae, is usually caused by gram negative organisms and responds slowly to intensive intravenous antibiotic therapy. The initial antibiotic suggested for the condition is cephalin.

Other fairly common salivary gland diseases of older people are Sjögren's and the Mickulicz syndrome, both of which effect the parotid and the submaxillary glands. These chronic collagen diseases create serious morbidity. Sjögren's syndrome, which includes rheumatoid arthritis, is not curable but may be attenuated by steroid therapy. A diagnosis may be confirmed by biopsy of a minor salivary gland from the lip. It is particularly important to differentiate salivary gland disease from acute odontogenic infection.

There are two significant differences between young and old people with odontogenic infection. The geriatric patient may have less resistance to infection because of concomitant disease and, therefore, needs agressive treatment. Also, the source of infection may be occult in edentulous elderly patients. Careful examination, including extraoral x-rays, may be required to identify an infected unerupted tooth, a retained root, or a cyst as the source of infection. Treatment is no different from that required in any odontogenic infection, though it may be necessary to treat the condition more vigorously and to utilize hospital care.

Facial neuralgia can be confused with infection and tumor, since pain may be the predominant presenting symptom for all three types of disease. Facial pain must be diagnosed as either atypical or as true tic douloureux. Either affliction is devastating and is, unfortunately, seen fairly frequently in geriatric patients. Atypical facial neuralgia occasionally responds to medication with diphenylhydantan while tic douleureux, or true facial neuralgia, does not. An important and recent advance in the neurosurgical approach to tic douloureux is the interruption of pain transmissions by the creation of a radiofrequency lesion (RFL). The RFL is a benign surgical procedure performed on an ambulatory basis under light general anesthesia. The results have been so successful that alcohol injection no longer has a place in the long-term treatment of such patients.

Atypical facial pain is a much more difficult problem. Unfortunately, medication is not always successful in treating the pain; sometimes it can be so devastating that patients submit to and even demand oral surgery to alleviate their symptoms. Many teeth can be unnecessarily lost in a futile attempt to relieve pain.

It is imperative that the most scrupulous diagnostic processes be followed when facial pain is being studied. Unless there is recognizable disease, surgery should not be performed. Concurrently, it must be remembered that facial pain may be the presenting symptom of an obscure tumor whose presence must be carefully sought by all available diagnostic means.

Cancer is a frequent finding among geriatric patients. Oral cancer may be primary or it may represent metastasis. It is always important to remember that tumors of the lung, kidney, thyroid, and breast sometimes metastasize to the oral structures. Primary tumors, such as squamous carcinoma, are often seen in patients who are heavy smokers and drinkers. Dentists are the first line of defense in the treatment of oral cancer, for they diagnose more than half of all such patients. Consequently, early detection by the dentist is often the patient's best hope for cure. Lesions that are detected early, which are one to two cm in size and without detectable nodes, have a potential cure rate of approximately 70 percent.

A final category of surgical problems with which the oral surgeon must deal is facial trauma. Auto accidents do not spare the elderly any more than they do the young. The only difference between treating young and old patients is the generally greater fragility of the geriatric population. There are obvious problems inherent in caring for the elderly, since they are frequently medically compromised. Careful attention must be given to their treatment when surgery is performed to repair the ravages of facial trauma. All relevant consultative sources should be utilized to provide each patient with the optimum treatment and the best possible prognosis.

As health care improves, the geriatric population will increase in numbers. With the development of more sophisticated surgical procedures, there will be a greater ability to safely treat older patients. The treatment of geriatric patients should be a normal part of oral surgical practice that is accepted without apprehension and carried out with confidence.

References

Davis, W.H., Delo, R.I., and Ward, W.B. Long-term Ridge Augmentation with Rib Graft. *J Maxillofac Surg* 3:103-106, 1975.

Evaluation of Drug Interaction, 2nd ed. (Washington, DC: American Pharmaceutical Association, 1976).

Goldberg, N.I. and Gershkoff, A. Fundamentals of the Implant Denture. *J Prosthet Dent* 2:40-48, 1952.

Goodman, L.S. and Gilman, A. The Pharmacological Basis of Therapeutics, 5th ed. (New York: Macmillan, 1975).

MacIntosh, R.B. and Obsgeser, H.L. Preprosthetic Surgery: A Scheme for Its Effective Employment. *J Oral Surg* 25:397-413, 1967.

Small, I.A. Metal Implants and the Mandibular Staple Bone Plate. *J Oral Surg* 33:571-585, 1975.

15 Correlation of Biologic, Psychologic, and Clinical Aspects of Dental Care for the Aging

Sidney L. Silverman

Therapeutics for the aging is a unique, patient-specific process where treating the symptoms and sequences of any disease or disorder must integrate competence and a humanistic approach (Halstead and Halstead, 1978). Competence-based therapy refers to the measures of reliable clinical knowledge or procedures established either experimentally or pragmatically, demonstrating predictable and generalized guidelines. On the other hand, humanist-based therapy must focus on the uniqueness and individuality of each patient and his or her interaction with others within the context of social realities. This requires the dentist's knowledge and sensitivity to individual conflicts between personal identity and impersonal bureaucratic practices, understanding of a patient's feelings, values, creativity, spontaneity, and disturbances within his or her chosen life style.

Therapeutics is thus a function of several biologic and social processes in interaction. It is also a function of a patient's illness and the duration, location, and intensity of the condition and the physiologic adjustment to that disease. Furthermore, a diagnostic skill must be based on sound biomedical knowledge to coordinate the identification, synthesis, and evaluation of the signs and stigmata of the dental disease with existent disorders and any psychophysiologic processes present.

Figure 15-1 illustrates the spectrum of sciences and arts required for treatment (Silverman, 1972). Figure 15-2 presents the interaction between the structures, organ systems, and functions which reveal the transition from health to disease regarding therapeutics (Silverman, 1961). In Figure 15-3, column 1 describes the system disorders that interact in tandem with the dental disorder symptoms and tissue alterations presented in column 2. Together, these disorders mediate the oropharyngeal functions in column 3, which adversely affect the quality of life listed in the last column.

Any valid therapy program should be designed to start with an assessment of the patient's coping ability on the following three levels: 1. Psychologic level of adjustive behavior to the stress inherent in the diagnostic procedures (the examination, impressions for study casts, and the minor pain or trauma during periodontal evaluation, radiographs, and prophylaxis); 2. Visceral and metabolic coping skills for pain control and wound healing following restorative,

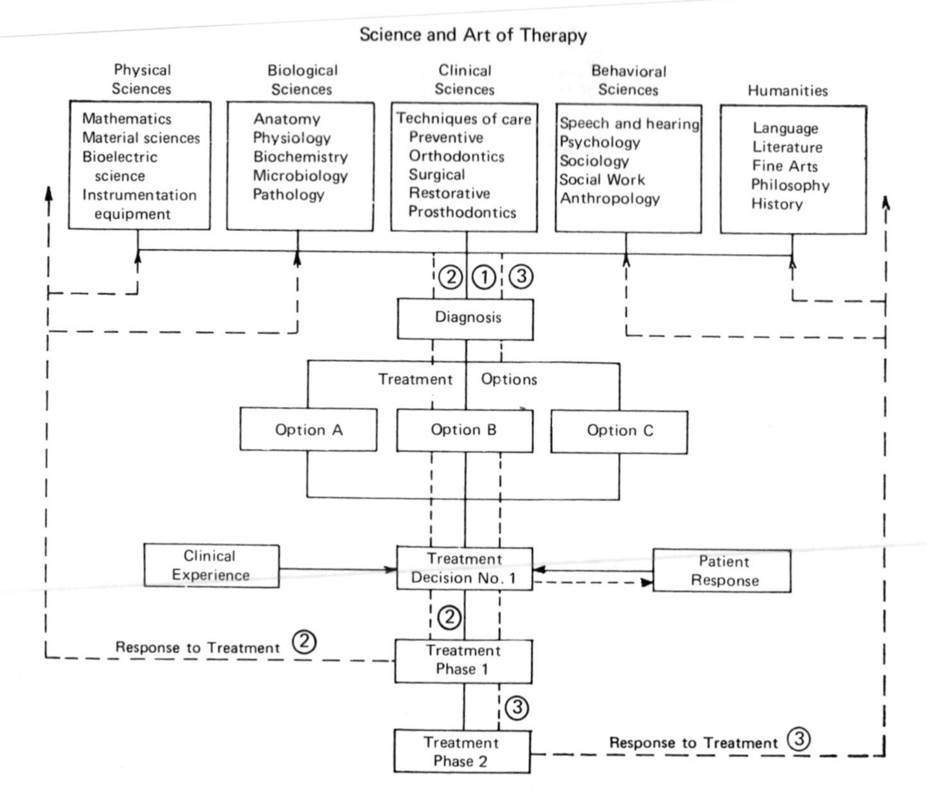

Figure 15-1. Schema for correlating the spectrum of knowledge in science and the arts appropriate for the processes of diagnosis, treatment, response to treatment, and reconfirmation of diagnosis and treatment plan.

prosthodontic, endodontic, periodontic, and surgical therapy; 3. Somatic voluntary skill for the management of dental occlusion and oral function associated with interim and long-term prosthodontic care.

An awareness of the interrelationship between dental and systemic disease is essential in treating the aged because of the high incidence of major dental problems and the increased frequency of chronic illness and pharmacotherapy. Recurring episodic disorders that may compromise dental treatment include cardiovascular disease, muscoloskeletal degeneration, neuropathology, endocrine disorders, and psychopathology. Table 15-1 summarizes the degree and frequency of chronic illnesses associated with age. Although dentists are able to identify caries, pulp pathology, periodontal disease, and oral tumors, they frequently have problems identifying symptoms arising from the disorganized occlusion because of increased edentulousness in the aged. In turn, dental disorders may be intensified by systemic problems that affect the biological

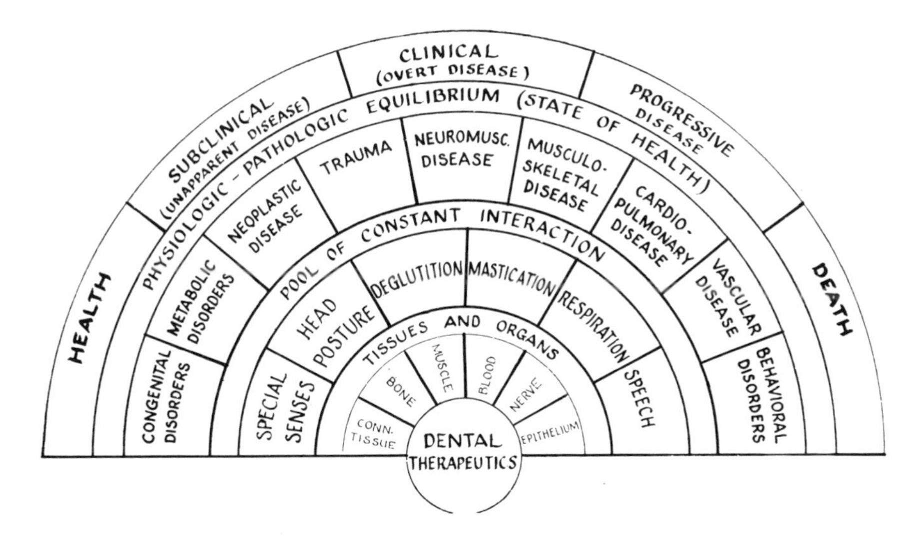

Figure 15-2. Health represents a state of equilibrium between normal physiologic activity and pathologic processes of disease.

processes associated with dental disease and may create an environment wherein the dental disease is intensified.

Pathologic Considerations in Dental Therapeutics

The following are the most prevalent systemic disorders affecting dental therapeutics.

Skeletal Disorders

Disturbances in the skeletal system accompanying osteoarthritis, rheumatoid arthritis, acromegaly, generalized osteoporosis, and osteomalacia. In addition, congenital deformities of the bones and joints may cause myofascial pain, limitation of jaw motion, disturbances in occlusion, and impaired hand-mouth skills (figures 15-4, 15-5, 15-6).

Sensory Disorders

Sensory loss or distortion may accompany aging (Litvak, Silverman, and Garfinkel, 1971) and are frequently associated with cerebrovascular accidents. Also,

Systematic Disorders		Oral Tissue Disorders		Oral Function Disorders		Measures of Quality of Life Affected by Systematic or Dental Disease
Cardiovasculare	Pool of interaction	Caries	Pool of interaction	Mastication	Pool of interaction	Nutrition
Cardiorespiratory		Pulp degeneration		Deglutition		Self-concept
Cerebrovascular		Periodontal disease		Speech		Communication skills
Peripherovascular		Edentulousness		Head posture and gait		Socialization
Musculoskeletal		Occlusion disorders		Head posture and special sense		Recreation
Neuropathy		Sensory distortion		Hand-mouth skills		Adjustive behavior
Metabolic		Mucosal alteration		Esthetics		Self fulfillment
Psychogenic		Secretory dysfunction				
Gastrointestinal		Osteogenic changes				
Genitourinary		Joint disorders				
Epithelial						
Tumor						
Trauma						
Infection						
Hematopoetic						

Figure 15-3. Interaction of systemic, oral tissue, and oral function disorders on the quality of life of aging patients.

Table 15-1
Health Status of the Civilian Noninstitutional Population of the Continental United States

			Persons With One or More Chronic Conditions[a]			
Age (Yr) (Both Sexes)	*All Persons*	*Persons with No Chronic Condition*	*Total*	*With no Limitation of Activity*	*With Partial*[b] *Limitation of Activity*	*With Major*[c] *Limitation of Activity*
All ages	100.0	68.6	41.4	31.3	8.0	2.1
Under 15	100.0	82.5	17.5	16.0	1.2	0.2
15-29	100.0	65.1	34.9	30.3	4.0	0.6
30-44	100.0	50.8	49.2	41.2	7.2	0.8
45-54	100.0	43.1	56.9	43.9	11.3	1.7
55-64	100.0	34.6	65.4	43.4	17.6	4.4
65-74	100.0	24.4	75.6	38.4	27.8	9.4
75	100.0	26.9	83.1	28.2	31.1	23.7

Source: From *United States Public Health Bulletin No. 584 B 1.* Washington, D.C., U.S. Government Printing Office.

[a]Chronic conditions: asthma, any allergy, dental disease, tuberculosis, chronic bronchitis, reported attacks of sinus trouble, rheumatic fever, hardening of arteries, high blood pressure, heart trouble, stroke, trouble with varicose veins, hemorrhoids or piles, gallbladder or liver trouble, stomach ulcer, any other chronic stomach trouble, kidney stones or other kidney trouble, arthritis or rheumatism, prostate trouble thyroid trouble or goiter, diabetes, epilepsy or convulsions of any kind, mental or nervous trouble, repeated trouble with back or spine, tumor or cancer, chronic skin trouble, hernia or rupture.

[b]Limited in amount or kind of major or outside activities.

[c]Unable to carry on major activity.

chronic peripheral vascular disease associated with diabetes or Berger's disease, degenerative neuropathy, and pharmacotherapy for psychopathology. The sensory distortion may be manifested as the "burning mouth syndrome" (Silverman, 1971), or facial pain. A new clinical syndrome of head posture hallucination, "Verkrumte Kupf syndrome" (VKS), (Silverman, 1975) related to severe personality disorders can occur. Sensory deprivation is almost universal in the aging. These special sense losses impair communication skills, posture, gait, and esthetic judgments.

Motor Disorders

Motor dysfunction is associated with a wide spectrum of disorders ranging from atrophy to hypertrophy of skeletal muscles, hypotonicity to hypertonicity, and various dyskenesias. Degenerative neuropathology such as parkinsonism, cerebral

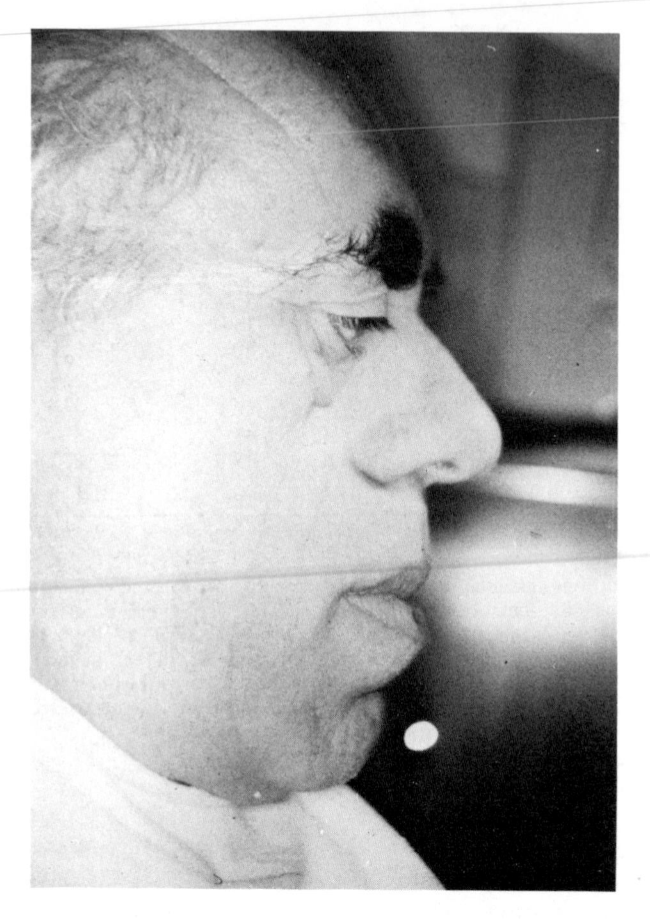

Figure 15-4. Profile of patient with acromegaly. Note the elongated facial skeleton and thickened soft tissues of the lips.

palsy, Bell's palsy, neurogenic tumors, and cerebrovascular accidents also result in muscular or motor disorders in mastication, and deglutition.

Communication Disorders

Organic brain syndrome and cerebrovascular accidents can cause both semantic and dysarthric speech as well as language disorders. They impede communication between the practitioner and the patient by affecting cooperation. These disorders may also create a delayed response time which, while not necessarily associated with confusion, requires additional time for integrating response

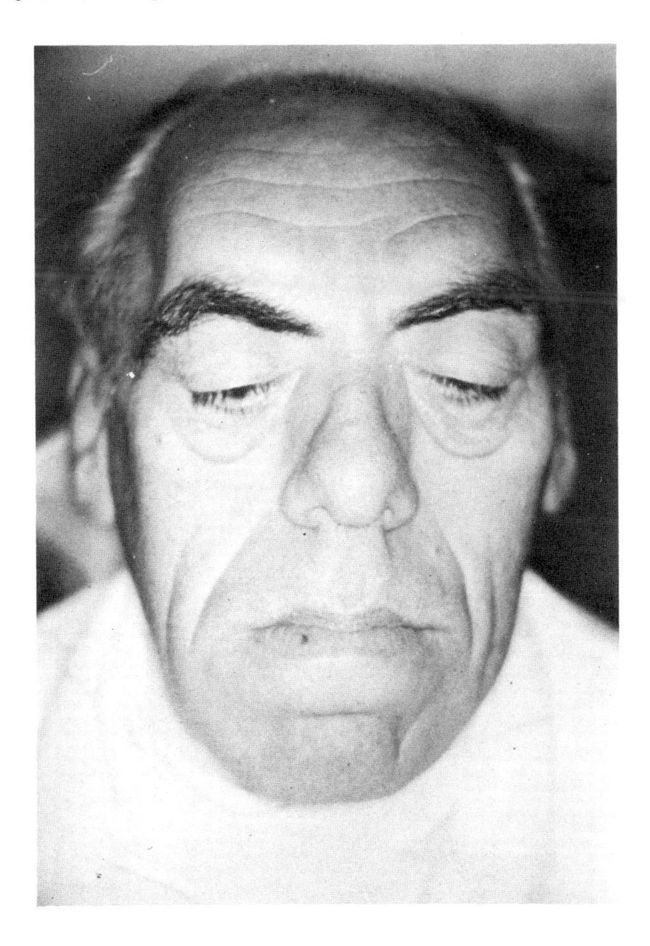

Figure 15-5. Full-face view of acromegaly patient. Notice that vertical length is increased to a relatively greater linear distance than is the width of the face.

sequences. Patients with a history of stroke often require simple or concrete language, the avoidance of distracting factors in the dental environment, and supportive sympathetic management for effective treatment.

Personality Disorders

Personality traits are frequently exaggerated with acute and chronic disease in the elderly. These include phobias, anxiety, depression, hostility, short-term

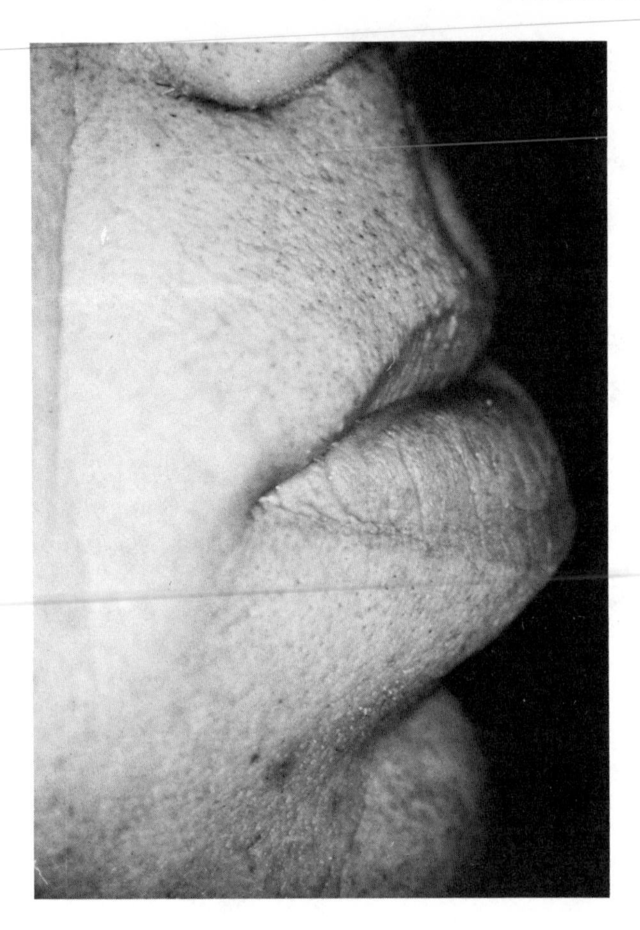

Figure 15-6. The lips are markedly thickened in acromegaly, as is the tongue. This increased bulk is associated with degenerative processes. There is a loss of strength and speed of motion even though there is an increase in bulk. There is a pathologic hypertrophy often associated with distortion of speech.

memory loss, nonconforming behavior, and appearance. These may be transitory, because of the stress of treatment, or may be permanent personality disturbances. Their origin should be identified by the practitioner. In addition, coping strategy for both the patient and the dentist should be established. It is also essential that the practitioner assess his or her own prejudices and resultant effect on therapy. Self concept studies by Silverman et al. (1976) have indicated that field dependent patients who continuously seek corroborative support for symptom complaints require a greater number of adjustments for their dental prostheses than field independent patients who readily make independent decisions.

Biologic Functions of Head Posture and Special Senses

The intimate relationship between head posture, gait or locomotion, hand skills, and the special senses can be seriously disordered by muscular, skeletal, and sensory motor disturbances. Insight into the coordination of vision, vestibular function, and the stretch reflex of muscles and tendons in regulating body posture can help reduce inappropriate muscle tension and jaw movement during clinical procedures. The clinician should stand in front of the patient when speaking, or instruct the patient to keep his or her eyes open during dental impression and occlusion recording procedures. These simple precautions help reduce muscle tension in the lip, tongue, and neck muscles.

Oral Function Characteristics

The morphogenesis of the orofacial complex consisting of the skeletal, muscular, and epithelial structures sustains the design of the digestive and respiratory systems (figure 15-7). The oropharyngeal components with a valving mechanism expedite the sequential and almost simultaneous activity of breathing, speaking, chewing, and swallowing. The skeleton supports muscular activity through a system of lever mechanisms (figure 15-8). These elements facilitate the speed and specificity of motion necessary to perform the highly selective movements of communication and food ingestion.

The variety of muscle groups (figure 15-9) and their distribution, as well as fiber arrangement, the number and location of attachments, and contiguous facial and connective tissue connections create the requisite movements within the spacial contour of sound production and trituration of foods for the ingestion of nutritional substances. The valving mechanisms (figure 15-10) with their neurologic components are a remarkable synthesis for creating activity in the orofacial structures. The cranial nerves that serve these orofacial structures are the apotheosis of the evolutionary history of the bronchial arch derivatives. The cranial nerve complex, which includes an autonomic nervous system component, mediates the visceral function of the jaws, lips, tongue, and soft palate. The hierarchy of evolutionary development allows swallowing to persist even when speech and chewing skills are impaired or lost.

Mastication is a learned function usually associated with unilateral jaw motion. The characteristic motion of the mandible is wide excursive lateral

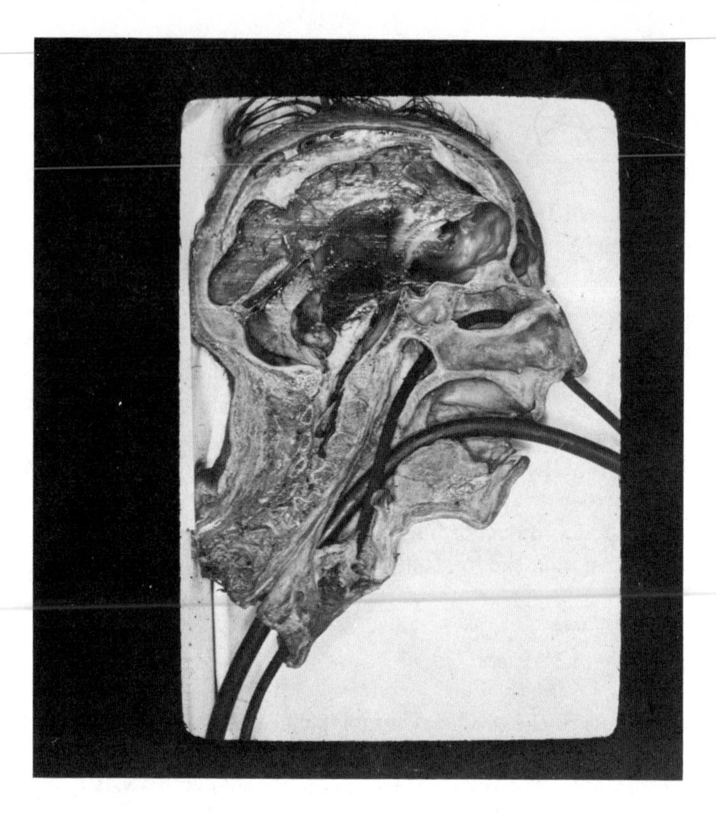

Figure 15-7. Midsagittal section of cadaver. The tubes demonstrate the airway passage and the food crossing anteroposteriorly in the oropharynx.

displacement (figure 15-11). Chewing is a voluntary sensorimotor function which is dependent on the available occlusive contact surfaces which, in turn, neurologically condition both the static and dynamic position of the mandible during mastication. Hence, the chewing pattern is intimately associated with centric occlusion and the patterns of occlusion can be altered by clinically modifying occlusion contact. These modifications can be the result of an interim prostheses, orthodontic procedures, or tooth form alteration because of extensive wear (figure 15-12).

On the other hand, deglutition and respiration appear to be innate biologic functions present at birth. They are symmetric, bilateral motions. Occlusal schema because of unilateral premature contacts that interfere with simultaneous bilateral movement are often rejected. Teeth may become abraded and masticating function diminished by a unilateral occlusal disorder.

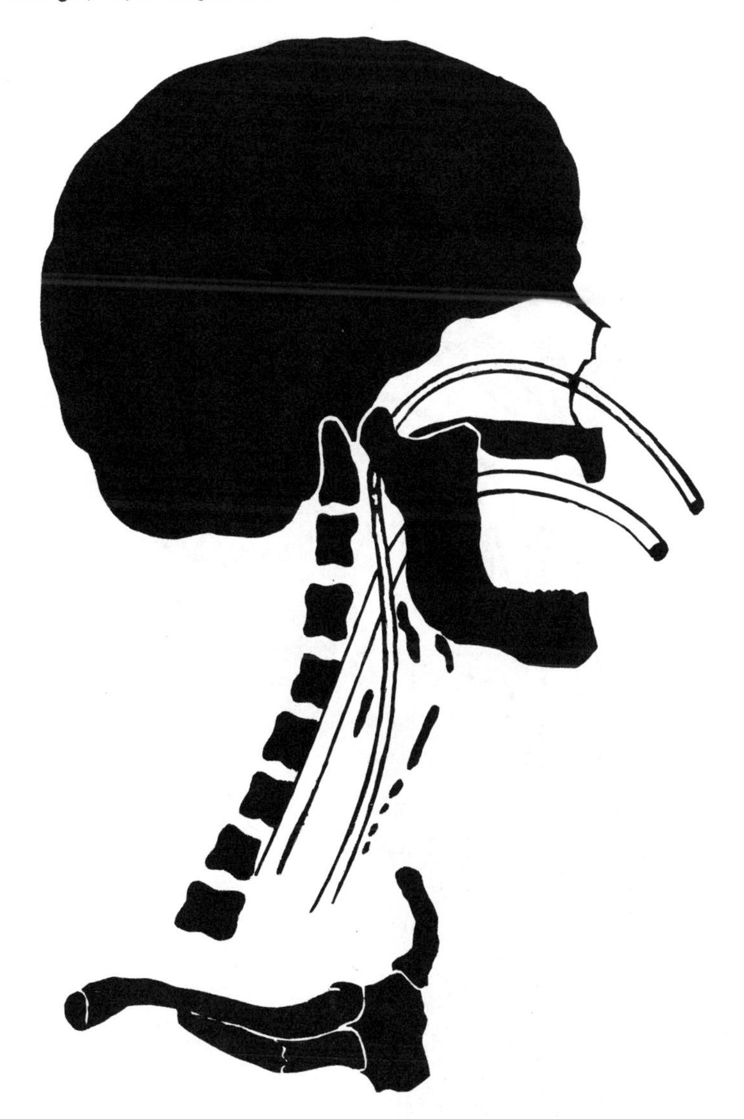

Figure 15-8. Schematic illustration demonstrating skeletal scaffolding supporting the airway and food passages.

Speech is a learned function dependent on respiration and is easily impaired by dental disorders. It is a bilateral movement and is characterized as a forward and downward movement rather than a lateral movement (figure 15-13).

With or without teeth, swallowing and respiration are retained as effective vital functions. Their effectiveness may range from a limited motor coordination

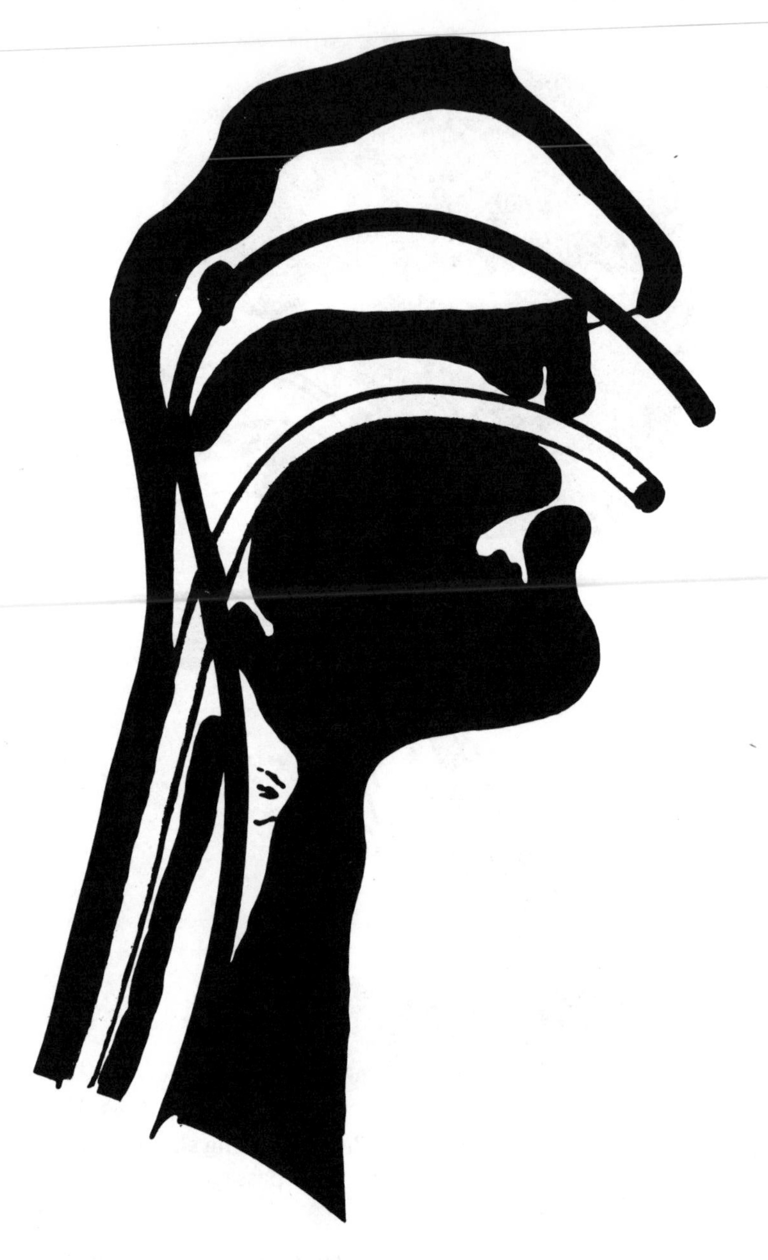

Figure 15-9. Schematic illustration demonstrating airway and food tubes in relation to the soft tissue mass and its oropharyngeal topography.

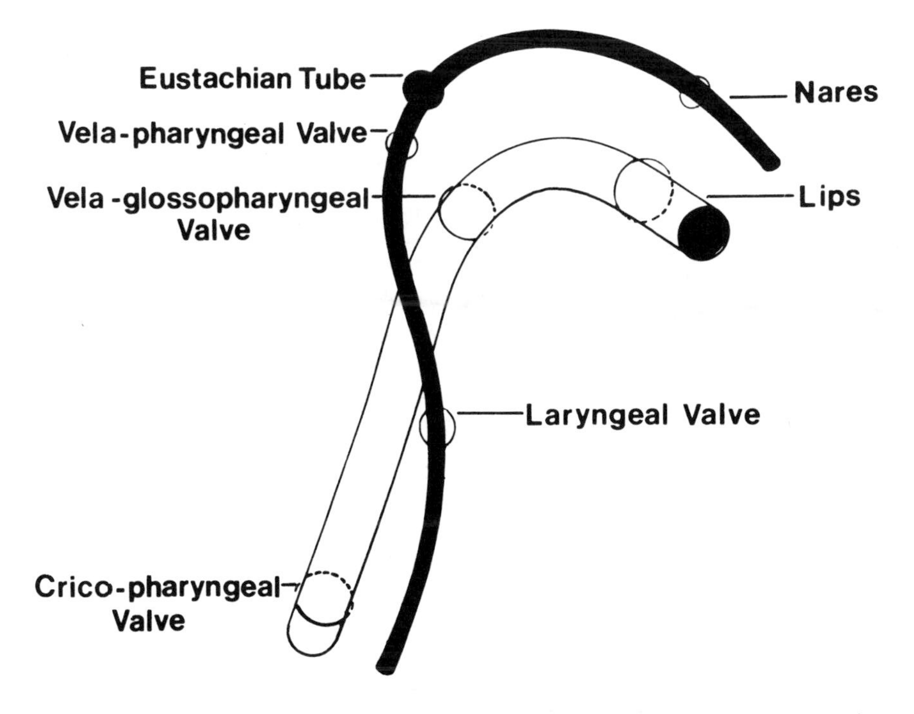

Figure 15-10. Schematic illustration demonstrating the valving mechanisms in relation to airway and food passages.

as in an arthritic condition of the TMJ to a wide variety of motions in the normal joint. Mastication and speech, however, require a relatively large number of natural or prosthetic teeth, in proper form and position, for an effective performance. The absence of teeth or substantial loss because of dental disease can adversely alter both the selection and trituration of food. Similarly, speech is equally affected because the production of consonants in speech requires teeth to produce the differentiated acoustic sounds in the column of expired air. The labiodental sounds (V, f), the linguadental sounds (t, d), and the interdental sounds (s, z) require teeth for clear production.

Oral functions are related to the esthetic self-image of the patient who perceives and evaluates the static and dynamic topography of the facial contour. The normal tonicity of facial musculature and the histochemical composition of the skin, replete with collagen and elastic fiber content, reflect the facial configurations that remain throughout life. When teeth are lost or disease alters the skin, the tubercle, the junction between the skin and vermillion border of the lips, the position and planes of the nasiolabial and geniolabial sulci are either lost,or distorted (figure 15-14).

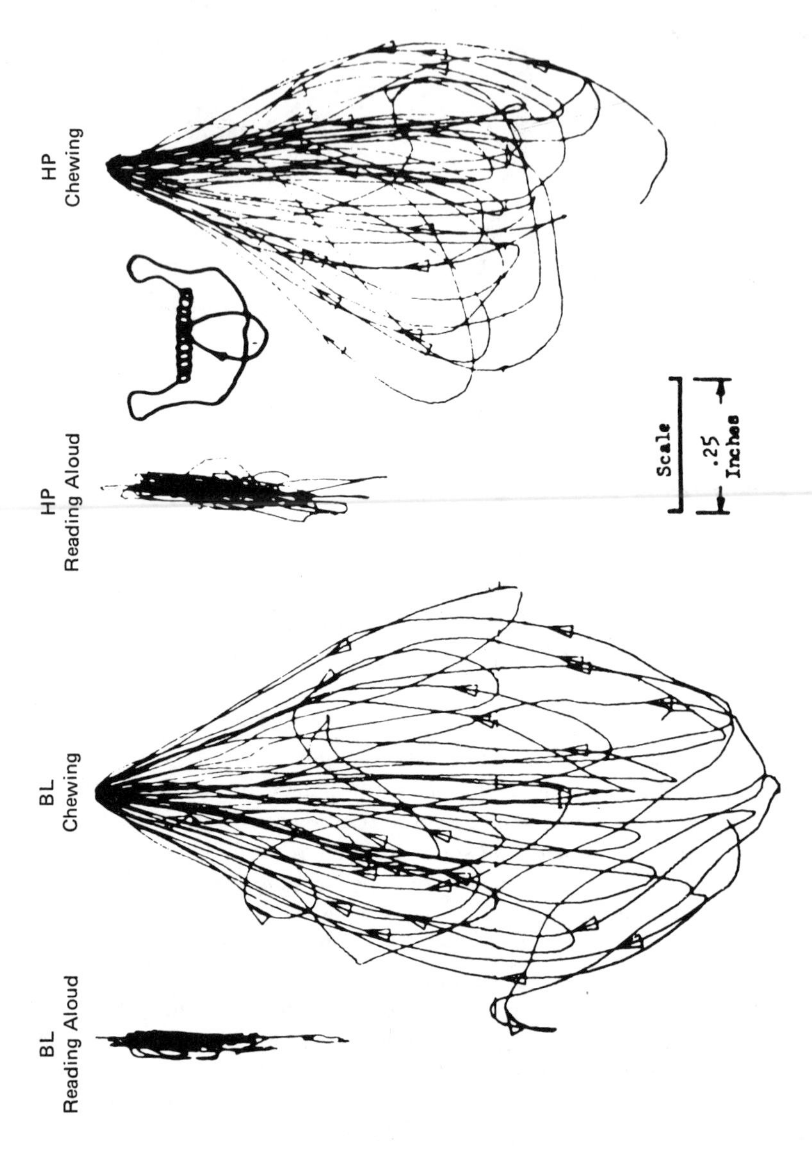

Figure 15-11 Orbits of motion of the central incisor in the frontal plane for speech and chewing.

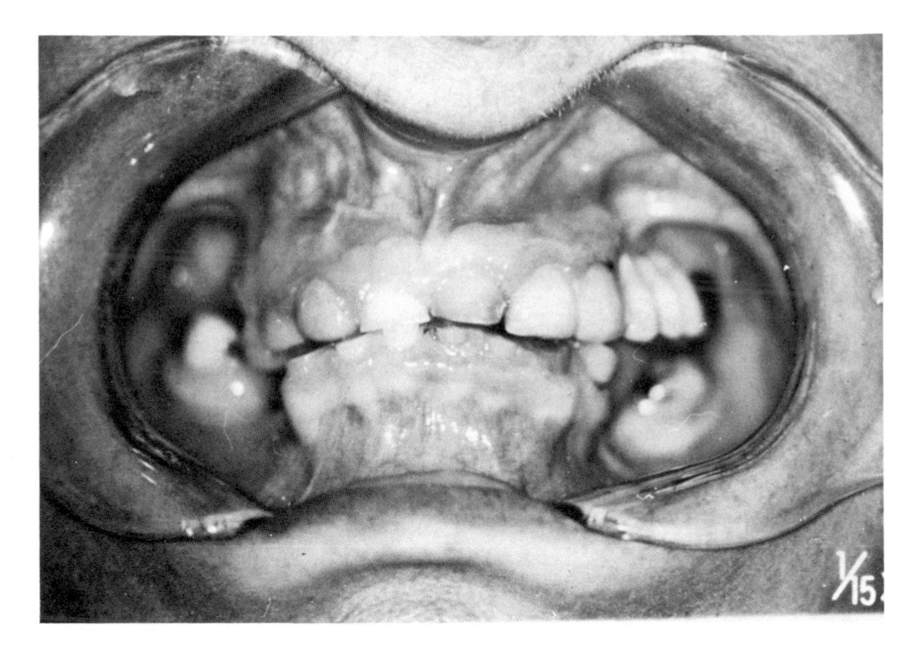

Figure 15-12. Excession attrition because of flexed head and neck posture when only anterior occlusion existed in opposition.

These functions of the oral pharyngeal tissues, mastication, deglutition, respiration, speech, and esthetics together crease an deglutition, respiration, speech, and esthetics together create an interdependent system, each diminishing or reinforcing one another.

Aging and Oral Tissue Changes

The clinical signs and symptoms of aging observed in oral tissues can not only be the consequences of a discrete pathologic disorder, but can also be the result of changes in many organs and tissues. To the practicing dentist, the most significant degenerative change is a diminished capacity for cell growth and tissue repair.

Modification of the tooth and the investing tissues including the periodontal membrane and the alveolar bone frequently occurs. Occlusal attrition, marked formation of secondary dentin, apical migration of the periodontal attachment, increased cementum deposition, root transparency, gingivitis, deepening of

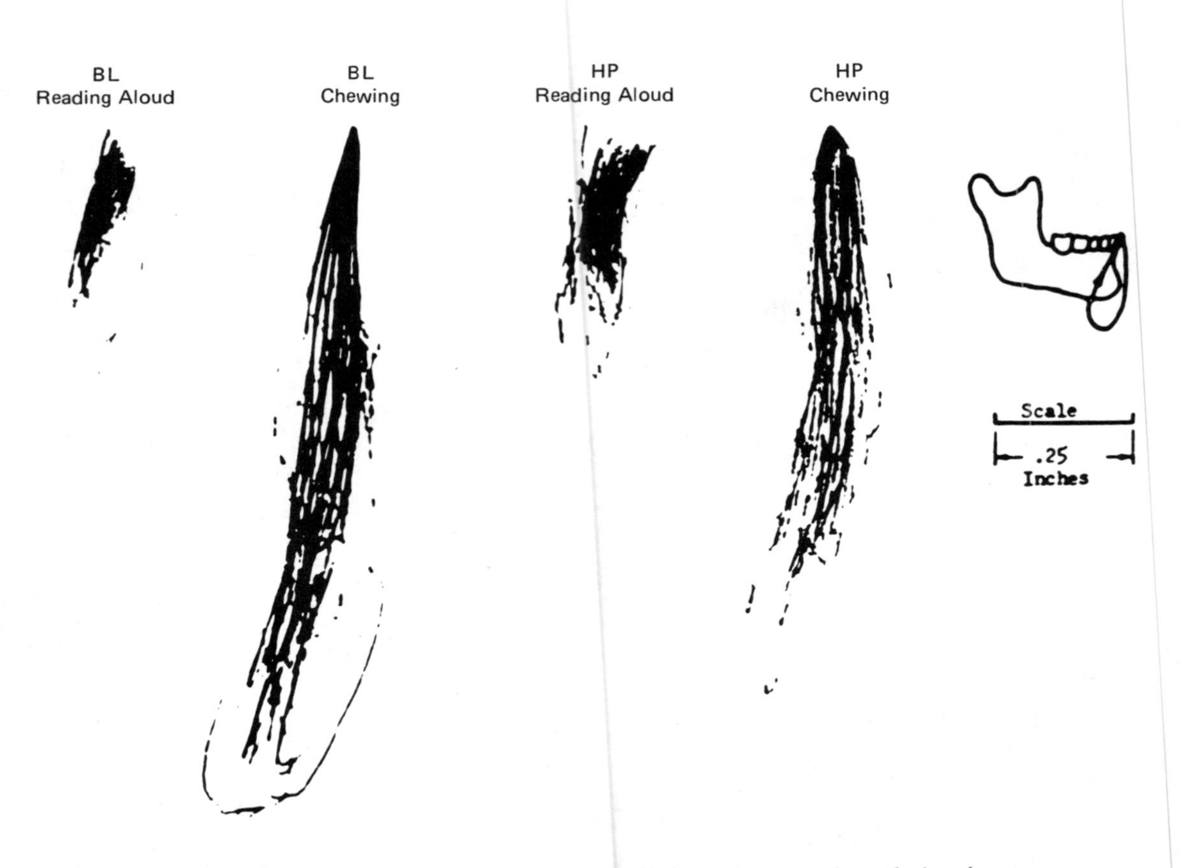

Figure 15-13. Orbits of motion of the central incisor in the sagittal plane for speech and chewing.

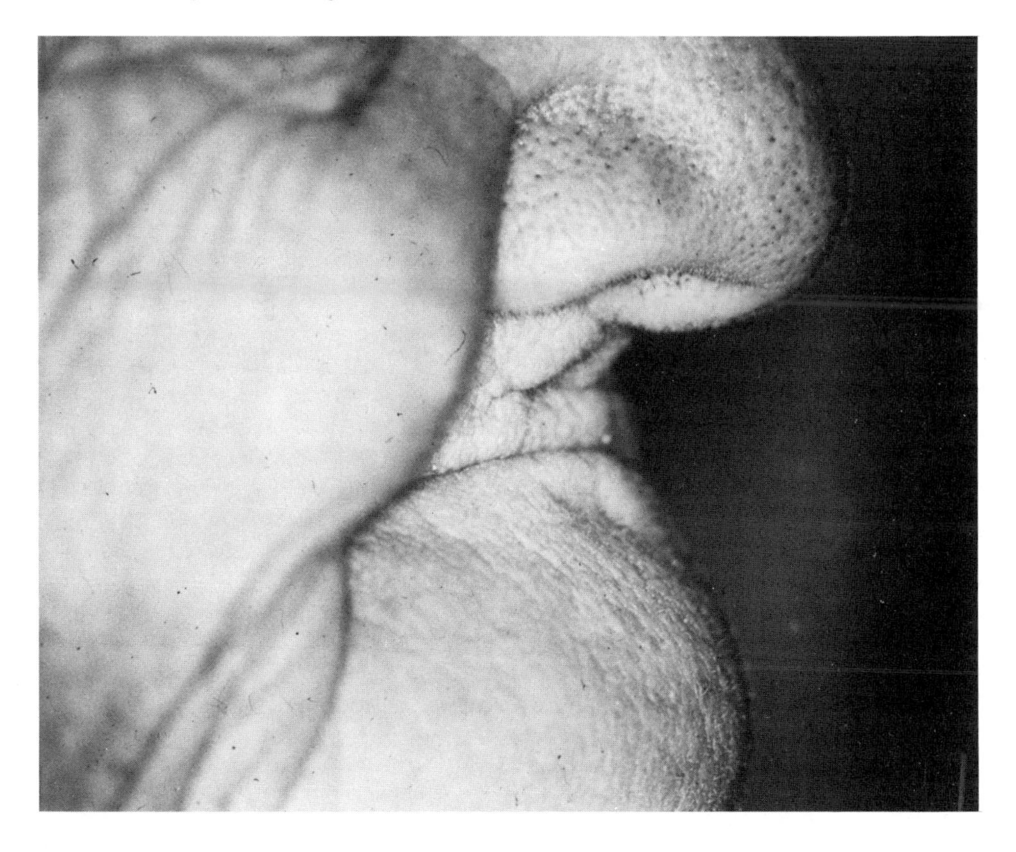

Figure 15-14. Collapse of facial musculature associated with a neurologic problem.

gingival pockets, and increased tooth mobility and migration are prevalent in the aging patient (figure 15-15).

Degenerative changes in the oral mucosa may take the form of hyperkeratosis, diminished secretion, loss of elastic properties, or tissue fragility. Ischemia and an associated increased predisposition to traumatic ulceration subsequent to therapy or when a prosthesis is used may also be encountered. Extensive ulceration may be present without pain. Conversely, hypersensitivity to minimal trauma may occur without overt signs of tissue damage.

Degenerative changes of the maxilla, mandible, and temporomuscular joint are frequently noted. The jaws often present signs of aging osteoporosis,

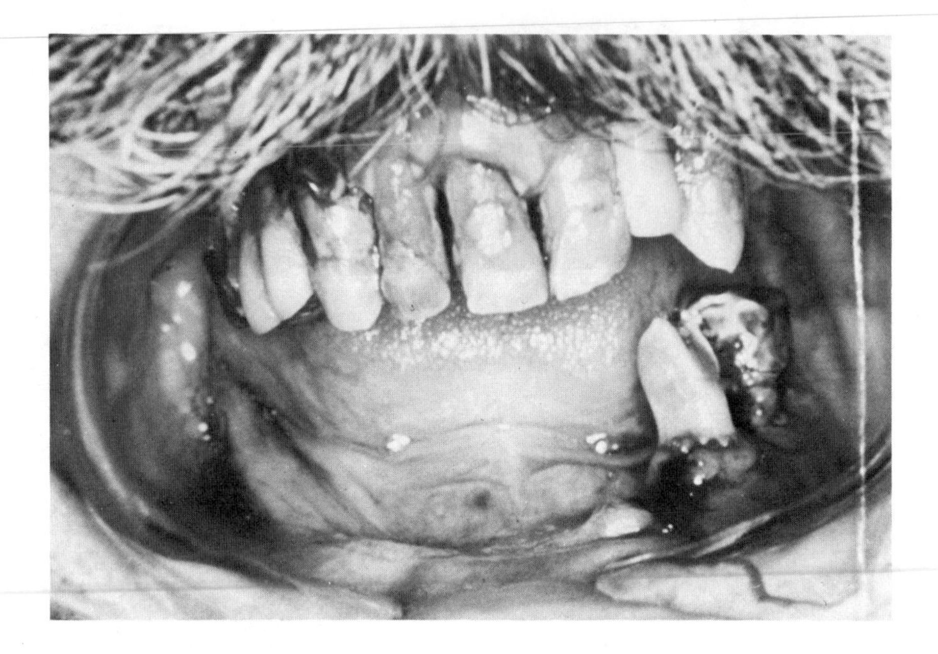

Figure 15-15. Patient with extensive caries, periodontal disease, partial edentulousness.

although this may be because of hormonal or nutritional disorders. There is considerable controversy over whether osteoporosis is a metabolic disorder, a degenerative disease, or a natural manifestation of aging. The temporomandibular joint is frequently observed in varying states of subluxation, and may be associated with poor muscular tone, malocclusion, or arthritis.

Distortion of neuromuscular response is generally associated with a loss in regulating and maintaining jaw posture. The loss of teeth also causes a reduced tonus of the facial musculature so that facial landmarks become distorted, displaced, or missing in both the static state of respiratory rest or the dynamic state of swallowing, speaking, and chewing. Landmarks that may be disturbed are the philtrum, the tubercle, and the vermillion border of the lips as well as the nasolabial sulcus and the commissure of the mouth. The skin may be markedly corrugated as elasticity is diminished because of changes in the elastic fibers and ground substance of the connective tissues.

Elevation in the overall threshold for perceived touch, pressure, temperature, and pain stimulation may produce loss or distortion of these thresholds which are associated with tooth contact and occlusion. Thus, excessive or asynchronous motor discharges during the contraction of masticatory muscles may result in trauma to the dental structures. This reduction in sensory perception may create problems in communication skills and personality.

Psychologic Effects of Aging

The aging patient often presents a number of personality changes. Stubbornness and inflexibility may occur. These changes may represent a weakening of ego function, wherein the patient reveals an increasing inability to repress and regulate antisocial impulses. Usually changes in special sense perception such as impaired hearing leave many patients suspicious and with paranoid tendencies. A decline in hearing is often a convergence point for a feeling of rejection. Many patients have loss of vision and may require better illumination or auditory or touch impulses to comprehend and react appropriately to diagnostic or therapeutic procedures. Older people burdened with systemic disorders and a history of oral disease require a sympathetic attitude to effect an accurate diagnostic interpretation.

Dental Care Procedures

The aging patient usually has dental concerns in addition to multiple biomedical, psychologic, and social problems. While these dental disorders may appear to offer no unusual difficulty because of their objective nature, they differ from similar conditions in younger individuals. The primary caries rate may not be of great importance since chronic periodontal disease is almost universal, and problems arising from edentulousness are at their highest level. Furthermore, mucosal degenerative changes are frequently evident and require careful diagnostic judgment. Treatment difficulties relate to a greater degree on medical and psychologic factors that affect motivation to seek care, manual skills in self-care, perceptual or motor problems, and, finally, self-concept and socialization needs.

The optimal treatment program provides acute care, prophylaxis, diagnosis, and a definitive treatment plan. The examination and acute care procedures are generally reliable predictors of patient capacity to accept treatment. Patients who cope well with these initial phases will benefit from periodontal, endodontic, and even minor orthodontic care. Temporary prosthetic devices may be provided by modifying old prostheses or constructing new short-term prostheses. Once good function, healthy periodontal tissue, and caries reduction have been achieved, a long-term fixed or removable prosthesis can be constructed.

An incremental care program should be planned so that treatment can be interrupted or terminated without complication. Economic hardship, illness, retirement, and migration to other regions are frequent events. Options for dental care of the aging usually include the full spectrum of treatment procedures available to all age groups. They include endodontic, periodontic, orthodontic, surgical, restorative, and prosthodontic procedures. One of the most prevalent disorders is the complete or partial state of edentulousness. This alters mastication, deglutition, as well as speech and language skills and can affect self-image and self-esteem of patients who often perceive their facial esthetics as faulty and unsightly.

The selection, sequence, and extent of dental procedures are patient specific. They should not be generalized by dental disorder, but treated by a tandem concept: dental problems qualified by the medical and psychosocial condition and with respect to any pharmacotherapeutic regimen. In essence, dental treatment is done as a selective response to the unique biologic, psychologic, and sociocultural status of each patient in consort with the nature and extent of any degenerative processes, maladaptive response in function, and the general coping skills of the patient.

References

Halstead, L.S. and Halstead, M.G. Chronic Illness and Humanism: Rehabilitation as a Model for Teaching Humanistic and Scientific Health Care. *Arch Phys Med Rehabil* 59:53-57, 1978.

Litvak, H., Silverman, S.I., and Garfinkel, L. Oral Sterognosis in Dentulous and Edentulous Patients. *J Prosthet Dent* 25:139-151, 1971.

Silverman, S.I. *Oral Physiology, 1st ed. (New York: Mosby, 1961).*

Silverman, S.I. The Burning Mouth Syndrome—Restorative and Prosthetic Treatment. *NY State Dent J* 33:459-466, 1971.

Silverman, S.I. Degeneration of the Dental and Oral Facial Structures. In American Speech and Hearing Association Report #7: *Orofacial Function: Clinical Search in Dentistry and Speech Pathology* (Proceedings of the Conference, Ann Arbor, MI, March 1-3, 1971). Washington, DC: American Speech and Hearing Association, 1972, pp. 33-67.

Silverman, S.I. The Burning Mouth Syndrome. *J Dent Assoc S Africa* 20:162-166, 1975.

Silverman, S., Silverman, S.I., Silverman, B., and Garfinkel, L. Self-Image and Its Relation to Denture Acceptance. *J Prosthet Dent* 35:131-141, 1976.

Part III
Psychologic and Socioeconomic Aspects

16 The Psychologic Significance of the Mouth in the Geriatric Patient

Donald B. Giddon

The psychologic significance of the face and the mouth may be conceptualized into three levels: survival, socialization, and self-fulfillment (Giddon, 1978). All three are important throughout life, but their relative importance depends, to a great extent, on the age of the individual.

From birth to death the mouth is essential for the intake of nutrients and the initial stage of food processing. The survival function is thus probably of greatest importance until adulthood, when it reaches a peak and plateaus. This is overlapped by a period when the orofacial area is essential for socialization. In turn, the latter is overlapped by the sensory apparatus incorporated in the mouth, which moves towards self-actualization, or the appreciation and enjoyment of taste and other aspects of life.

To clarify this concept, first consider the pain experience of the infant when food is not available or during teething. The pain associated with dental disease occurs throughout the entire life span of the individual (Giddon, 1978). The role of the face and the mouth in the process of socialization begins in infancy, both with perceptual development and differentiation of self from others. The development of the oropharyngeal muscels and the tongue enables the individual to communicate with others both by facial expression and speech.

In self-actualization and the hedonistic aspect of the mouth both the quantity and quality of oral stimulation are significant. The food industry has recognized that, in addition to flavor, the texture and sound associated with foods are important for acceptance. Foods with a slick or mushy texture pose control problems while in the oral cavity and may provoke survival anxiety actions such as gagging and choking, which can be exaggerated in elderly patients. Crunchy foods, on the other hand, provide reassurance of control for each discrete portion (Szczesniak and Kahn, 1971; Szczesniak, 1971).

Perhaps the most important role of the face and the mouth is its central feature. This is interpersonal attractiveness and communication. First impressions are formed by observing the face. This is where the entire gamut of human needs, intentions, and emotions are reflected. As might be expected, the face, and the mouth in particular, assume great importance in perceived physical attraction and self-concept. Speech leads to communication of feeling, which for both men and women of any age can lead to self-fulfillment.

In addition to serving biologic needs, there appears to be a basic need for oral activity, which may decrease with age. It has been noted that the total amount of smoking, drinking, and eating activity occurs in rhythmic cycles averaging ninety-six minutes in waking patients (Friedman and Fisher, 1967). These peaks of activity appear to be directly related, in some subjects, to alertness and reading activity. They may occur as a waking counterpart of rapid eye movement (REM) sleep, possibly increasing in frequency, similar to gastric secretion and muscle contractions, with deprivation of REM sleep. Since the sleep requirement may decrease with age, it might be expected that oral activity would also be lowered as the individual ages.

Certain relevant findings (Giddon and Bikofsky, 1973) provided the basis for an attempt to utilize this information to predict the overall response of elderly individuals obtained from a group of "average geriatric patients." This was done recognizing that individuals within any age group vary considerably, and that it is not possible to predict individual responses from group data.

Frequently, changes observed during a prior stage of development for any given modality are of greater importance than the present level of functioning. Changes in gustatory sensitivity are presumably related to a decreased number of functioning taste receptors, particularly in the anterior portion of the tongue (Birren, 1959). Yet the reduction in taste receptors is not sufficient to account for the loss of denture wearers to discriminate sweetness in solid foods. This loss of sensitivity was found to be related to a reduction in ability to effectively manipulate the food bolus (Giddon, et al., 1954; Kapur and Soman, 1964; Kapur, Soman, and Yurkstas, 1964). Although all responsible factors have not been defined, it is possible that the proprioceptive reflex involved in chewing is diminished. Aged individuals chew longer. This is indicated by the increased amount of time required to reach the swallowing threshold with a test food (Feldman, et al., 1964; Kapur, Chauncey, and Sharon, 1966). Similarly, more time was required to decide whether a sample of food was sweeter or less sweet than a standard stimulus (Giddon et al., 1954).

Furthermore, various studies have indicated that denture wearers are less responsive to the olfactory component in flavors. This appears to be a result of palatal coverage which interferes with touch receptors that enhance olfactory sensitivity (Chauncey, Shannon, and Feller, 1967; Feller and Shannon, 1970; Shannon, Terry, and Chauncey, 1969).

The ability to appreciate texture, another important attribute of food, is also diminished with age and in denture wearers (Birren, 1959; Manly et al., 1952; Kapur and Collister, 1967). This difference in discriminative ability appears to be, at least in part, because of a decrease in tactile sensitivity. In addition, the diminution in the hedonistic aspect of food ingestion may be a result of changes in the vibratory and auditory senses or temperature sensitivity (Birren, 1959).

Pain is probably one of the most complex sensory modalities affected by aging. As with certain other modalities, there is a diminution in the functional capability of neurophysiological components associated with pain. This decrease, however, is not a simple phenomenon. The threshold for cutaneous pain may be increased (Schluderman and Zubeck, 1962), but tolerance of deep pain, such as that produced by pressure on the Achilles tendon, appears to be decreased in the aged individual (Woodrow et al., 1972).

The interpretation of laboratory data and comparison of these findings with clinical reports of pain is complicated by the differences between the awareness of sensation or "I feel it," the perception of the sensation as pain, or "I hurt," and tolerance, or "I can't stand it." The first, sensation threshold, is unlearned and is basically a neurophysiological given; the second, perceptual threshold, has both learned and unlearned components; while the third, tolerance threshold, is almost completely learned and is related to social behavior. Tolerance threshold has been recently reanalyzed utilizing a psychologic technique, sensory decision theory (Lloyd and Appel, 1976). Variations in threshold are attributed to difference in willingness to report pain. For the elderly individual, particularly those vulnerable to depression, the mouth becomes a target for pain, organic or functional, as well as for real or imagined disease, psychosomatic disease, or conversion reactions. The reduction in sensation and pain perception by the aging individual partially offsets certain degenerative problems.

In addition to the factors involved in self-perception by the individual, there are sensory processes that relate to the perception of others and to perception of self by others. As stated previously, the orofacial area is key to interpersonal relations. Since the sensorimotor functions of the face and adjunct structure are involved in both the sending and receiving of messages, changes with age are significant. This definition includes almost all the senses and can relate to fading vision, with a lessened ability to see facial expressions or detail in others, or to the image of self in a mirror, even to a lessened ability to hear sounds that emanate from that individual.

The contributions of the other senses to interpersonal relationships involving the orofacial area are less obvious. The importance of a reduction in odor detection may relate to the social needs of the individual for distinguishing ethnic similarities or differences.

It must be emphasized that tolerance to these changes is very much related to the rate at which they occur. If they are gradual, and generally parallel other aspects of the aging process, there can be fewer adaptation problems; however, if these changes are sudden, because of trauma or disease, coping frequently can be more difficult. In general, the adequacy of coping behavior and related emotional responses depends on the balance between available resources and environmental demands. The resource pool may include assets such as physical attributes (health, strength, and appearance); intellectual capacity; socioeconomic assets (family, friends, avocations, prestige, social status, respect, economic security, income, or occupation); and personal characteristics (life style, emotional stability, and resiliency). To predict the adequacy of the coping behavior or the magnitude of adverse emotional response, it is necessary to determine the extent or value that has been placed on the lost asset and the degree of retention of that and the other remaining assets (Giddon and Bikofsky, 1973).

If flexibility is one of the remaining resources, it is likely that the reduction in one or more of the other resources may be offset by attributes or skills that have accrued to the individual. These may include any of the assets previously indicated. If we can gain an understanding of how the individual has adjusted to previous adversities and the demands of the current environment, a good basis for predicting the ability of the individual to cope with age-related changes may be obtained. Coping behavior at any point in time is often related to preexisting personality, as reflected by life style (Neugarten, Crotty, and Tobin, 1964).

Perception of health and resultant behavior are particularly relevant factors. The clinician is aware of the great concern that aging individuals have for their bodies. Whatever the cause, waning ability, ill health, or depression, this concern is most likely to occur where there is a withdrawal of interest in other persons or objects. Hypochondriasis is not a disease, but is a syndrome consisting of anxious preoccupation with the body or its component parts, which the patient believes are diseased or not functioning properly (Busse and Reckless, 1961). Whether or not organic disease actually exists may not be as important as what the patient believes, which may reinforce an incorrect interpretation of real, but normal, tissue changes.

Adjustment to full dentures has been shown to parallel overall adjustment to health changes (Emerson and Giddon, 1955). Since self-image is of particular concern, the loss of natural teeth aggravates feelings of deteriorating body image. The loss of teeth has been equated with loss of youth, and for the female, femininity; for the male, virility. When dentures are requisite, every effort should be made to encourage the patient to use them and enhance their self-image. Without adequate attention, the patient may reject dentures either because of the effort involved in maintenance or for other reasons. Popular myths to the contrary, self-image and attractiveness are also important to the aging individual since our culture endorses it.

Thus, increasing the attractiveness of the orofacial area can have a very important role in self-actualization and even erotic behavior by the elderly. If we cut through the underbrush of social taboo and failure to understand what the geriatric patient does or does not want, as well as can and cannot do, we would be surprised to find that although physiologic signs and frequency of excitement may be less pronounced (Masters and Johnson, 1970), interest in erotic activity is not lost. In fact, 20 to 25 percent of men have an increased interest in sexual activity with advancing age, particularly if they are not married (Pfeiffer, 1975). Data available regarding women over 50 years of age indicate that their capacity for response remains undiminished (Masters and Johnson, 1970). Middle-aged men with all this capacity and interest often believe that they have something for the future. The question asked then is "What are they supposed to do in the meantime?"

In view of these findings it should be obvious that the three stages: survival, socialization, and self-fulfillment, cannot be readily separated. In the maturing individual the face and the mouth are used for satisfaction of the high-order needs of self-actualization or fulfillment once biologic and social needs are met. It is not what the orofacial apparatus actually is, but what it appears to be, that is important. In viewing the significance of the face and its contributions to the quality of life, the magnitude of psychologic disparity, rather than physical disparity, between what was and what is, is often the essential component in the adjustment to age-related changes.

References

Birren, J.E. (Ed.) *Handbook of Aging and the Individual: Psychological and Biological Aspects.* (Chicago: University of Chicago, 1960).

Busse, E.W. and Reckless, J.B. Psychiatric Management of the Aged. *JAMA* 175:645-648, 1961.

Chauncey, H.H., Shannon, I.L., and Feller, R.P. Effect of Oral and Nasal Chemoreception and Parotid Secretion. In Schneyer, L.H. and Schneyer, C.A. (Eds.), *Secretory Mechanism of Salivary Glands* (New York: Academic, 1967), pp. 351-364.

Emerson, W.H. and Giddon, D.B. Psychologic Factors in Adjustment to Full Denture Prostheses. *J Dent Res* 34:683-684, 1955.

Feldman, R.S., Kapur, K.K., Alman, J.E. and Chauncey, H.H. Aging and Mastication: Changes in Performance and Swallowing Threshold with Natural Dentition. *J Am Ger Soc* (in press).

Feller, R.P. and Shannon, I.L. Taste, Tactile Stimulation and Parotid Flow in the Human. *J Oral Med* 25:87-88, 1970.

Friedman, S. and Fisher, C. On the Presence of a Rhythmic, Diurnal, Oral Instinctual Drive Cycle in Man: A Preliminary Report. *J Am Psychoanal Assoc* 15:317-343, 1967.

Giddon, D.B., Driesbach, M.E., Pfaffman, C., and Manly, R.S. Relative Abilities of Natural and Artificial Dentition Patients For Judging the Sweetness of Solid Foods, *J Prosthet Dent* 4:263-268, 1954.

Giddon, D.B., and Bikofsky, C.G. Socio-Psychological Aspects of Aging. In Fishman, N. and Bikofsky, C.G. (Eds.), *Proceedings of the Conference on Dentistry and the Geriatric Patient,* April 10-12, 1972. Harvard School of Dental Medicine and the American Society for Geriatric Dentistry, 1973.

Giddon, D.B. The Mouth and the Quality of Life. *NY J Dent* 48:3-10, 1978.

Kapur, K.K. and Soman, S.S. Masticatory Performance and Efficiency in Denture Wearers. *J Prosthet Dent* 14:687-694, 1964.

Kapur, K.K., Soman, S.S., and Yurkstas, A. Test Foods for Measuring Masticatory Performance of Denture Wearers. *J Prosthet Dent* 14:483-491, 1964.

Kapur, K.K., Chauncey, H.H., and Sharon, I. Oral Physiological Factors Concerned with Ingestion of Food. In Nizel, A.F. (Ed.), *Nutrition in Clinical Dentistry* (Philadelphia: W.B. Saunders, 1966), pp. 296-304.

Kapur, K.K., Collister, T., and Fischer, E.E. Masticatory and Gustatory Reflex Secretion Rates and Taste Thresholds of Denture Wearers. *J Prosthet Dent* 18:406-410, 1967.

Kapur, K.K. and Collister, T. A Study of Food Textural Discrimination in Persons with Natural and Artificial Dentitions. In Hayashi, T. (Ed.), *Second Symposium on Oral Sensation and Perception* (London: Pergamon Ltd., 1967), pp. 307-320.

Lloyd, M.A. and Appel, J.B. Signal Detection Theory and Psychophysics of Pain: An Introduction and Review. *Psychosom Med* 38:79-94, 1976.

Manly, R.S., Pfaffman, C., Lathrope, D., and Kaiser, J. Oral Sensory Thresholds of Persons with Natural and Artificial Dentitions. *J Dent Res* 31:305-315, 1952.

Masters, W.H. and Johnson, V.E. *Human Sexual Inadequacy* (Boston: Little, Brown & Co., 1970).

Neugarten, B.L., Crotty, W.J., and Tobin, S.S. Personality Types in an Aged Population. In Neugarten, B.C. and associates (Eds.), *Personality in Middle and Late Life: Empirical Studies* (New York: Atherton, 1964), pp. 158-187.

Pfeiffer, E. Sexual Behavior. In *Modern Perspectives in the Psychiatry of Old Age* (New York: Brunner/Mazel, 1975), pp. 313-325.

Schluderman, E. and Zubeck, J.P. Effect of Age on Pain Sensitivity. *Percept Mot Skills* 14:295-301, 1962.

Shannon, I.L., Terry, J.M., and Chauncey, H.H. Effect of a Maxillary Mouthguard on the Parotid Flow Rate Response to Flavored Solutions. *Proc Soc Exp Biol Med* 130:1052-1054, 1969.

Szczesniak, A.S. and Kahn, E.L. Consumer Awareness of and Attitudes to Food Texture. I: Adults. *J Texture Stud* 2:280-290, 1971.

Szczesniak, A.S. Consumer Awareness of Texture and of Other Food Attributes. II. *J. Texture Stud* 2:196-206, 1971.

Woodrow, K.M., Friedman, G.D., Siegelaub, A.B., and Collen, M.F. Pain Tolerance: Differences According to Age, Sex, and Race. *Psychosom Med* 34:548-556, 1972.

17 Nutritional Needs of the Elderly

Donald M. Watkin

The nutrition-health-aging (NHA) triad is important in dealing with problems of the aged. The NHA triad is extremely relevant to the needs of the elderly, more so than preventive medicine (which this concept includes), since most older individuals already have one or more diseases or disabilities. Moreover, the health of these individuals can be improved through education and counselling, appropriate medical and dental care, and proper individualized nutrition.

The developments of these concepts within the framework of the NHA triad is a priority of the nutrition program authorized by Title VII of the Older Americans Act of 1965 (Administration on Aging, 1976a, 1976b; Watkin, 1977). The Nutrition Program for Older Americans (NPOA) has indicated that improvement of health status should not be confined solely to NPOA project sites, but should also be established in community settings. NPOA project sites serve to integrate loci for teaching, counselling, and referrals.

NPOA and its network of associated service providers now form a microcosmic model which other comprehensive health systems may adopt. There are several problems that must be resolved by the NPOA before promoting a program on a national or international scale.

The Large Number of People Involved

There are approximately 32 million people aged 60 and over in the United States today. A realistic view shows that many men and women are physiologically older than 60 years of age, despite their younger chronological age. Included among these are people under 60 who are incapacitated to some extent by prior disease or disability. When this definition of the term "aged" is applied, the number of old persons approaches 50 million. Not only are the absolute numbers of those 60 years and over very large, but over one-third are already ill or disabled. An indication of this is that 28.9 percent of the 420 to 431 million dollar personal health care expenditures in fiscal year 1976 was paid by or for persons 65 years of age or more, who comprise 10.5 percent of the total population (Gibson, Mueller, and Fisher, 1977).

Unfortunately, the elderly are notorious underutilizers of available health services. Probability samples such as the Ten State Nutrition Survey (Center for Disease Control, 1972) and the Health and Nutrition Examination Survey (HANES) (Abraham, Lowenstein, and O'Connell, 1975) indicate that disease or disability or both afflict over one-third of older individuals. Within the framework of NPOA, the few studies of health status conducted under state auspices have produced similar results.

From the nutrition-oriented health care perspective, 100 percent of the malnutrition seen in the elderly today is secondary to disease or disability—physical, emotional, or attitudinal. Examples of this include altered metabolism accompanying disease (Watkin and Steinfeld, 1965; Levenson and Watkin, 1959) and the inability to obtain food, prepare meals, or even feed oneself because of a physical handicap (Watkin, 1972; 1977a). Other impairments to food consumption by the elderly are the absence of teeth, or poorly fitting dentures, the lack of desire to feed oneself, the avoidance of protective foods, and the ingestion of harmful foods through habit.

Ineffective Dietary Intervention

Available evidence appears to indicate that dietary intervention introduced late in life has little significant effect. Data derived from studies in Framingham, Massachusetts (Gordon and Kannell, 1972), Tecumseh, Maryland (Nichols et al., 1976) and Seattle, Washington (Hazzard, 1976) when viewed uncritically seem to indicate that dietary interventions initiated at age 55 or later have no beneficial effects. This interpretation has discouraged medical and dental scientists from promoting the NHA triad among the aged population. This unrealistic attitude, adopted by the old, the young, and scientific community, must be overcome.

Educating the Young Regarding Aging Issues

Another problem is directly related to the previous one: long-range answers to all aging issues involve influencing the young and affecting their life styles at a time when it can make a difference in their health care. This creates a conflict for those involved in supporting aging research and medical services. It may be difficult to justify allocating large portions of our national resources for the aged if they will gain only minimal benefits. The issue is two-sided: how to reach the young and how to meet the needs of those already old.

Separating the NHA Triad

Nutrition is only one part of the NHA triad and cannot be treated separately from the other two components. Nor can the other two be treated apart from nutrition. Everyone knows that something called "good nutrition" is required for attractive hair, skin, nails, eyes, teeth, and figures, and strong bones and muscles. The mass media relates the message daily, but how many people know that almost all malnutrition in this country is related to disease or disability—physical, emotional, or attitudinal? How many also realize that primary malnutrition in the United States no longer exists?

The goal of the NPOA is to resolve these immediate problems. However, the needs of two constituencies must be recognized—persons already old and younger persons who are aging. Our aged population needs attention. The number of people suffering from diseases, disabilities, and associated secondary malnutrition increases every year and demands a share of government-supported health services. The second group comprises the vast "silent majority." These are individuals not yet 60 years old who will continue to join the old in increasing numbers. The question is how best to help everyone realize their potential life span.

Local, state, and federal agencies have become increasingly interested in the nutritional needs of the elderly. Some recent legislation-related action includes the promulgation of *Dietary Goals for the United States* (McGovern, 1977a) by the Select Committee on Nutrition and Human Needs, U.S. Senate; the hearings on diet and killer diseases before the Senate Select Committee (McGovern, Chairman, 1977b); the communications from state agencies on aging, state health departments, and federal regional offices asking how to improve the health of those already old and to maintain or improve the health of all those who are aging. There are indications that the general population is developing a genuine concern for improving present and future health status. NPOA participants are utilizing diagnostic screening tests, demanding more readily accessible and more varied health services, emphasizing their desire to stay out of institutions, seeking more advice and counselling in their own communities, questioning the outrageous claims of food faddists and medical quacks, and engaging vigorously in physical and mental health programs.

Younger age groups are espousing consumer activism, questioning the marketing practices of food and medicine providers, abandoning fatalistic approaches to physical and mental diseases, adopting more favorable dietary habits, emphasizing physical and mental exercise, and demonstrating a total health awareness. The decrease in mortality rate from cardiovascular diseases exemplifies that a change is taking place regarding public health attitudes (U.S. Bureau of the Census, 1977).

The federal government is constantly investigating a wide range of health care issues as shown by congressional hearings on diet and killer diseases, promulgation of dietary goals, the saccharin controversy, the reorganization of the Department of Health, Education, and Welfare, the Administration on Aging (AoA)—VA Shared Responsibility Studies, the investigations of alleged scandals in Medicaid, and the rising concern of the high, continuously increasing costs of health care.

One major accomplishment of the NPOA, over the past four years, has been the implementation, growth, and maturation of the "Aging Network." Components of this network comprise NPOA, the area agencies on aging, the state-level agencies on aging, the federal regional offices on aging, and the central office of the Administration on Aging (AoA). In 1977, NPOA was comprised of 972 projects and 8,122 project sites. Subsequently, there has been a modest increase in projects and a substantial expansion of existing sites. In addition, 538 planning and service areas out of a total 596 had area agencies on aging with approved plans. Finally, more than one thousand senior citizen centers will have been financed with funds authorized by Title V of the Older Americans Act of 1965, as amended.

The planning, organization, and staffing of this NPOA network has involved the training of more than twenty thousand paid staff and one hundred thousand volunteers. These staff and volunteers comprise a large group dedicated to improving the needs of the elderly. Their efforts enable the Aging Network to effectively implement new approaches to the resolution of problems of the aged. However, relatively few trained and dedicated persons have attempted to resolve the major problem of health among the elderly. This is attributed, in part, to the relatively insignificant number of professionally trained health care personnel affiliated with Aging Network programs.

Another accomplishment has been the community development operation of the entire Aging Network. Figure 17-1 illustrates major features of this conceptualization, particularly of NPOA. The columns to the left, right, and at the bottom show that dining together serves as the focal point from which or to which most people congregate and where they have an opportunity to participate in health service, educational, counselling, recreational, and social activities.

Those in leadership roles in the Aging Network realize that nutrition, health, and aging form an inseparable triad. Many states have enacted programs directed at evaluating the health of the elderly and training personnel to cope with health conditions prevalent among the aged. A state-sponsored study in Maryland revealed that 34 percent of NPOA participants and 41 percent of nonparticipants described health as the major problem of old age. Eight out of sixteen dropouts from the NPOA cited health as the prime reason. One-third of the participants who had difficulty getting to the project sites gave poor health as the reason. One-third of the nonparticipants gave health as their reason for nonattendance.

A screening project funded by the state division of aging (Lintz, 1975) in Ogden, Utah analyzed and compared objective health measures of NPOA participants with the participants' self-evaluations of their respective health status. Only 18 percent recognized they had some health problems. However, health screening results indicated that 42 percent had hypertension, 42 percent had abnormalities detectable by physical examination, 16 percent required podiatric care, 56 percent had abnormal hematologic and blood chemistry

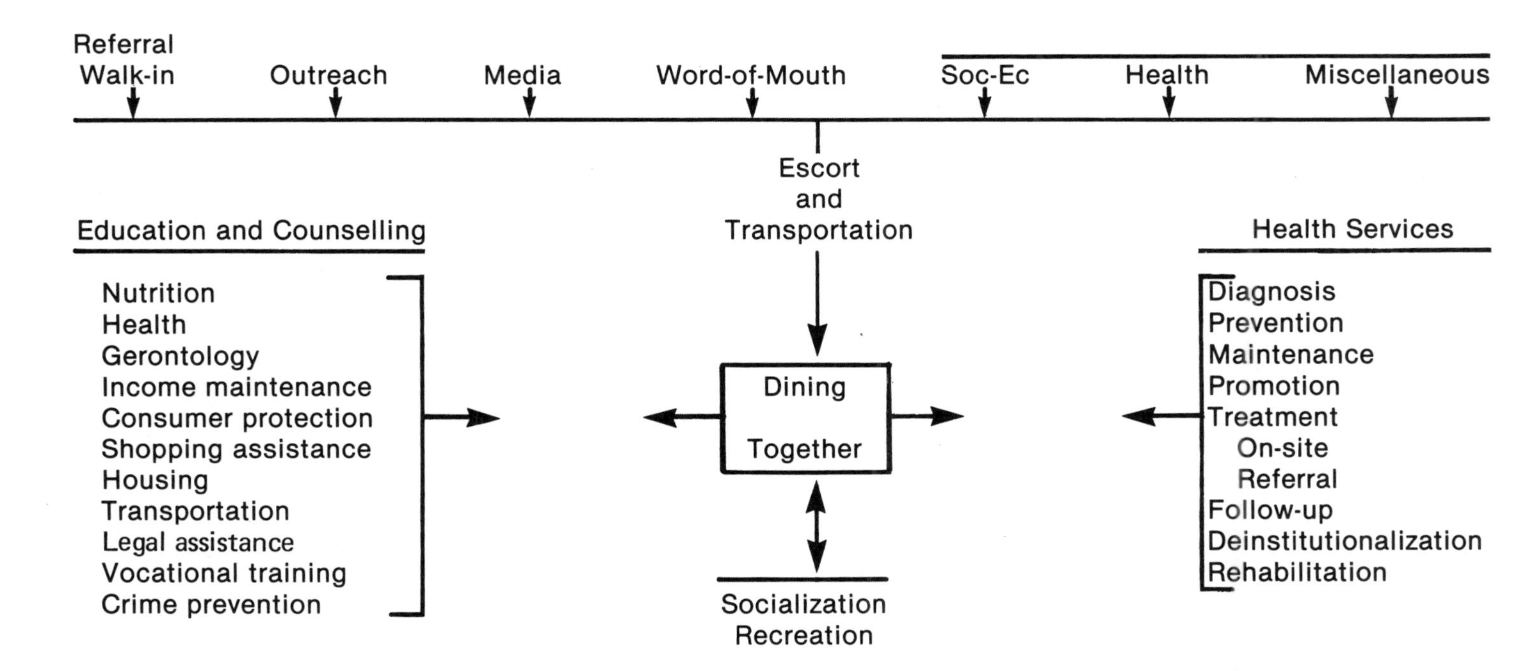

Figure 17-1. Conceptualization of the Nutrition Program for Older Americans (NPOA) authorized by Title VII of the Older Americans Act of 1965, as amended. (Reproduced with permission from *Nutrition, Longevity, and Aging*, edited by M. Rockstein and M.L. Sussman. New York: Academic Press, 1976.)

values, 26 percent were hard of hearing, 22 percent had abnormal pulmonary function tests, 31 percent were diabetic, and 30 percent had abnormal urinalyses. There was no reported data on dental pathology. Percentages of individuals with abnormalities for any given test were essentially the same in all age quintiles from 60 through 95. Many people had as many as six concurrent problems, whereas few had only one.

The results of Kohrs' (1976) nutritional study conducted in central Missouri showed that daily dietary calorie and calcium intake was less than the National Academy of Sciences-National Research Council (NAS-NRC) Food and Nutrition Board's recommended dietary allowances (RDAs) for both participants and nonparticipants. Moreover, protein, iron, vitamins A, B_1, and B_2, niacin, and ascorbic acid were consumed in amounts equal to or above the RDAs. Blood samples indicated that about half of the participating men and 10 percent of the women were anemic. Serum iron concentrations were deficient in only 5 percent of both men and women, suggesting that iron deficiency was not the cause of the anemia. Low levels of vitamins A and C were found in more nonparticipants than participants. No deficiencies of vitamin B_2 were found. Albumin, used as an index of protein nutriture, was low in about 5 percent of the subjects tested and seemed unrelated to participation in the meal program.

These findings in Missouri strongly suggest that factors other than nutrition influence hemoglobin, hematocrit, and albumin values. When combined with results from the Maryland and Utah studies, they suggest that disease factors must be considered when evaluating the nutritional status of the elderly. The studies indicate lucidly the need for integrating nutrition, health, and aging into a single, inseparable triad.

Large national organizations have favorably publicized NPOA programs developed in response to the needs of the elderly. Unfortunately, problems exist in meeting the demands of these programs. Rising costs of health care for the nation's older population (60 or more) accounts for one-third of the estimated $160 billion health care bill. The Aging Network is involved with expediting programs that will diminish the cost of health care. AoA has worked closely with interested federal departments and agencies to develop programs on a national level that will serve as prototypes for use at the state and intrastate level. Twenty-four such programs are now in operation.

Action plans designed to consolidate the information and promote the NHA tenets will stress nutritional education and provide medical service for those already afflicted with one or more physical, emotional, or attitudinal disabilities. NPOA sites, senior citizen centers, and various elderly housing projects will provide the setting for these programs. Trained personnel will be employed to provide basic medical services such as rendering diagnoses, advising and counseling, giving minor therapy, and referring individuals with serious illness, as well as training the families and friends of the elderly.

The inseparable triad of nutrition, health, and aging requires constant attention and continual focus. Ironically, the health status of many mature adults, still physiologically young, reflects an appalling ignorance about health and nutrition principles. The promotion of health among the young should be a top priority. Among old persons, prescribed nutrition is a beneficial therapeutic aid in many diseases, and is a major prophylactic role in the early management of disease. Health-related aspects of nutrition demand better application of known nutritional principles. However, nutrition is no panacea. The interrelationships between nutrition, health, and aging must be considered as an inseparable triad, each one being of equal importance.

References

Abraham, S., Lowenstein, F.W., and O'Connell, D.E. *Preliminary Findings of the First Health and Nutrition Examination Survey. United States 1971-72: Anthropometric and Clinical Findings.* HEW Publication No. (HRA) 75-1229. (Washington, D.C.: U.S. Government Printing Office, 1975).

Administration on Aging. *National Nutrition Program for Older Americans.* DHEW Publication No. (OHD) 76-20230. (Washington, D.C.: U.S. Government Printing Office, 1976a).

Administration on Aging. *Older Americans Act of 1965. As Amended, and Related Acts.* DHEW Publication No. (OHD) 76-20170. (Washington, D.C.: U.S. Government Printing Office, 1976).

Center for Disease Control. *Ten State Nutrition Survey, 1968-1970.* Vols I-V Plus Highlights. HEW Publication Nos. (HSM) 72-8130, 8131, 8132, 8133, and 8134. (Washington, D.C.: U.S. Government Printing Office, 1972).

Gibson, R.M., Mueller, M.S., and Fisher, C.R. Age Differences in Health Care Spending, Fiscal Year 1976. *Social Security Bulletin* 40:3-14, 1977.

Gordon, T. and Kannel, W.B. Predisposition to Artherosclerosis in the Head, Heart and Legs: The Framingham Study. *JAMA* 221:661-666, 1972.

Hazzard, W.R. Aging and Atherosclerosis: Interactions With Diet, Heredity, and Associated Risk Factors. In Rockstein, M. and Sussman, M.L. (Eds.), *Nutrition, Longevity, and Aging* (New York: Academic, 1976).

Hollander Associates. Nutrition and Social Experience: A Descriptive Evaluation of Title VII Lunch Program in Maryland. Prepared for the Maryland Office on Aging. Baltimore: Sidney Hollander Associates, 1976.

Kohrs, M.B. Influence of the Congregate Meal Program in Central Missouri on Dietary Practices and Nutritional Status of Participants. Lincoln University, Jefferson City, 1976, unpublished report.

Levenson, S.M. and Watkin, D.M. Protein Requirements in Injury and Certain Acute and Chronic Diseases. *Fed Proc* 18:1155-1190, 1959.

Lintz, L.P. Weber County Health Screening Project. Weber County Department on Aging. Ogden, Utah, 1975.

McGovern, G., Chairman. *Dietary Goals for the United States.* Select Committee on Nutrition and Human Needs of the United States Senate. Committee Print No. 81-605 0. (Washington, D.C.: U.S. Government Printing Office, 1977a).

McGovern, G., Chairman. *Diet and Killer Diseases with Press Reaction and Additional Information.* Select Committee on Nutrition and Human Needs of the United States Senate. Committee Print No. 79-283 0. (Washington, D.C.: U.S. Government Printing Office, 1977b).

McGovern, G., Chairman. *Diet Related to Killer Diseases.* II. Part 1: Cardiovascular Disease, Committee Print No. 83-693 0. Part 2: Obesity, Committee Print No. 84-107 0. III. Response to Dietary Goals for the United States Regarding Meat, Committee Print No. 90-845. IV. Dietary Fiber and Health, Committee Print No. 89-772. Select Committee on Nutrition and Human Needs of the United States Senate. (Washington, D.C.: U.S. Government Printing Office, 1977).

National Center for Health Statistics. Unpublished computation. Rockville, 1973.

Nichols, A.B., Ravenscroft, C., Lamphiear, D.E., and Ostrander, L.D., Jr. Daily Nutritional Intake and Serum Lipid Levels. The Tecumseh Study. *Am J Clin Nutr* 29:1384-1392, 1976.

U.S. Bureau of the Census. Current Population Reports, Series P-25, No. 643. Estimates of the Population of the United States by Age, Sex, and Race: July 1, 1974 to 1976. (Washington, D.C.: U.S. Government Printing Office, 1977).

U.S. Bureau of the Census. Current Population Reports, Series P-25, No. 704. Projections of the Population of the United States: 1977 to 2050. (Washington, D.C.: U.S. Government Printing Office, 1977).

Watkin, D.M. and Steinfeld, J.L. Nutrient and Energy Metabolism in Patients With and Without Cancer During Hyperalimentation with Fat Administered Intravenously. *Am J Clin Nutr* 16:182-212, 1965.

Watkin, D.M. Practical Solutions to Malnutrition in Spinal Cord Dysfunction. In *Proceedings of the Joint Meeting of the 18th Spinal Cord Injury Conference of the Department of Medicine and Surgery of the United States Veterans Administration and the International Medical Society of Paraplegia,* Boston, October 1971. (Washington, D.C.: U.S. Government Printing Office, 1972).

Watkin, D.M. The Nutrition Program for Older Americans: A Successful Application of Current Knowledge in Nutrition and Gerontology. *World Rev Nutr Diet* 26:26-40, 1977.

Watkin, D.M. Aging, Nutrition, and the Continuum of Health Care. *Ann Ny Acad Sci* 300:290-297, 1977.

18 Dollars and Sense About the Economics of Geriatric Dental Care

Robert Morris

Any discussion of dental health care policy requires inclusion of both fiscal and ethical considerations. Both must be dealt with on a long-term basis. On a short-term basis, dental disease is inappropriately considered similar to elective surgery. The loss of teeth, while troublesome, does not appear life-threatening, and the individual usually subtly adapts to the altered condition. As with other apparently undramatic health conditions, a remedy is usually sought by persons who are perceptive of the eventual consequences or patients who can afford to pay for the supposedly elective remedial services. There is, however, justification for considering the long-term consequences. We know that a strong chain links tooth loss, inadequate nutrition, and poor health. Two-thirds of persons over 65 have at least one edentulous arch (Public Health Service, 1974). While we have not yet been able to prove unequivocally that preventive measures such as topical or water fluoridation provided only when the individual is a child will reduce tooth loss at all ages, we are justified in focusing on the loss of teeth as a major insidious health threat to the older population.

At all ages, tooth loss also has immediate psychologic, social, and economic as well as physical consequences. Physical appearance is damaged, self-image is usually battered, and the development or maintenance of normal social relationships can be adversely affected, either because of the embarassment of the patient or withdrawal by others. The literary description of the toothless old crone has done much to shape our image of old age.

It has thus far proven difficult to confront the serious consequences of dental disease. In contrast to the recurrent common cold and other minor ailments, immediate restorative treatment appears costly. This tendency to delay treatment cannot be condoned unless we sincerely believe that it is acceptable to ignore the effects of a condition that will eventually contribute to ill health. This dilemma is especially pertinent to low-income individuals who will suffer from the erosion of self-respect and a normal social life if we permit this condition to continue without active intervention. Prevention requires the investment of an increased proportion of our health budget on dental health care services for persons of all ages. This adjustment in health care priorities is justified if we take a long-term view regarding ill health, and simultaneously adopt a more activist view regarding psychologic and social problems that can occur from inadequate masticatory ability.

The extensive nature of the problem is indicated in the Ten-State Nutrition Survey, 1968-1970 (1972) which shows that approximately one-half of the population age 50 years and above has chronic destructive periodontal disease. In addition, the Health, Education and Welfare National Health Survey on Eduntulous Persons (1974) documented that 22 million Americans have lost all their teeth. Furthermore, as of 1969, only 50 percent of the population received a periodic dental check-up during the previous twelve months (Public Health Service, 1972).

An examination of 3705 Kansas City residents found that 78 percent required dental care and 50 percent had a condition that could be treated. It is shocking to find that more than 60 percent of persons over 65 years have lost all the teeth in at least one arch. Of even more importance is the observation that 21 percent were under 45 years of age (U.S. Public Health Service, 1961).

To have any meaningful effect on this vast problem requires a shift in public health care policy and priority rating. A reasonable basis for health resource allocation might utilize some formula that multiplies the numbers of affected persons by some rating factor that measures the immediate severity of the condition as well as the long-range outcome. Any formula that employed these factors would indicate that the allocation of health resources toward dental care should be significantly increased.

The National Academy of Science report on veterans (1977) gives strong support for an enlarged approach of this nature. It also suggests, at least indirectly, how the current attitude of dental vis-à-vis medical and surgical programs has diverted attention from this problem. The report indicates that there is a high rejection rate (40 percent) of applications for dental care by veterans. The ambulatory care program relies heavily on patient-motivated initiatives rather than on professional activitism; and there appears to be an underutilization of existing dental resources compared with the rate found in private offices.

In addition, the report intimates that quite possibly the overall procedure for utilization of dental resources in the Veterans Administration may be linked too closely with medical decisions made about nondental conditions. Dental treatment is too frequently authorized only as an adjunct to a medical treatment plan. This suggests that a more active and independent role be given to dental treatment programming. The National Academy of Science report suggests that all eligible veteran patients secure comprehensive dental care, including prosthetic replacements.

Any comprehensive approach, whether for a specific age segment or the entire populace, is complicated by the ease with which dental health needs can be diffused and removed from public and professional attention. Any valid program cannot depend on patient initiative. Many of the patients with major dental needs live in nursing homes. They can readily be lost from sight. Many nursing homes are not visited by dentists, nor are arrangements made for patients to obtain dental care. Medicaid, a major resource for individuals with limited incomes, has been buffeted by state pressure to control costs, usually by reducing fees and services. Roghman, Haggerty, and Lorenz, (1971) found that between 1967 and 1969 the proportion of eligible children receiving dental examinations declined from 57 to 43 percent. Between 1967 and 1972 Medicaid dollars spent on dental care for all ages declined from 3.2 percent to 2.7 percent of the total funds available, although the dollars spent for dental care doubled (Lewis, Fein, and Mechanic, 1976). Administrative decisions to reduce provider fees or devise stricter eligibility requirements are subtle ways of controlling costs. This also serves to hide the dental health problem which is thereby excluded from entry into the program.

For these and a variety of other reasons, the dentally crippled individual will continue to be crippled until a public program assumes the responsibility for attacking this problem. Any comprehensive program for the general population, either national or regional, can appear to have formidable logistics: population dispersion, funding strictures, and the very insidious nature of dental disease. However, two strategic populations that can be readily focused on are children and the elderly.

The VA has the opportunity to initiate and determine the optimal comprehensive approach for adults. An assertive program could reduce the rate of edentulousness in the veteran population. It involves determination to provide extended care to all veterans as they enter an eligibility system at outpatient clinics, during an acute hospital stay, as well as veterans in nursing homes and domiciliaries, whether operated by the VA or private providers. An assertive approach would give the dental service responsibility for pursuing this goal without concentrating the majority of the dental effort on a limited number of individuals with a condition deemed treatable because it is associated with certain specified medical problems.

The resources to attack this problem involve dollars and labor, but the cost can be far less than estimated. There may be a vast untapped resource potential available in the VA. The approach would undoubtedly require a different deployment of professionals and equipment than now exists. But the foundation is already present. On a national basis, the Health Professions Educational Assistance Act of 1976 made a substantial effort to expand the pool of available dentists. For example, under Title V, "Grants for Health Professions Schools," 20 percent of the authorizations of appropriations for fiscal years 1978-1980 have been allocated to dental schools (U.S. Congress, 1976). However, of all funds appropriated and spent under the act in fiscal year 1978, only 10.4 percent of the total went to dentistry (Lawrence, 1978). Information gained from the VA program can be readily translated to public programs.

At present, administrative officials for the most part understand the need; scientific advances have provided the requisite information, and certain necessary resources are available to provide a favorable climate for this major effort.

The only obstacles are outdated tradition and a reluctance to reorder our priority regarding insidious causes of illness that affect many millions of people but do not offer the drama of more visible problems that frequently involve only a small proportion of the populace.

References

Lawrence, R.M. Personal communication. U.S. Public Health Service, Department of Health, Education, and Welfare, Boston, MA, 1978.

Lewis, C., Fein, R., and Mechanic, D. *A Right to Health: The Problem of Access to Primary Medical Care* (London: John Wiley & Sons, 1976).

National Academy of Sciences. *A Study of Health Care for American Veterans.* Report submitted to the Committee on Veteran's Affairs, U.S. Senate. June 7, 1977. (Washington, DC.: U.S. Government Printing Office).

Public Health Service, Division of Dental Public Health and Resources, U.S. Department of Health, Education, and Welfare. *Dental Care For the Chronically Ill and Aged: A Community Experiment.* DHEW Publication No. 899. (Washington, DC.: U.S. Government Printing Office, 1961).

Public Health Service, U.S. Department of Health, Education, and Welfare. *Dental Visits: Volume and Interval Since Last Visit.* DHEW Publication No. (HSM) 72-1066. (Washington, DC.: U.S. Government Printing Office, 1972).

Public Health Service, U.S. Department of Health, Education, and Welfare. *Edentulous Persons.* DHEW Publication No. (HRA) 74-1516. (Washington, DC: U.S. Government Printing Office, 1974).

Roghman, K., Haggerty, R., and Lorenz, R. Anticipated and Actual Effects of Medicaid on the Medical Care Pattern of Children. *New Engl J Med* 285:1053-1057, 1971.

Ten-State Nutritional Survey in the United States, 1968-1970. III. Clinical Dental. DHEW Publication No. (HSM) 72-8131. Center for Disease Control, Atlanta, GA, Health Services and Mental Health Administration, 1972.

U.S. Congress, Public Law 94-484, Health Professions Educational Assistance Act of 1976.

19 Planning for Dental Services—Impact of an Expanding Elderly Population

Lois K. Cohen

The planning process for dental services should be an integral part of the planning for general health services. This, in turn, should be an integral part of the comprehensive social and welfare services to be provided. Health care is one of many competing priorities and dental health is but one of the competitors for available resources when the health budget is allocated (Hicks and Doherty, 1977).

As the world's population grows, even larger proportions of valuable resources are being spent on health care. There is a growing awareness that the capability of the populace to use health resources is almost limitless; yet the resources available are limited. It is requisite to plan programs that deal with significant health problems in the most efficient and effective manner. Evaluation, the mirror image of planning, must be included to reveal the efficacy of the program employed and how much various problems have been lessened.

The concept of "most significant health problem" should be given emphasis, especially when considering the prospect for a national health insurance program in a time when economic resources are scarce. Will all health services be considered for inclusion? If only certain conditions are considered, which will be deemed more critical to the overall well-being of the population? Which illnesses might have a catastrophic effect on usual and necessary societal functions? How do dental illnesses and oral malfunction rate in terms of disabling the population? How much time is lost from work, school, or any productive pursuit as a result of oral disability? Answers to these and other pertinent questions must be considered and at least estimated prior to the first planning decision.

The six planning steps presented are taken from the *Report of the World Health Organization Expert Committee on Planning and Evaluation of Public Dental Health Services* (World Health Organization, 1976). They include situation analysis; problem identification and formulation of objectives; formulation and analysis of alternative strategies; identification of special efforts; strategy selection; and program formulation and evaluation.

If these steps are followed sequentially in planning for a population with a large segment of geriatric persons, the situation analysis should reveal problem areas reflecting the dental health needs characteristic of an aging population. Problems of mastication, nutrition, and speech become more apparent and important than problems related to caries. Except when prevented early, the consequences of oral diseases might emerge as the most significant problem.

The initial step of situation analysis may well be the most critical and revealing. This information forms the base on which all subsequent steps depend. If that analysis is incomplete, relevant intervention points that are essential for important strategies will be missed. For example, if the analysis of a situation defines the health needs of a given population but fails to define the numbers, types, and characteristics of the care providers, the means to reimburse the provider, and the physical access of patients to the provider, the entire program could collapse under the crush of arbitrary ad hoc planning decisions.

A schematic view of the elements to be considered in the analysis is shown in figure 19-1. The circle represents the social, economic, and political context describing the target population. "C" represents the potential consumers of dental services in the target area. "P" represents all available providers, including dental professionals and associated indigenous health personnel. So-called "illegal" dental workers should be counted or estimated, they do provide certain services and must be considered since they could not exist if there were no demand for their services. "A" represents administrators, decision makers, politicians, insurance company representatives, or other individuals whose function is to facilitate the provision and receipt of dental care services. Finally, the triangles represent oral health products, services, payment, and information. Oral health products include oral hygiene aids such as toothbrushes, toothpaste, floss, and similar items. Treatment services include oral cancer screening programs and traditional services such as restorative, periodontal, prosthetic, and surgical treatment.

This model reflects how these elements describe special situations in populations with a large proportion of elderly persons (Kegeles, Lotzkar, and Andrews, 1966). The social, economic, and political environment may take on a conservative or liberal characteristic dependent on the predominant political constituency. If the area being considered is economically well-off the status quo might be advocated. But, if the area is economically depressed, a demand for social welfare and health services might be expressed politically. Other factors such as leisure activities may proliferate in the social environment of older populations. Institutionalized living or, if current national efforts have an impact, extended care or foster family care may predominate. These differences are important to note, if only to be utilized to pinpoint the location of forces supportive of, or antagonistic to, program development (U.S. Congress, 1976).

In considering the administrative elements that may affect or be affected by an aging population, it should be realized that general health and oral health policies are often established by central or local governmental agencies. It is necessary, therefore, to request that these offices, specifically those focused on programs for the aged, the chronically ill, and the handicapped, provide

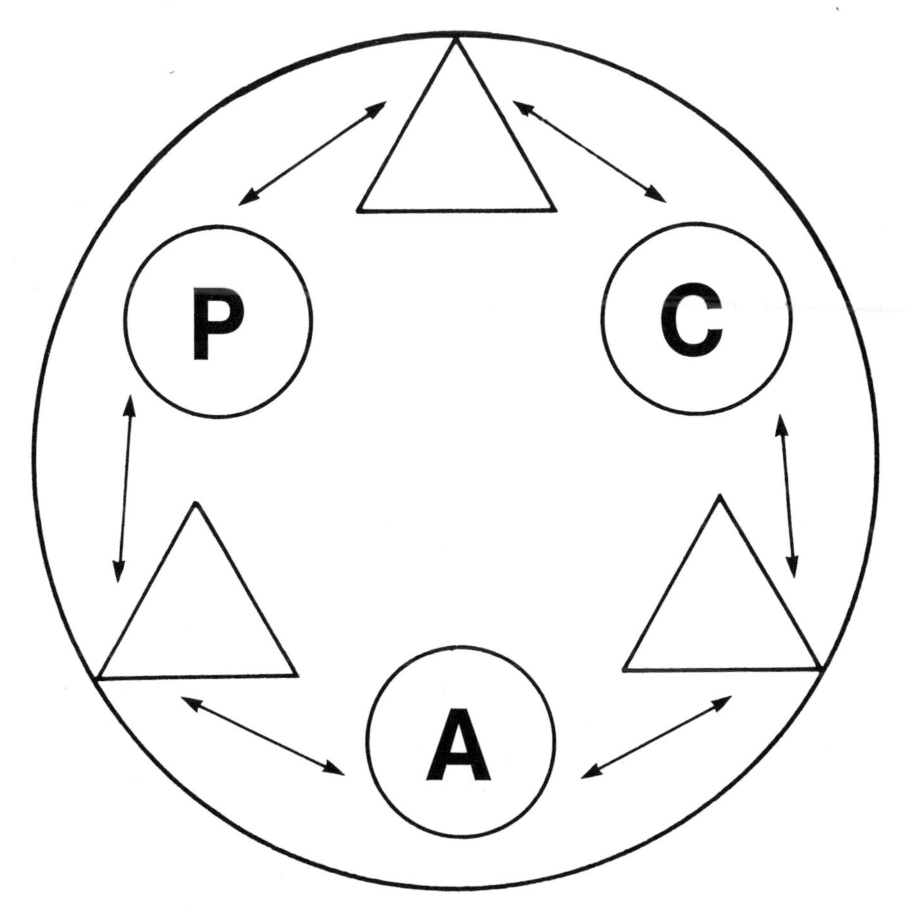

○ = Social, economic and political context of the population
C = Consumers
P = Providers
A = Administrators
△ = Oral health goods and service
↔ = Communication channels

Figure 19-1. Schematic model of a dental care system.

information about their particular priorities and the available resources (Waldman, 1964; Mobley, 1967; Soble, 1974).

Existing third party coverage in both the public and private sectors should be examined and described according to the amount, type, and scope of services. The volume of expenditures for dental services delivered to specific age groups can be particularly helpful in planning unit costs with a greater degree of precision than figures derived from fee schedules for typical services to the aged, such as dentures.

Analysis of administrative elements of exiting programs can help in estimating the personnel requirement for any new venture with a special population. Similarly, the number and size of facilities used to provide care must be assessed. These include mobile units, private facilities, and public clinics. Their distribution in relation to population density should be mapped, as well as their capacity to handle patients. If there are large home bound or nonmobile groups, satellite facilities may be inadequate. Eventually the facility may have to come to the patient. This occurs in certain parts of the United States and in other countries. The need for simplified dental equipment which can be operated in a residence might become a priority item.

Data must be obtained concerning the current and potential consumer. It is advisable to collect information about age-sex distributions, urban-rural distribution, size of households (by area of residence), population density and distribution, immigration and emigration, occupational distribution, and memberships in special oral health care eligibility groups (Soble, 1974). Data on individual and family income levels for each residential area as well as type and distance of transportation to care facilities are desirable. Local expectations about oral health service systems and past experience regarding receipt of services is helpful information. In addition, it is necessary to consider the intended usage of such services, assessment of ability to pay, frequency of visits, and desired changes in the delivery systems (Banting, 1971). A geriatric population is likely to have a longer history of involvement with dental care systems by virtue of having lived longer, and may be more critical and demanding of specific care. Their needs must be considered in collecting planning data. It is essential to know the proportion of people in various age groups with specific treatment needs (Banting, 1972; Kovar, 1977).

Providers of care should be described in both the private and public sectors by type of practice specialization, membership in insurance programs, location of practice, patient load, and potential use of auxiliary personnel. Facts about income (by type of service), opinions about working conditions, reimbursement arrangements and views about delivering care to the aged are also extremely useful (Waldman, 1964).

These data elements are not exhaustive. Nor are all of them essential. However, they do help to identify problems and rank them by priority.

The World Health Organization (WHO) has suggested criteria to help order priorities for oral conditions. They are problems of an emergency nature; that threaten large numbers of people; that cause public concern or cause death; and that can be prevented or controlled. Certain general criteria have also been suggested (World Health Organization, 1976). Some are relevant to meeting politically expressed needs, increasing social equity, economic development, and the quality of life.

Perhaps the quality of life criterion is the crux for planning services to areas with an expanding elderly population. Although dental diseases rarely increase the mortality of a population, they usually affect daily comfort. Dental problems can inhibit normal regular activities such as eating, sleeping, speaking, working, and participating in leisure activities. Quantification of these functions is frequently discussed but rarely presented. Unless the impact of these factors is measured and described, few decision makers will pay attention to a plan for dental services in general, and especially for a geriatric population.

Throughout the world there has always been a certain pragmatic attraction for categorical approaches to the planning of dental services. No category appears to exceed child health in popularity. In various surveys of national dental health activities the child population nearly always emerged as the top priority (Cohen, 1978). This may be attributed to the concept that preventing oral disease among the young will eventually decrease the need for huge dental treatment programs among the older segments of the population. Incremental care programs assume that reductions in cost and personnel will be a result of keeping the target population at a maintenance care level. Even considering the vast amount of information now known about prevention, such programs have not provided proof that they do not defer the need for treatment rather than truly preventing the need for professional care at a later age.

Categorical approaches based on age grading are incompatible with comprehensive, family-oriented care. There appears to be inherent discrepancies between isolated planning for treatment of an easily identified group and the concept that oral health status results from a complex of sociocultural influences on the individual who generally belongs to a family group. It is true that a large proportion of the elderly no longer belong to a closely cohesive, or even extended, family group. These isolates form a special group which should be considered apart from the family. Some of these individuals are in institutions that serve as surrogate family groups (Kegeles, Lotzkar, and Andrews, 1966). Others who live alone with few meaningful social supports may be contacted through social and welfare agencies that reach them through other services. Moreover, as our entire population ages the need for noninstitutional settings probably means that the family will have to take increasing responsibility for the care of the elderly.

As society increases its efforts to keep the elderly out of institutions, more resources must be allocated to develop family-oriented comprehensive health services. From the sociologist's point of view, this approach is more reasonable than the traditional age-graded approach. Certain countries use this method and their polyclinic health services are available to all on demand. They have nationalized the concept of the neighborhood health center.

The U.S. Public Health Service/World Health Organization International Collaborative Study of Dental Manpower Systems in Relation to Oral Health Status is now collecting data from Eastern Europe that will be added to information from several western nations and an asian population (Cohen, 1978). With this basic data, we will have beginning evidence to test the effect of family-oriented care on the status of long-term oral health.

Once the special characteristics of the aged have been identified, it might seem logical to create separate programs for this group. Yet, whenever care is provided in separate settings, each one develops stereotypic virtues and disadvantages. Separate geriatric programs run the risk of stigmatization–private hospital rooms versus ward care and separate systems for the rich and poor. The negatives tend to relate to the delivery of partial services and a dislike for treating the old and the chronically ill. It may, therefore, be better to integrate the elderly into the predominant system of care available for the rest of the population. Conceivably, integrating oral health services into the predominant medical care system might improve health practices, provide reinforcement from other health providers, and avoid social stigmas.

Neither a completely public nor a completely private system is likely to work. Both planning extremes ignore socially differentiated patterns to which the population has grown accustomed, and which the care providers prefer. Ignoring existing structures and building entire new programs invites implementation problems.

Finally, preventive as well as restorative services must be provided. The common assumption is that aging populations require only repair or replacement services. The fact that new carious lesions or gingival disease may occur, and that certain preventive programs could either delay or deter these as well as other problems is rarely considered.

Although some surveys suggest that dental services are underutilized by the elderly, the need for care is in many ways more acute than among younger age groups (Banting, 1972). Over half of the elderly population have no natural teeth. A great many elderly persons with dentures need replacements or refitting (U.S. Congress, 1976). To reduce this backlog, it is essential that time by spent on prevention. The prevention message must be reinforced, even after the occupationally productive years, or the need for replacements will increase as will the danger that the dental profession will be unable to meet this burgeoning demand. This segment of the population may be forced to seek low-priced, nonprofessional alternatives that are potentially injurious.

All investigators, planners, clinicians, administrators, and educators have biases. Normal pride in our occupation leads to this subjectivity. But it is important to express these biases so that others can analyze and evaluate them. In this manner we can hope that resolution of these differences will result in the evolution of plans and decisions suited to the situation. We can also hope that this process will provide information that will allow us to be more sensitive to the needs of citizens of all ages, to the providers of health care, and to administrators or intermediates who facilitate the flow and exchange of oral health goods and services throughout our society.

References

Banting, D.W. Dental Care for the Aged. *Can J Public Health* 62:503-508, 1971.

Banting, D.W. A Study of Dental Care Cost, Time, and Treatment Requirements of Older Persons in the Community. *Can J Public Health* 63:508-514, 1972.

Cohen, L.K. Dental Care Delivery in Seven Nations. In J.I. Ingle and P. Blair (Eds.), *International Dental Care Delivery Systems: Issues in Dental Health Policies.* (Cambridge: Ballinger, 1978), pp. 201-214.

Hicks, B. and Doherty, N. Comprehensive Dental Services for the Elderly Under Medicare. *J Dent Res* 56(Special Issue B):B95, 1977.

Kegeles, S.S., Lotzkar, S., and Andrews, L.W. Predicting the Acceptance of Dental Care by Residents of Nursing Homes. *J Public Health Dent* 26(1):290-302, 1966.

Kovar, M.G. Health of the Elderly and Use of Health Services. *Public Health Rep* 92(1):9-19, 1977.

Mobley, E.L. Dental Program for the Chronically Ill and Aged. *J Tenn State Dent Assoc* 47(2):137-154, 1967.

Soble, R.K. Sociologic and Psychologic Considerations in Special Patient Care. *Dental Clin North Am* 18(3):545-556, 1974.

U.S. Congress (94th, second session, 1976). Report by the Subcommittee on Health and Long-Term Care of the Select Committee on Aging. *Medical Appliances and the Elderly: Unmet Needs and Excessive Costs for Eyeglasses, Hearing Aids, Dentures, and Other Devices.* (Washington, DC.: U.S. Government Printing Office, 1976).

Waldman, H.B. Report of a Demonstration Dental Care Program for Homebound Chronically Ill and Aged Patients. *J Am Dent Assoc* 69(6):722-729, 1964.

World Health Organization. Report of a WHO Expert Committee, Technical Report series 589. Planning and Evaluation of Public Dental Health Services. Report of a WHO Expert Committee, Geneva, Switzerland, 1976.

20 Overview of the Practitioner-Patient Relationship in Aged Persons

Norton Fishman

Our predecessors in geriatric dentistry had a totally humanistic motivation for providing services to the elderly which we still adhere to today. We must continue this tradition, utilizing the entire array of newly acquired scientific information, clinical techniques, management procedures, as well as state and federal support to provide optimal dental care for our elder citizens.

Many roadblocks inhibit the delivery of care to this segment of our population, most particularly to the advanced elderly. Although chronological age is not always significant, I wish to place emphasis on persons over 75 and individuals not within the mainstream of programs that provide health care services. These extremely elderly persons do not view dentistry as "the smile of beauty or plaque-free teeth." Most are crisis-oriented, as evidenced by the large percent who wear dentures. Furthermore, their perception of dentistry and its broader ramifications is classically low. They view the ability to maintain dentition into the later stages of life as a rare occurrence. In the not too distant past decisions relative to dental treatment were limited to "Should I have the rest of my teeth out now and get my dentures, or should I wait, lose them one at a time, and suffer before finally getting dentures?" Today the elderly find themselves receiving preventive maintenance, fluoride applications, periodontal therapy, and, on occasion, complicated restorative treatment.

Dentistry for the elderly may be extremely tedious and time consuming. It often requires a level of effort that may make the cost factor prohibitive. For the most part, whether the patient is wealthy or destitute, their assessment of value in dentistry is usually low. No matter what the fee, it is often considered to be much greater than its actual value. Unfortunately, this assessment is frequently based on a dental fee that occurred many years ago. It can also be related to a feeling that they are old, so why bother wasting money. Certain treatment compromises and transitional procedures are usually requisite, but it is important to make sound compromises. Do not place yourself or the patient in situations that are either nonmaintainable or nonresolvable.

Regardless of the finances available, the insecurities associated with advancing age are very serious, and the desire for dental care tends to rapidly diminish with most individuals. Another important factor is the mobility of this population, both in the sense of physical capability and the availability of public or private transportation. The number of stairs to climb, the safety of the neighborhood, and presence of wheelchair ramps, and lighting all tend to be very important features relative to whether care is sought on a continuous basis.

Many psychologic problems are inherent in this age group. They include involuntary changes, low self-esteem, intensified personality disorders, and the anxiety associated with being old, without having accomplished all the desired life goals.

Consider the patient who is not interested in the maintenance of his dental health, cannot afford dental fees, and continues to relate dentistry to acute episodes of pain. This person is mentally and physically exhausted by the trip to the dentist, and is upset after waiting fifteen minutes for a treatment, even though he is one hour early for the appointment. The dentist is relatively young, sensitive about the costs of his or her education, the office equipment, and loan and interest payments. He is taking continuing education courses, both on new clinical techniques and practice management. He is proud of his office efficiency. He is, however, uncomfortable with older people, but doesn't really know why. He becomes quite concerned after reading the patient's medical history and discovers that the patient used both the front and back side of the printed forms as well as an extra sheet of paper to complete the medical history, including medications currently being used. The young dentist really becomes apprehensive when this patient chokes and gasps upon being placed in the horizontal four-handed lap position and cannot rise to clear his throat.

The oral examination reveals a miscellaneous assortment of teeth and spaces, with an even more miscellaneous array of crowns, amalgams, and plastic restorations, even an old "added-onto" removable appliance. What does the patient really want or expect? Does this require a comprehensive examination with a Panorex survey, full mouth individual radiographs, diagnostic study models, bite registration, and an appointment to discuss an extensive treatment plan? The patient has a minor problem which requires immediate attention and probably will not return after this problem is resolved, and he is relatively comfortable. This is the moment of truth for the busy health care practitioner. Does the dentist listen patiently, reassure the individual, instill confidence, and attempt to explain why comprehensive treatment is necessary? Or does he accede to the patient's request for only treatment of the immediate problem? Or does the dentist avoid any treatment because the individual does not fit into the pattern of his practice? Are we willing to lower our goals, expectations, and in doing so compromise the prognosis to serve only the patient's immediate needs, which may be relatively minor and of no real long-term value?

Although our expectation from treatment may be vast, the ultimate service delivered is often limited and the satisfaction obtained may be doubtful and infrequent. However, if the clinician assumes the attitude that he has attained a degree of professional maturity which allows flexibility in his treatment plan, he can be confident and undertake a positive approach toward treating the total needs of these patients. He can even understand why they often cancel at the last minute because transportation is not available or illness has occurred or the pain has eased. He is aware of the difficulty encountered by formerly independent vital people who now see themselves slipping into dependency, no matter how hard they try to continue as independent individuals. Unfortunately, the professional often does not provide support when these people most need it.

This text has succinctly indicated the multitude of dental problems that the elderly encounter. In many cases comprehensive care becomes very tedious, and the restoration of oral function is a major challenge, even for the best prosthodontist. Tissue and bone atrophy, diminished salivary flow with altered consistency, decreased elasticity and resilience of the soft tissue, a poor healing rate, decreased masticatory ability, and gross neglect of oral hygiene are the norm for the elderly. A lifetime of use and abuse with medical, psychologic, and socioeconomic problems which have accumulated over many decades produce a patient who requires special care—not the care of a specialist, but "special care." This care must be rendered with understanding, patience, and sympathy, in addition to providing full dentures or restoring a few remaining anterior teeth and fabricating removable partial dentures.

One of the most important factors in the delivery of care to the elderly is an understanding of the aging process and the attendant social, economic, behavioral, and medical ramifications. Often a sympathetic and understanding approach can expedite provision of the individualized attention these people need. Establishing a feeling of rapport is most important. Short appointments may be an important consideration. Some patients, however, would rather nap in a comfortable chair and have more work done at each visit. A simple explanation of the intended work will frequently gain added patient cooperation. Maintaining a calm attitude is important. Many patients can be very trying, uncooperative, and suspicious. They will take delight in elevating your stress threshold and then will carefully back off. You are being tested and these patients are very clever.

Geriatric dentistry must be based on a comprehensive preventive program, but a different type of preventive program. Preventing problems is a very serious consideration for the elderly, where change, by itself, can present problems they may be unable to handle. It means that every new patient must be examined and a complete dental record obtained. In addition, this record should indicate language ability, ability to verbalize, ability to provide for personal and oral hygiene, capacity for ambulation, as well as major medical diagnoses, medication taken, special problems, and special precautions which may include the presence of a pacemaker. A geriatric history may be extensive and can often involve other information sources such as children, friends, and physicians, but this can be essential to the development of an optimal treatment plan.

All denture patients should receive an annual recall with a screening for oral cancer and instructions on denture care. Dentures should be labelled in the event that the patient becomes hospitalized. Patients with natural teeth should have more frequent recalls and receive a prophylaxis, a topical fluoride treatment, and a review of hygiene and plaque control. These patients, if capable, are taught preventive techniques.

Adequate, well-defined treatment planning is the most important first step. Decisions will involve the amount of treatment, the rate of treatment, as well as the desired goal. Patient ability to biologically and emotionally cope is a prime consideration and, often, an incremental treatment plan must be evolved. Preventive care requires attention to the possibility of serious interruptions during any treatment sequence, and alternate plans must be made for continued function during delays.

These procedures are appropriate both in the private office and the health care facility. Many appear to follow our day-to-day routine, but all too frequently routine techniques are inappropriate for the elderly patient. Moreover, all problems encountered in geriatric dentistry are completely within the bounds of the interested general practitioner.

Name Index

Subject Index

About the Contributors

Albert J. Aaronian, D.D.S., Assistant Chief Medical Director for Dentistry, Veterans Administration Central Office, Washington, D.C.

Lois K. Cohen, Ph.D., Special Assistant to the Director, National Institute of Dental Research, National Institutes of Health, Bethesda, Maryland.

I. Leon Dogon, L.D.S., R.C.S., D.M.D., Professor and Head of the Department of Operative Dentistry, Associate Dean for Administrative Affairs, Harvard School of Dental Medicine; Head of the Department of Dental Materials, Forsythe Dental Center, Boston, Massachusetts.

Norton Fishman, D.M.D., Assistant Clinical Professor of Prosthetic Dentistry, Harvard School of Dental Medicine, Boston, Massachusetts; Chief of Dental Service, Hebrew Rehabilitation Center for Aged, Roslindale, Massachusetts.

Donald B. Giddon, D.M.D., Ph.D., Former Dean, New York University Dental Center; Professor of Behavioral Sciences and Community Health, New York University Medical Center; Professor of Anesthesiology, New York University Medical School; Professor of Psychology, New York University Faculty of Arts and Sciences.

Ralph Goldman, M.D., Assistant Chief Medical Director for Extended Care, Veterans Administration Central Office, Washington, D.C.

Walter C. Guralnick, D.M.D., Professor and Chairman, Department of Oral and Maxillofacial Surgery, Harvard School of Dental Medicine; Chief, Oral and Maxillofacial Surgery Service, Massachusetts General Hospital, Boston, Massachusetts.

Krishan K. Kapur, D.M.D., M.S., Chief, Dental Service, Veterans Administration Medical Center, Sepulveda, California; Professor-in-Residence of Removable Prosthodontics, UCLA School of Dentistry, Los Angeles, California.

Morley R. Kare, Ph.D., Director, Monell Chemical Senses Center, University of Pennsylvania, Philadelphia, Pennsylvania.

Florence Mahoney, Member, President's Commission on Mental Health, Washington, D.C.; Member, Advisory Council, National Institute on Aging, National Institutes of Health, Bethesda, Maryland.

Takashi Makinodan, Ph.D., Director, Geriatric Research, Educational and Clinical Center, Wadsworth Veterans Administration Health Center, Los Angeles, California.

Michael J. Malone, M.D., Director, Geriatric Research, Educational and Clinical Center, Veterans Administration Medical Center, Bedford, Massachusetts; Professor of Neurology and Psychiatry, Boston University School of Medicine, Boston, Massachusetts.

Robert Morris, D.S.W., Kirstein Professor of Social Planning; Director, Levinson Gerontological Policy Institute, Florence Heller Graduate School for Advanced Studies in Social Welfare, Brandeis University, Waltham, Massachusetts.

Morris Rockstein, Ph.D., Professor of Physiology and Biophysics, University of Miami School of Medicine, Miami, Florida.

Thomas D. Sabin, M.D., Director of Neurology, Boston City Hospital, Boston, Massachusetts; Associate Professor of Neurology and Psychiatry, Boston University School of Medicine, Boston, Massachusetts.

Ira L. Shannon, D.M.D., M.S., Director, Oral Disease Research Laboratory, Veterans Administration Medical Center, Houston, Texas.

Gerald Shklar, D.D.S., M.S., Charles A. Brackett Professor of Oral Pathology, Head, Department of Oral Medicine and Oral Pathology, Harvard School of Dental Medicine, Boston, Massachusetts.

Jeremiah E. Silbert, M.D., Director, Normative Aging Study, Veterans Administration Outpatient Clinic, Boston, Massachusetts; Associate Professor of Medicine and Biochemistry/Pharmacology, Tufts University School of Medicine and Dental Center, Boston, Massachusetts.

Sidney I. Silverman, D.D.S., Professor, Department of Removable Prosthodontics, New York University Dental Center, New York, New York.

Paola S. Timiras, M.D., Ph.D., Professor and Chairman, Department of Physiology/Anatomy, University of California, Berkeley, California.

Edgar A. Tonna, Ph.D., Professor of Histology, Director, Laboratory for Cellular Research in Aging, Director, Institute for Dental Research, New York University Dental Center, New York, New York.

Donald M. Watkin, M.D., M.P.H., Former Special Assistant to the Director, Office of State and Community Programs, Administration on Aging, Department of Health, Education, and Welfare, Washington, D.C.

About the Editors

Howard H. Chauncey, Ph.D., D.M.D. is Associate Chief of Staff for Research and Development of the Veterans Administration Outpatient Clinic, Boston, and Associate Professor of Oral Pathology at the Harvard School of Dental Medicine. Prior to this he was Chief, Research in Oral Diseases, Medical Research Service, VA Central Office, Washington, D.C. He has held positions as Professor, in the Department of Oral Pathology, Tufts University School of Dental Medicine, Visiting Professor, Division of Oral Biology, University of Miami School of Medicine, Visiting Investigator, The Systematic Ecology Program, the Marine Biological Laboratory, Woods Hole, and was a Member, FDA, Bureau of Drugs, OTC Panel on Dentifrices and Dental Care Agents.

Dr. Chauncey received his dental degree from Tufts University School of Dental Medicine. He earned his Ph.D. degree in biochemistry from Boston University and his M.S. (biochemistry) and B.S. (chemistry) degrees from Boston University and Tufts University, respectively.

Kalidas Nandy, Ph.D., M.D., is the Associate Director, Geriatric Research, Educational and Clinical Center, Edith Nourse Rogers Memorial Veterans Hospital, Bedford, Massachusetts, and Professor of Anatomy and Neurology, Boston University School of Medicine. Dr. Nandy received the M.D. degree from the University of Calcutta and the Ph.D. degree in neurobiology from Emory University. He is a member of a number of scientific societies, including the Gerontological Society, the American Aging Association, and the American Geriatric Society.

He has published extensively in the field of aging, particularly of the nervous system, and has contributed chapters in numerous books in the field. He has also edited *The Aging Brain and Senile Dementia* (Nandy and Sherwin), *Senile Dementia: A Biomedical Approach*, and *Geriatric Psychopharmacology*.

Carl J. Toga, D.M.D., is Chief of Dental Service at the Edith Nourse Rogers Memorial Veterans Hospital, Bedford, Massachusetts, and is a faculty member, Department of Operative Dentistry, Harvard School of Dental Medicine, Boston, Massachusetts.

He served as chairman of the VA-Harvard Symposium on the Geriatric Dental Patient held in Boston in 1977, and has made numerous presentations on geriatric dentistry.

He was elected a Fellow of the Academy of General Dentistry in 1975, and his current memberships include the American Association of Hospital Dentists, and the American Society of Geriatric Dentistry.

Dr. Toga received his dental degree from Tufts University School of Dental Medicine and the B.S. degree in chemistry from Tufts University.